STRANGERS
AMONG US

STRANGERS AMONG US

How Latino Immigration
Is Transforming America

ROBERTO SURO

 ALFRED A. KNOPF   NEW YORK   1998

THIS IS A BORZOI BOOK
PUBLISHED BY ALFRED A. KNOPF, INC.

Copyright © 1998 by Roberto Suro

Library of Congress Cataloging-in-Publication Data
Suro, Roberto.
Strangers among us : how Latino immigration is transforming America / Roberto Suro.—1st ed.
p.   cm.
Includes bibliographical references and index.
ISBN 0-679-42092-4 (alk. paper)
1. Hispanic Americans—History—20th century.
2. Immigrants—United States—History—20th century.
3. Hispanic Americans—Social conditions.   4. Latin America—Emigration and immigration—History—20th century.   5. United States—Emigration and immigration—History—20th century.   I. Title.
E184.S75S86   1998
305.868073—dc21   97-36676   CIP

Manufactured in the United States of America
First Edition

Con cariño para mis papás,

Guillermo y Piedad,

who taught me how to be an American

CONTENTS

PART I

◆·◆·◆·◆·◆·◆·◆·◆·◆·◆·◆·◆·◆·◆·◆·◆·◆·◆·

THEY ARE HERE

And if a stranger sojourn with thee in
your land, ye shall not vex him.
But the stranger that dwelleth with you
shall be unto you as one born among you,
and thou shalt love him as thyself, for ye
were strangers in the land of Egypt . . .

—LEVITICUS 19:33–34

❖•❖•❖•❖•❖•❖•❖•❖•❖•❖•❖•❖•❖•❖•❖•❖•

Children of the Future

❖•❖•❖•❖•❖•❖•❖•❖• **O**n Imelda's fifteenth birthday, her parents were celebrating everything they had accomplished by coming north to make a new life in the United States. Two short people in brand-new clothes, they stood in the driveway of their home in Houston and greeted relatives, friends, and neighbors, among them a few people who had come from the same village in central Mexico and who would surely carry gossip of the party back home. A disc jockey with a portable stereo presided over the backyard as if it were a cabaret instead of a patch of grass behind an overcrowded bungalow where five people shared two bedrooms. A folding table sagged with platters of tacos and faji-tas. An aluminum keg of beer sat in a wheelbarrow atop a bed of half-melted ice cubes. For Imelda's parents, the festivities that night served as a triumphant display of everything they had earned by working two jobs each. Like most of the other adults at the party, they had come north to labor in restaurants, factories, warehouses, or construction sites by day and to clean offices at night. They had come to work and to raise children in the United States.

Imelda, who had been smuggled across the Rio Grande as a toddler, wore a frilly dress ordered by catalog from Guadalajara, as befits a proper Mexican celebrating her *quinceañera,* which is the traditional coming-out party for fifteen-year-old Latin girls. Her two younger sisters and a little brother, all U.S. citizens by birth, wore new white shirts from a discount store. Their hair had been combed down with sharp, straight parts and dabs of pomade.

When it came time for Imelda to dance her first dance, her father took her in his arms for one of the old-fashioned polkas that had been his favorite when a band played in the town square back home. By tradition, boys could begin courting her after that dance. Imelda's parents went to bed that night content they had raised their children according to proper Mexican custom.

The next morning at breakfast, Imelda announced that she was pregnant, that she was dropping out of school, and that she was moving in with her boyfriend, a Mexican-American who did not speak Spanish and who did not know his father. That night, she ate a meal purchased with food stamps and cooked on a hot plate by her boyfriend's mother. She remembers the dinner well. "That night, man, I felt like an American. I was free."

This is the promise and the peril of Latino immigration. Imelda's parents had traveled to Texas on a wave of expectations that carried them from the diminishing life of peasant farmers on a dusty *rancho* to quiet contentment as low-wage workers in an American city. These two industrious immigrants had produced a teenage welfare mother, who in turn was to have an American baby. In the United States, Imelda had learned the language and the ways. In the end, what she learned best was how to be poor in an American inner city.

Latino immigration delivers short-term gains and has long-term costs. For decades now, the United States has engaged in a form of deficit spending that can be measured in human lives. Through their hard work at low wages, Latinos have produced immediate benefits for their families, employers, and consumers, but American society has never defined a permanent place for these immigrants or their children and it has repeatedly put off considering their future. That future, however, is now arriving, and it will produce a reckoning. The United States will need new immigration policies to decide who gets into the country. More importantly, the nation will need new means of assuring political equality and freedom of economic opportunity. Soon Americans will learn once again that in an era of immigration, the newcomers not only demand change; they create change.

When I last met Imelda, she was just a few weeks short of her due date, but she didn't have anything very nice to say about her baby or her boyfriend. Growing up in Houston as the child of Mexican immigrants had filled her with resentment, especially toward her parents, and that was what she wanted to talk about.

"We'd get into a lot of yelling and stuff at home because my parents, they'd say, 'You're Mexican. Speak Spanish. Act like a Mexican girl,' and I'd say, 'I'm here now and I'm going to be like the other kids.' They didn't care."

Imelda is short and plump, with wide brown eyes and badly dyed yellow hair. She wore a denim shirt with the sleeves ripped off, and her expression was a studied pout. Getting pregnant was just one more way of expressing anger and disdain. She is a dime-store Madonna.

Imelda is also a child of the Latino migration. She is a product of that great movement of people from Latin America into the United States that is older than any borders but took on a startling new meaning when it gradually gained momentum after the 1960s and then turned into something huge in the 1980s. Latino immigrants were drawn north when America needed their services, and they built communities known as barrios in every major city. But then in the 1990s, as these newcomers began to define their permanent place here, the ground shifted on them. They and their children—many of them native-born Americans—found themselves struggling with an economy that offered few opportunities to people trying to get off the bottom. They also faced a populace sometimes disconcerted by the growing number of foreigners in its midst. Immigration is a transaction between the newcomers and the hosts. It will be decades before there is a final tally for this great wave of immigration, but the terms of the deal have now become apparent.

Imelda's story does not represent the best or the worst of the Latino migration, but it does suggest some of the challenges posed by the influx. Those challenges are defined first of all by demography. No other democracy has ever experienced an uninterrupted wave of migration that has lasted as long and that has involved as many people as the recent movement of Spanish-speaking people to the United States. Twelve million foreign-born Latinos live here. If immigration and birth rates remain at current levels, the total Hispanic population will grow at least three times faster than the population as a whole for several decades, and Latinos will become the nation's largest minority group, surpassing the size of the black population a few years after the turn of the century. Despite some differences among them, Latinos constitute a distinctive linguistic and cultural group, and no single group has ever dominated a prolonged wave of immigration the way Latinos have for thirty years. By contrast, Asians, the other large category of immigrants, come from nations as diverse as India and Korea, and although the Latino migration is hardly monolithic, the Asian influx represents a much greater variety of cultures, languages, and economic experiences. Moreover, not since the Irish potato famine migration of the 1840s has any single nationality accounted for such a large share of an immigrant wave as the Mexicans have in recent decades. The 6.7 million Mexican immigrants living in the United States in 1996 made up 27 percent of the entire foreign-born population, and they outnumbered the entire Asian immigrant population by more than 2 million people. Latinos are hardly the only immigrants coming to the United States in the 1990s, but they will define this era of immigration, and this country's response to them will shape its response to all immigrants.

Latinos, like most other immigrants, tend to cluster together. Their enclaves are the barrios, a Spanish word for neighborhoods that has become part of English usage because barrios have become such a common part of every American city. Most barrios, however, remain a place apart, where Latinos live separated from others by custom, language, and preference. They are surrounded by a city but are not part of it. Imelda lived in a barrio named Magnolia Park, after the trees that once grew along the banks of the bayou there. Like other barrios, Magnolia is populated primarily by poor and working-class Latinos, and many newly arrived immigrants start out there. Magnolia was first settled nearly a hundred years ago by Mexicans who fled revolution in their homeland and found jobs dredging the ship channel and port that allowed Houston to become a great city. Latinos continued to arrive off and on, especially when Houston was growing. Since the 1980s, when the great wave of new arrivals began pouring into Magnolia, it hasn't mattered whether the oil city was in boom or bust—Latinos always find jobs, even when they lack skills and education. Most of Magnolia is poor, but it is also a neighborhood where people go to work before dawn and work into the night.

Like other barrios, Magnolia serves as an efficient port of entry for Latino immigrants because it is an easy place to find cheap housing, learn about jobs, and keep connected to home. Some newcomers and their children pass through Magnolia and find a way out to more prosperous neighborhoods where they can leave the barrio life behind. But for millions like Imelda who came of age in the 1990s, the barrios have become a dead end of unfulfilled expectations.

"We could never get stuff like pizza at home," Imelda went on, "just Mexican foods. My mother would give me these silly dresses to wear to school. No jeans. No jewelry. No makeup. And they'd always say, 'Stick with the Mexican kids. Don't talk to the Anglos; they'll boss you. Don't run around with the Chicanos [Mexican-Americans]; they take drugs. And just don't go near the *morenos* [blacks] for any reason.'"

Imelda's parents live in a world circumscribed by the barrio. Except for the places where they work, the rest of the city, the rest of America, seems to them as remote as the downtown skyline visible off in the distance on clear days. After more than a dozen years, they speak all the English they need, which isn't much. What they know best is how to find and keep work.

Imelda learned English from the television that was her constant childhood companion. Outside, as Magnolia became a venue for gangs and drug sales, she learned to be streetwise and sassy. Growing up fast in Magnolia, Imelda learned how to want things but not how to get them.

Many families like Imelda's and many barrios like Magnolia are about to become protagonists in America's struggles with race and poverty. Latino immigrants defy basic assumptions about culture and class because they undermine the perspective that divides the nation into white and nonwhite, a perspective that is the oldest and most enduring element of America's social structure.

Are Latinos white or nonwhite? There is only one correct answer, though it is often ignored: They are neither one nor the other. This is more than a matter of putting labels on people. Americans either belong to the white majority or to a nonwhite minority group. That status can determine access to social programs and political power. It decides the way people are seen and the way they see the world. White and nonwhite represent two drastically dissimilar outcomes. They constitute different ways of relating to the United States and of developing an American identity. Latinos break the mold, sometimes entering the white middle-class mainstream, often remaining as much a group apart as poor blacks.

Most European immigrants underwent a period of exclusion and poverty but eventually won acceptance to the white majority. This process of incorporation occurred across generations as the immigrants' economic contributions gained recognition and their American-born children grew up without foreign accents. Too many Latinos are poor, illegal, and dark-skinned for that path to serve as a useful model.

African-Americans traveled an even greater distance to achieve levels of material and political success unthinkable fifty years ago, but as a racial group, they remain juxtaposed to the white majority. Blacks have formally become part of the body politic, but they remain aggrieved plaintiffs. Latino immigrants lack both the historical standing and the just cause to win their place by way of struggle and petition. And these newcomers are not likely to forge an alliance with blacks, but instead, these two groups are already becoming rivals.

Neither the European ethnics nor the African-Americans were free to choose the means by which they became part of American society. Their place in this country is a product of history, and in each case it is a history of conflict. After centuries of slavery and segregation, it took the strife and idealism of the civil rights era to create a new place for African-Americans within the national identity. The Irish, the Italians, and other European ethnics had been coming here for decades but did not win full acceptance until after the Great Depression and World War II reforged and broadened the American identity to include them. Now the Latinos stand at the gate, looking for a place in American society, and the conflict that will inevitably attend their arrival is just beginning to take shape.

Latinos are different from all other immigrants past and present because they come from close by and because many come illegally. No industrialized nation has ever faced such a vast migration across a land border with the virtual certainty that it will continue to challenge the government's ability to control that border for years to come. No immigrant group has carried the stigma of illegality that now attaches itself to many Latinos. Unlike most immigrants, Latinos arrive already deeply connected to the United States. Latinos come as relations, distant relations perhaps, but familiar and connected nonetheless. They seem to know us. We seem to know them, and almost as soon as they are in the house, they become part of our bedroom arguments. They are newcomers, and yet they find their culture imbedded in the landscape of cities that have always had Spanish names, such as Los Angeles and San Antonio, or that have become largely Spanish-speaking, such as Miami and New York. They do not consider themselves strangers here because they arrive to something familiar.

They come from many different nations, many different races, yet once here they are treated like a pack of blood brothers. In the United States, they live among folk who share their names but have forgotten their language, ethnic kinsmen who are Latinos by ancestry but U.S. citizens by generations of birthright. The newcomers and the natives may share little else, but for the most part they share neighborhoods, the Magnolias, where their fates become intertwined. Mexican-Americans and Puerto Ricans account for most of the native-born Latino population. They are the U.S.-made vessel into which the new immigration flows. They have been Americans long enough to have histories, and these are sad histories of exploitation and segregation abetted by public authorities. As a result, a unique designation was born. "Hispanics" became a minority group. This identity is an inescapable aspect of the Latino immigrant experience because newcomers are automatically counted as members of the group for purposes of public policy and because the discrimination that shaped that identity persists in some segments of the American public. However, it is an awkward fit for several reasons. The historical grievances that led to minority group designation for Latinos are significant, but compared to slavery or Jim Crow segregation they are neither as well known nor as horrible. As a result, many Americans simply do not accept the idea that Latinos have special standing, and not every native Latino embraces this history as an inescapable element of self-concept. Moreover, Latinos do not carry a single immutable marker, like skin color, that reinforces group identity. Minority group status can be an important element of a Latino's identity in the United States, but it is not such a clear and powerful element of American life that it automatically carries over to Latino immigrants.

"Hispanic" has always been a sweeping designation attached to people of diverse cultures and economic conditions, different races and nationalities, and the sweep has vastly increased by the arrival of immigrants who now make up about 40 percent of the group. The designation applies equally to a Mexican-American whose family has been in Texas since before the Alamo and a Mexican who just crossed the Rio Grande for the first time. Minority group status was meant to be as expansive as the discrimination it had to confront. But now for the first time, this concept is being stretched to embrace both a large native Latino population with a long undeniable history of discrimination and immigrants who are just starting out here. The same is occurring with some Asian groups, but the Latino phenomenon has a far greater impact because of the numbers involved. Latino immigrants are players in the old and unresolved dilemma of race in America, and because they do not fit any of the available roles, they are a force of change.

Like all other newcomers, Latino immigrants arrive as blank slates on which their future course has yet to be written. They are moving toward that future in many directions at once, not en masse as a single cohesive group. Some remain very Latino; others become very American. Their skin comes in many different colors and shades. Some are black, and some of them can pass very readily as white. Most Latinos arrive poor, but they bring new energy to the labor force even as they multiply the ranks of the chronically poor. Latino immigrants challenge the whole structure of social science, politics, and jurisprudence that categorizes people in terms of lifetime membership in racial or ethnic groups. The barrios do not fit into an urban landscape segregated between rich and poor, between the dependent and the taxed.

Latino immigrants come in large numbers. They come from nearby. They join fellow Latinos who are a native minority group. Many arrive poor, illegally, and with little education. Those are the major ingredients of a challenge unlike any other.

. . .

Listening to Imelda complain about how her parents tried to impose Mexican ways on her, I remembered arguments over language with my own parents. They were both bilingual, but they preferred we speak Spanish with them. I can still hear them instructing me that I should never allow my first name, Roberto, to be rendered as "Bob," no matter how much trouble it caused me on the playground.

But that was a very different time and place. My father came from Puerto Rico in the 1920s, my mother from Ecuador in the 1940s. My father found his place here when the Depression and World War II forged a new nationalism in the United States. He reluctantly gave up his first name, Guillermo, and became "Bill" in the company of Anglos who could not be bothered to learn the pronunciation of such a foreign name. My mother found her place with him, though she never broke her ties to home and has never changed her citizenship. They made their family together in the 1950s in the optimism of a new suburban Cape Cod cottage in the Maryland suburbs of Washington, D.C.

Just as my father practiced rhymes with my sister and me so we could properly roll our r's in Spanish, he was equally adamant, even fierce, in insisting that our English had to be perfect at school. He had just about erased the accent from his voice, but the effort still showed. He told us good English and an education would save us from having to change our names.

There was no barrio in Washington then. There was one grocery store on Columbia Road where we bought Latino foodstuffs like *plátanos* (plantains), and at some point the old Ontario Theater started featuring the slapstick Mexican comedian Mario Moreno, whose pants were always falling down and who was best known by his stage name, Cantinflas. But I don't think the word Hispanic had been invented yet, and in Washington, at least, there was not an identifiable group that needed a label.

For me, Spanish and everything that went with it belonged at home and with family friends and relatives; and the language came to life most powerfully on our trips back to Puerto Rico and Ecuador. English belonged in all the other places. And it was not hard going back and forth. The mostly Irish kids at the Catholic schools I attended played rough with what they got from TV— "Alberto VO5," "*con* Gleem," and "José Jiménez," and eventually plain old "spic." My name, "Robert with an o on the end," was a laughable oddity for the Americans I grew up with, but everyone suffered some teasing, and being a Latino was not grounds for complete exclusion, like being black.

For me, Spanish could belong to one world and English to another, and the door between them was open. We were light skinned and middle class, and I could switch from one language to another, from one world to another. By becoming culturally ambidextrous, I fulfilled my parents' aspirations. When I passed through the door into America from my Spanish-speaking home, I did it quietly and no one much noticed.

It was not a time of large-scale immigration and so there was no backlash. That made it easier. Also, when I came of age in the 1960s, people still assumed that each new generation of Americans would do better than the last. Talking to Imelda thirty years later, so much was different. For her, growing up between two worlds produced ambivalence and alienation. For her and her friends in Magnolia and for many other children of Latino immigrants coming of age in the 1990s, there were no grounds for easy optimism.

More than a third of all Latinos are younger than eighteen years old. This vast generation is growing faster than any other segment of the population. It is also failing faster. While dropout rates among Anglos and African-Americans steadily decline, they continue to rise among Latino immigrants, and mounting evidence suggests that many who arrive in their teens simply never enter American schools at all. A 1996 Rand study of census data found that high school participation rates were similarly high—better than 90 percent—for whites, blacks, and Asians, native and immigrant alike, and for native Latinos, as well. Latino immigrants, especially from Mexico, were the only group lagging far behind, with less than 75 percent of the school-age teens getting any education. Only 62 percent of the Mexican immigrant seventeen-year-olds were in school, and these young people are the fuel of U.S. population growth into the twenty-first century.

Dropout rates are only one symptom. This massive generation of young people is adapting to an America characterized by the interaction of plagues. Their new identities are being shaped by the social epidemics of youth homicides, pregnancy, and drug use, the medical epidemic of AIDS, and a political epidemic of disinvestment in social services. These young Latinos need knowledge to survive in the workforce, but the only education available to them comes from public school systems that are on the brink of collapse. They are learning to become Americans in urban neighborhoods that most Americans see only in their nightmares. Imelda and a vast generation of Latino young people like her are the victims of a vicious bait and switch. The United States offered their parents opportunities. So many of the children get the plagues.

For the parents, movement to the United States almost always brings tangible success. They may be poor by U.S. standards, but they measure their accomplishments in terms of what they have left behind. By coming north, they overcome barriers of race and class that have been insuperable for centuries in Latin America. Meanwhile, the children are left on the wrong side of the barriers of race and class that are becoming ever more insuperable in the United States. With no memory of the *rancho,* they have no reason to be thankful for escaping it. They look at their parents and all they see is toil and poverty. They watch American TV, and all they see is affluence. Immigrant children learning to live in this dark new world face painful challenges but get little help. Now, on top of everything else, they are cursed by people who want to close the nation's doors against them. The effects are visible on their faces.

"I can tell by looking in their eyes how long they've been here," said the Reverend Virgil Elizondo, rector of San Fernando Cathedral in San Antonio, Texas. "They come sparkling with hope, and the first generation finds that hope rewarded. Their children's eyes no longer sparkle. They have learned only to want jobs and money they can't have and thus to be frustrated."

The United States may not have much use now for Imelda's son, but he will be eighteen and ready to join the labor force in the second decade of the next century, just as the bulk of the baby-boom generation hits retirement age. Then, when the proportion of elderly to young workers is going out of whack, this country will have a great need for him and the other children born in the barrios, who will contribute financial sustenance in the form of their payroll deductions and other taxes. This is already an inescapable fact because of the relatively low birth rates among U.S.'s whites and African-Americans for the past several decades. Women of Mexican ancestry had fertility rates three times higher than non-Hispanic women in the 1990s (and they were the least educated mothers of any group). Mexican immigrant women account for more than a quarter of all the births in California and nearly a third of the births to teenage mothers. The United States may not care about the children of the barrios, but it must start to address their problems now. If it lets them fail, there will be a great price to pay.

Not all immigrants are in such straits. Social scientists have taken to describing an "hourglass effect" in the distribution of income, education, and skills among recent immigrants because they are bunched at the extremes. At the top, an extraordinary two-thirds of all immigrants from India arrive with at least four years of college. Newcomers from Korea, the Philippines, China, and several other Asian nations also arrive with more education than the average native-born American. At the bottom of the hourglass are most of the Latino nationalities that have recently produced large inflows. Less than 8 percent of the immigrants from the Dominican Republic or El Salvador and less than 4 percent of the Mexicans have four years of college. Many Latino immigrants lack not only the credentials to prosper but also the minimum education necessary to survive in the U.S. economy. Less than a quarter of all Mexican immigrants have a high school degree.

The immigrants at the top—mostly Asians—generate a few policy controversies that generally fall under the heading "embarrassment of riches," such as when they contribute to a glut of medical specialists. A considerable number of Latino immigrants have achieved middle-class stability and are unlikely to cause much concern. However, the real social, political, and economic challenges arising from immigration today are posed by those at the bottom, and they are overwhelmingly Latinos. Again demography defines the challenge because the top and the bottom of the hourglass are not the same size. At the top, 760,000 Indian immigrants contribute exceptional skills. At the bottom, 6.7 million Mexicans represent extraordinary needs.

About a third of all recent Latino immigrants live below the official poverty line. More than a million and a half Mexicans who entered the country legally and illegally since 1980—43 percent of the total—were officially designated as poor in 1994. With little education and few skills, they have nowhere to start but low on the economic ladder, and in America today, people who start low tend to stay low and their children stay low as well unless they get an education. For two decades now, immigration has quietly added to the size of that perennially poor population and it has changed the nature of poverty in the United States. Twenty years ago there were nearly three times more poor African-Americans in this country than poor Latinos, but those numbers have been converging during the economic expansion of the 1990s with the African-American poverty figures trending down and the Latino numbers rising so that they are now nearly equal. However, they represent strikingly different forms of poverty. In 1996 the workforce participation rate for Latinos was higher than for blacks, indeed it was even higher than for whites, but Latinos also had the highest poverty rate of any group. Latinos suffer the poverty of the working poor. While that is not unusual in the immigrant experience, it marks a historic departure from the kind of poverty that has plagued American cities for the past several decades. William Julius Wilson, the Harvard sociologist who invented the concept of the underclass, argues that "the disappearance of work and the consequences of that disappearance for both social and cultural life are the central problems in the inner-city ghetto." That diagnosis from Wilson's 1996 book, *When Work Disappears,* applies to urban African-American communities, but not to the barrios. As Wilson himself notes, nearly a decade of detailed research in Chicago showed that poor Mexican immigrants can share the same kind of dilapidated neighborhoods as poor blacks, but the Mexicans will be surrounded by small businesses owned by fellow immigrants and will benefit from tightly knit social networks that help them find jobs.

Latino poverty will not be remedied by the welfare-to-work programs that are now virtually the sole focus of U.S. social policy, and it will not be fixed by trying to close the nation to further immigration. The Latino poor are here and they are not going to go away. Unless new avenues of upward mobility open up for Latino immigrants and their children, the size of America's underclass will quickly double and in the course of a generation it will double again. That second generation will be different than the first. It will not only suffer the economic and political disenfranchisement that plagues poor blacks today but it will also be cut off from the American mainstream in even more profound and dangerous ways.

·   ·   ·

"I call it the 'East L.A. short circuit,'" said Art Revueltas, "and the way it goes is that if you come to East L.A. from Mexico and you have kids, the clock is ticking on how long you've got to make it out. If you get stuck there, the kids don't make it through school. So they don't make it out. Then you get teenage parents, and their kids won't make it out, either. All of a sudden, you're talking about third-generation gang members."

Revueltas is the son of a Mexican immigrant who came to East Los Angeles, America's oldest and largest barrio, during World War II. About a quarter of the Latino families there live in poverty now and some of the street gangs do indeed trace their lineage back more than three generations. Revueltas and his family got out. He became the vice-principal of an intermediate school in Montebello, a Latino middle-class suburb of Los Angeles. With its pastel-colored bungalows set back on small lawns, Montebello is just the sort of place that many Latinos, native-born and immigrant alike, head for as soon as they have the money to leave the inner city.

Revueltas is deeply worried that an ever greater number of immigrants are getting short-circuited. He knows that the immigrants of his parents' generation established themselves in the 1950s and 1960s, when the industrial economy was still strong. His parents worked their way to blue-collar economic stability, which was plenty. "They developed enough equity to allow me to become vested in the system."

Getting that foothold was much easier just three decades ago. For the children of Revueltas's generation, it was a simpler, less dangerous time. State and local government poured money into public education as part of a deliberate strategy to build California's fortunes on the quality of its workforce. College attendance was not limited to the rich or academically minded. Instead, the state had a great "master plan" to make higher education broadly accessible. As a key element of that plan, the California State University system expanded rapidly to serve as an engine of upward mobility for people of modest means and for students of average abilities who desired a profession. The Cal State Los Angeles campus was built on an escarpment overlooking East L.A. and became a vital way station for thousands of smart and aggressive barrio kids like Revueltas who went up the hill to educate themselves, usually while working to pay their way. When they graduated, they emerged as fully credentialed candidates for the middle class.

Revueltas's parents labored with their hands, he went to college, and now his children have opportunities not just to participate in the system but also to prosper in it. That is the classic formula for successful immigration, and it is a formula that worked particularly well for those who came from Europe at the turn of the century. Simply put, it is supposed to take three generations to climb the ladder: The first generation works the low-wage entry-level jobs and lives in immigrant enclaves. The second generation moves up to blue-collar life and often makes it to the suburbs; they are hyphenated Americans, ethnically aware but thoroughly English-speaking. The third generation goes to college, enters the white-collar world, and carries the vestige of an ethnic identity, which is revived on holidays and family occasions. "Peddler, plumber, professional" was the plan.

As Revueltas's experience shows, the economic stepladder was available until recently. Many of the Mexican-Americans who moved from rural areas to cities in the 1950s and 1960s have done quite well. As with a portion of the black population that migrated north after World War II, those who became vested in the system before the 1980s moved up. These Mexican-Americans and their children are the core of the large Latino middle class that has been a key contributor to economic stability and growth in Southern California and parts of Texas and the Southwest.

Latino immigrants present more of a mixed picture than their native coethnics. Historically, immigrants start out earning less than native-born workers of a similar age and similar skills because the newcomer usually is facing a language barrier and lacks familiarity with the labor market, but over time that wage gap shrinks. The conventional benchmark is that immigrants who arrive when they are twenty-five or younger will close the gap and earn wages equivalent to those of a native worker after twenty years in the labor force. It is a long pull, but for many millions of people it has proved fruitful. Considerable evidence now shows that Latino immigrants, especially Mexicans, are not closing the gap. In the most extensive nationwide study of immigration's economic, fiscal, and demographic impacts on the United States, the National Research Council concluded in 1997 that Mexicans start out with the lowest wage levels of any immigrant nationality and that their wage gap actually widens substantially over time. Meanwhile, European and Asian immigrants are closing the wage gap at something like the traditional pace. A 1997 UCLA study found that Mexicans who had been in the United States for thirty years had achieved modest economic gains, while recent arrivals suffered actual declines in their earnings. Nearly three-quarters of the recent arrivals went to work in "low-skill occupations out of which there are few avenues of escape," writes the study's author, Vilma Ortiz, a UCLA sociologist. "Clearly, the traditional ethnic saga of hard labor followed by rewards does not apply to Latino immigrants."

The latest wave of immigrants has come to the United States only to find the ladder broken. Their arrival has coincided with changes in the structure of the U.S. economy that make the old three-generation formula obsolete. The middle rungs of the ladder, which allowed for a gradual transition into American life, are more precarious because so many jobs disappeared along with the industrial economy of smokestacks and assembly lines. In addition, the wages paid at the bottom of the labor force have declined in value steadily since the early 1980s.

The old blue-collar jobs are not the only rungs of the ladder that are now wobbly. The United States greatly expanded its system of public education in order to prepare the children and the grandchildren of the European immigrants for the workforce, extending it first to high schools and then to universities. Latino immigrants have arrived, only to find this education system dangerously in disrepair. As with the demise of the industrial economy, this reflects a fundamental change in the structure of American society. Government's priorities have shifted in ways that alter the nature of opportunity. The results have quickly become apparent. The State of California now pays better salaries to experienced prison guards than to tenured Cal State professors. The guards are more in demand. Labor unions, big-city political machines, and other institutions that helped the European immigrants are also less vigorous and far less interested in the immigrants' cause than in the early decades of this century. The Roman Catholic church gave vital help to the Europeans in establishing enclaves, gaining education, and developing ethnic solidarity, but it moved to the suburbs with the second and third generations and has played a minor institutional role—primarily as a lobbyist for liberal immigration policies—in helping the new Latinos gain a foothold in the United States.

Starting at the bottom has usually been an immigrant's fate, but

this takes on a new meaning in an increasingly immobile and stratified society. Skills and education have come to mark a great divide
in the U.S. workforce, and the gap is growing ever broader. The
entire population is being divided into a two-tier workforce, with a
college education as the price of admission to the upper tier. In the
new knowledge-based economy, people with knowledge prosper.
People without it remain poor. These divisions have the makings of
a new class system because this kind of economic status is virtually
hereditary. Very few Latino immigrants arrive with enough education to make it into the upper tier of the workforce. Their children,
like the children of all poor people, face the greatest economic pressures to drop out and find work. When they do stay in school, the
education they receive is, for the most part, poor.

Like Latinos today, the European ethnics built enclaves, and some
were places of exceptional misery and rejection. But the Europeans'
enclaves became places to make a gradual transition into American
life. As they built their communities, they could nurture ethnic
identity and cohesion until it evolved into a source of political
strength. The Europeans established their economic claims over
long periods of time, slowly moving into the mainstream as they
did so.

Blacks also built enclaves when they moved north, although their
separation was forced on them. A blue-collar class developed and in
another generation a middle class and a professional class of blacks
emerged. This upward mobility resulted from employment in the
industrial economy, antipoverty programs, and a concerted effort to
grant African-Americans at least minimal access to good schools
and universities. Even with these vehicles of upward mobility, it
took a long time to achieve limited success.

Today, Latinos do not have the luxury of time. Immigrants and
their children are no longer allowed missteps or setbacks. And there
are fewer programs to ensure that at least a few of the worthy move
up. Newcomers today either make it or they don't. Instead of a
gradual evolution, the process of finding a place in America has
become a sudden-death game.

The United States sits atop the Western Hemisphere like a
beacon atop a lighthouse, a sole source, powerfully distorting
everything it illuminates even as it points the way. For a hundred

years, it has exercised a powerful influence over Latin America, and whether the medium was the Marine Corps or the Peace Corps, the message has always been that Americans knew better, did better, lived better. Whenever the United States became scared of Nazis or Communists, it expended huge resources to portray itself as the paragon of civic virtue and a land of boundless economic opportunity. Meanwhile, the American consumer culture penetrated deep into the Latin psyche, informing every appetite and defining new desires. With TV shows, soldiers, and political ideals, the United States has reached out and touched people across an entire hemisphere. It has gotten back immigrants in return.

America beckons, but massive human flows occur only after migrant channels have evolved into highly efficient conduits for human aspirations. In Mexico's case, emigration to the United States developed out of proximity, shared history, and encouraging U.S. business practices and government policies. When the Mexican revolution displaced millions of peasants after 1910, railroad foremen greeted them at the border and recruited them into track gangs. Dispersed by the Southern Pacific and the Santa Fe railroads, they remained in hundreds of farm towns and built the first urban barrios. Aside from these permanent settlements, a kind of circular traffic developed. Many thousands of Mexicans came to the United States for sojourns of work often lasting no more than a harvesting season but sometimes stretching to years. This migration was expanded and legalized by an agricultural guest-worker program launched in 1942 to help with wartime labor shortages. American farmers liked the cheap, disposable labor so much that that program survived until 1964. By that time, 4.5 million *braceros,* as the workers were known, had learned the way north. The *bracero* program ended, but the traffic continued even as the United States started trying to control the flow. Many Mexicans had acquired some kind of legal status here, including those born in the United States to migrant-worker parents. Others came illegally and found shelter in such barrios as Magnolia and East L.A., which had become permanent Spanish-speaking enclaves. Major changes in U.S. immigration law enacted in 1965 raised the overall ceilings for legal immigration and removed biases that favored Northern and Western Europeans. The most important change in the long run, however, gave preference to immigrants who were reuniting with kin. Having a relative here became the key qualification for a visa, rather than a prospective employer or marketable skills, and immigrant flows became self-duplicating as every new legal immigrant eventually became a potential sponsor for others.

Saskia Sassen, a professor of urban planning at Columbia University, has defined two distinct stages in the history of a migration: the *beginning* of a new flow and its *continuation*. In *The Mobility of Labor and Capital,* a pioneering work on the global economy, Sassen argues that the beginning of a migration involves factors in both the sending and receiving countries that allow for "the formation of objective and subjective linkages . . . that make such migration feasible." Once migrant channels are established, Sassen believes, the continuation of the flow depends largely on the host country's demand for immigrant labor.

A long history of U.S. political and military intervention and of deep economic involvement established ties between the United States and Cuba, so that during the turmoil accompanying Fidel Castro's takeover in 1959, migration was not just feasible but natural and easy. Similar links facilitated a flow from the Dominican Republic when it underwent political upheavals in the 1960s. Although they arrived under very different circumstances, the early waves of Cubans and Dominicans prepared the ground for larger numbers of their countrymen who followed in later years.

The migrant channels from Latin America found their concrete manifestation in the barrios that began to develop in many U.S. cities in 1970s. These communities must be understood as both a cause and a result of immigration. Newcomers pour into the barrios because these communities make immigration accessible to a greater number of people by reducing the cost and difficulty of getting settled here. As the barrios grew larger and more permanent, new migrant channels evolved faster. By the 1980s, it took only a few years for robust flows to grow out of the political turmoil in Central America.

Once efficient linkages had developed, a variety of economic circumstances in the United States generated the demand for immigrant labor, which encouraged the continuation of migrant flows. Just as the rise of the industrial era created jobs for the great wave of European immigrants, the end of that era created opportunities for Latinos. Some manufacturers in old industries such as garments, furniture, and auto parts turned to low-cost immigrant labor as a way of remaining competitive with foreign producers. As the U.S. population shifted south to the Sun Belt, Latinos arrived to build the new cities. Immigrants filled hundreds of new job niches as the United States developed a postindustrial service economy that saw booms in light manufacturing and all manner of consumer and financial services.

In addition to economic demand, changes in U.S. immigration law have also promoted continued movement from Latin America. The Immigration Reform and Control Act of 1986 was meant to halt illegal immigration, but it actually encouraged its growth. It created amnesties that allowed nearly 3 million former illegal aliens—nearly 90 percent of them Latinos—to acquire legal residence and eventually become eligible for citizenship. They, in turn, have become hosts to about a million relatives, who have lived in the United States illegally while applying for legal status, and to uncounted others who have no claim on residency. The 1986 reform also imposed sanctions for the first time—mostly civil fines—on employers who hire illegal aliens. No mechanism was ever created to enforce the law, and so it eventually became a meaningless prohibition. Then in 1990, Congress raised the limits on several forms of legal immigration, thus ensuring a protracted influx.

Sassen's framework—beginning and continuation—does not take into account the sudden mass movements of people that characterize the history of emigration to the United States. The Irish, for example, came across the Atlantic as early as the seventeenth century and kept coming steadily for nearly two hundred years in response to demand for low-wage workers. This well-established linkage allowed for a massive, explosive migration during the potato famine in the middle of the nineteenth century and another huge wave in the 1880s during a period of rapid industrialization. Although the U.S. government now tries to regulate immigration, Mexico resembles the Irish case. As with the Irish in the nineteenth century, the migrant channels are abundant and efficient—there are large receiving communities here and the native-born descendants of immigrants have begun to penetrate the mainstream of American society. When Mexico suffered a devastating economic crisis in the 1980s and the U.S. economy boomed, the number of Mexican immigrants living in the United States doubled in a decade. That explosion continues so forcefully that the numbers might nearly double again in the 1990s. And the explosion does not involve just Mexicans now. The flows from the Dominican Republic and El Salvador are also running at a rate headed for a doubling by the end of decade.

Americans are only just waking up to the size of this immigrant wave, and yet the foreign-born already account for 9 percent of the total population—the highest proportion since World War II. For fifty years after the end of the European wave in the 1920s, there was no steady immigration, and then the long lull was followed by a demographic storm. Some 7 million more immigrants, counting the estimates of the illegal flow, came to the United States between 1975 and 1995 than during the preceding half-century hiatus. Now, like Rip van Winkle aroused from his slumber, the United States is trying to understand something that is at once familiar but changed. The nation's reference points for large-scale immigration are set in an era of steamships and telegraphs, yet the United States needs to manage a massive influx at a time of jet travel and global television. Moreover, the Latino immigration is not just unexpected and unfamiliar; many Americans consider it unwanted. No national policy debate and no clear process of decision making led to formal action opening the doors to a level of immigration unfamiliar in living memory.

When the counterreaction hit, it hit hard. In the early 1990s, an extraordinary variety of events combined to present immigration as a menacing force. It began quietly during the recession at the start of the decade and grabbed the public's attention with the nanny problems of Zoë Baird, President Clinton's first nominee for attorney general. Then came the World Trade Center bombing, perpetrated by evildoers who slipped through the immigration system. Chinese smuggling ships, Haitian boat people, Cuban rafters, and swarms of Tijuana border jumpers all fueled anxieties about a chaotic world infringing on America. Even though the United States remained more open to foreigners than any other nation, immigrants had come to represent mysterious and uncontrollable dangers.

Fears often reflect preexisting conditions in the mind of the victim, and fear of foreigners is no different. Immigrants served as emblems for perils that had already begun to gnaw away at this country's sense of confidence. The seemingly unregulated flow of people struck many Americans as another irrational product of feckless Washington. The immigrants themselves were seen as unworthy beneficiaries of American largesse, arriving unbidden to take advantage of jobs, welfare programs, and much else. Because they are nonwhite and because Hispanic civil rights groups had pushed relentlessly for more open admissions, Latino immigrants also became associated in the minds of some whites with the era of minority-group activism and fears of "reverse discrimination." The ease with which illegal aliens flaunted border controls haunted those who believed that the United States exists in a world full of unworthy but vexing adversaries.

The most virulent expressions of the backlash emerged, not surprisingly, from Southern California, where the economic downturn of the early 1990s was most severe and where immigration was most intense. But every national poll showed that immigration caused widespread if not well-articulated anxieties. Voters indicated they wanted something done, although they were not sure what. An election-year Congress responded in 1996 with measures to keep legal immigrants off welfare and to begin a massive buildup of the Border Patrol. Then, as the economy improved and demand for labor remained high, the rhetoric cooled. The underlying causes of anti-immigrant anxieties have not changed; rather, they have been building. If the U.S. economy sours, or if a crisis in Mexico, Cuba, or Central America produces a highly visible surge of migrants, the backlash will return with even greater fury. Then, Americans are likely to demand strict limits on both legal and illegal immigration and they will hold their leaders to account for failing to develop such controls when the flow was smaller and more manageable.

Devising effective immigration control is an important challenge because without a credible immigration policy the American people are unlikely to make the kind of effort necessary to ensure the successful integration of Latino immigrants and their children. Illegal immigration and high drop-out rates in barrio schools may seem like unrelated problems, but in fact it will be difficult to muster the political will and the resources necessary to deal with the looming crisis in the barrios without first gaining control of the borders. Over the next few decades, despite efforts to close the nation's doors, immigrants will continue to come and, along with the millions already here, many will form a new class of outsiders. No one knows where these new people are supposed to fit into American society, and yet their story has become an American one.

. . .

The aim here is to explore what has happened to Latinos now that they have been in the United States for several decades, and to look toward the future. It is important to describe some of the significant shapes and patterns that have emerged from this vast and varied demographic event, and to tell the stories of several different barrios—the Puerto Ricans in East Harlem who are U.S. citizens by birth but acted as harbingers for the rest of Latino immigration; the Cubans in Miami who erected the ultimate enclave; the Dominicans in Washington Heights who loved transience too much; and the newest Mexican and Central American arrivals in Los Angeles. Each depicts an aspect of how Latinos define their niches in an American city. It is important as well to focus on events in the first half of the 1990s, because this period marked a turning point—the time when Latinos began to realize the full price of their trip north and when the nation fully awoke to their presence.

Latinos are a people in motion. Coming from many different places, they are headed in many different directions, and it is the recent immigrants who travel the farthest and the fastest. America was changing when they got here, and they became part of that change. The new Latino immigration is the story of people struggling to adapt to an economy undergoing a prolonged and profound transformation. It is the story of communities trying to find their place in a society suffering confusion and conflict. Now, because of their energy and their numbers, Latino immigrants are helping determine where an era of change will take the nation.

Latinos are rapidly becoming the nation's largest minority group at a time when that term is quickly losing its meaning. Latino immigration can prompt the creation of a new civil rights framework that distinguishes between two distinct tasks—redressing the effects of past discrimination and providing protection against new forms of bias—and undertakes both tasks aggressively.

Latinos are also rapidly adding to the ranks of the working poor at a time when the nation is redefining the role of its lower classes. The divisions between rich and poor, between the knowledgeable and the unskilled, grow greater even as a broad political consensus favors reducing services and benefits for the poor. Understanding recent Latino immigrants, however, involves appreciating a very distinct kind of poverty. The ambition and optimism of the Latino poor could sour in the future, especially if the second generation gets nowhere, but in the meantime Latino immigration offers this country a chance to revise its attitudes toward the poor. Understanding the poverty of hard work will carry Americans beyond the common misperception that the poor are no more than an unsightly appendage to an affluent society. Instead they will be viewed as an integral part of the larger whole, one that must have opportunities to escape poverty in order for the whole to prosper.

These changes can occur, however, only if Latinos alter some attitudes of their own. Long-term residents of the barrios—natives and immigrants alike—must realize that they, more than anyone else, suffer the ill-effects of illegal immigration and that it is in their self-interest to turn illegals away from their communities. Latinos must also take a new approach to language. Instead of preserving Spanish as a way to redress past grievances with the education system, English-language training should be pursued as a means of securing a successful future in a new land.

Finally, Latino immigration will cause the United States to rethink the connection between the issues of race and poverty. For too long, the two have been linked in an easy but false equation that renders the problems of the poor as the problems of African-Americans and vice versa. This constitutes a form of prejudice and, like all prejudice, it is blinding. The arrival of Latino immigrants tangibly breaks the connection.

Addressing these challenges will require a cohesion and purposefulness that the United States has sorely missed for many years. By their numbers alone, the Latinos will require the country to find a place for them. Along the way, there is a chance that America might find itself again.

In the meantime, they will keep coming.

❖•❖•❖•❖•❖•❖•❖•❖•❖•❖•❖•❖•❖•❖•❖•❖•❖•

CHAPTER 2

Looking North

❖•❖•❖•❖•❖•❖•❖•❖•❖• At 10:30 p.m. on the night of August 18, 1994, Attorney General Janet Reno strode into the White House press room and in her practiced monotone announced new measures to halt the thousands of Cubans who were launching themselves into the Florida Straits aboard flimsy rafts every day that summer. The television pictures of navy ships rescuing water-weary hordes excited fears among many Americans that the United States no longer exercised the sovereign right to determine who could enter the country. As the number of rafters grew, so did the public's anxiety. Rather than be labeled a weakling on immigration, Clinton sent Reno before the cameras to declare that henceforth Cuban rafters picked up at sea would be detained at the Guantánamo Bay naval base until they could be sent home. Once regarded as the heroic victims of Fidel Castro's tyranny, the Cubans were now to be treated as just so many illegal aliens. Instead of receiving a generous welcome, they would end up behind barbed wire. This was more than an emergency plan. Unceremoniously and in the dark of night, Reno had reversed long-standing policies that embraced and celebrated people who risked their lives to escape communism. If Cubans could be shut out, then anyone could be rejected. The United States was closing its doors, and most Americans applauded.

Almost forty-eight hours later, on a beach about fifteen miles west of Havana, six men and two women, all in their late twenties or early thirties, carried a raft down to the water in the dark. White House pronouncements did not matter to them. They were committed to their journey.

They set the craft down on the sand and began their good-byes to several relatives and friends. The raft was made of three truck-tire inner tubes sandwiched between two thin pieces of plywood. By the light of a match, a man with a thick beard inspected the purple plastic cords that held it all together.

It was a ridiculous vessel, but thousands of people were setting out those days in similar craft. Some people washed back up on the beach, sunburned, exhausted, and vomiting. Sometimes rafts washed up empty. These travelers were not people of the sea. They readily admitted they knew nothing of currents and winds, but that did not matter to them, either.

The bearded man pulled the purple cords and nodded, satisfied. The raft was ready. He could care less about the U.S. flotilla and the new policies designed to halt his voyage north. Pointing his arm out to sea, he said in Spanish with loud bravado, "Florida is there and Florida is where we are going. The Americans will not keep us away."

For a moment, the bearded man stared to the north as if there was something to see other than the blackness. He knew what was there. He knew what he wanted to see: the lights of Miami glowing like the dawn. He had heard from friends and relatives who had gone before him about what lay across the water. He had seen the medicine, the T-shirts, and the bottles of shampoo that people sent back from that place. He had seen pictures of the food and the houses and the cars. Although the lure of the north was clear, the man on the beach was not happy to leave the island of flowering red jacarandas and ancient ceiba trees. Like all the other travelers that night, he was being pushed out by a life that had become intolerable in too many ways. As much as he desired his destination, the only certainty was his need to leave the one place he had ever known.

According to the inscription on the Statue of Liberty, immigrants are the "tired . . . poor . . . huddled masses yearning to breathe free, the wretched refuse of your teeming shore . . . the homeless, tempest-tossed." Unfortunately, those words did not apply when Emma Lazarus wrote them in 1883, and they are even less accurate today. The tempest-tossed were, and still are, just that. They are at the mercy of forces beyond their control. That describes most people. It is the others, the ones battling the storms, who end up taking trips. Over the centuries, immigration has reflected a continuity in human behavior, but it has always been an exception to the rule. Most people look around, see defeated expectations, and adjust. A few decide to move, undaunted by the tempests.

The bearded man would have preferred to stay in Cuba if it could be the place he wanted it to be. Like the others preparing to leave that night, he was an anxious but unwilling traveler. He buried the pain of departure and embraced the uncertain journey.

All along the Cuban coast that night, people waded into the sea. In Mexican mountain villages and city apartment buildings, in Guatemala and Colombia, all across the hemisphere, there were thousands of travelers that night, all heading north. Motives blurred with the motion.

Politics forced them to go. Their pocketbooks drove them. They had family and friends in the United States who pulled at them. They sought the freedom that comes with movement. They desired the liberating moment of reinvention. They also knew the anxious desire of wanting to join in something that thousands of others had already enjoyed. All that overwhelmed the pain of leaving.

The bearded man's wife, dressed in shorts and a short-sleeved polka-dot shirt, sat on the raft and did not take part in the exultant farewells. Her hands were shaking when she tried to light a cigarette. Her husband had to take the matches and help her.

"Don't worry. By dawn, we will be out with the Americans and they will find us," he said, but the woman kept shaking. Overhead, a full moon cast pale light through gauzy clouds. The wind was warm and moist and steady. In the distance, a squall lit the sky with lightning.

The woman held herself and shivered, even though it was not the least bit cold. Asked why she was leaving if she was so afraid, she said, "If I was not meant to die tonight, I won't. Death on land, death on sea—it's the same. I must go."

The dream of bright lights draws people north. Their homelands push them out. The bold set out on journeys, as they always have before. Laws and barbed wire do not deter the most determined. Not even the danger of death stops the boldest.

The woman and her husband and the other travelers climbed onto the raft, and several of their companions waded into the water to help them push off. The men started rowing. Beyond them, there was nothing but darkness and the sound of waves.

❖•❖•❖•❖•❖•❖•❖•❖•❖•❖•❖•❖•❖•❖•❖•❖•

CHAPTER 3

From One Man,
a Channel

❖•❖•❖•❖•❖•❖•❖•❖•❖• One morning in September 1978, Juan L. Chanax set out alone from the Guatemalan highlands of Totonicapán on a voyage of unimaginable consequences. A weaver's son and a good weaver himself, Juan made one of the few decisions allowed to ordinary men that has the power to change nations. He decided to move.

Juan and his people have lived in the valleys and hillsides of Totonicapán for more than two thousand years. They created Mayan civilization, saw it disappear, and abided the turmoil of modern Guatemala, escaping relatively untouched from the political violence that visited grief on other Mayan communities at various times in the twentieth century. They raised grains in terraced fields. The most adventurous made trips to southern Mexico or El Salvador to sell weavings.

By the time Juan was a young man, there was talk in Totonicapán of people who had gone to the United States and found jobs that paid a lot of money, but Juan never met anyone who had actually made the trip. In 1978, he decided to go north, traveling alone. He ended up in Houston, mopping a supermarket floor. He was not alone for long. His hometown, San Cristóbal, and the villages that surround it had a population of about four thousand people when he left. Within fifteen years, some two thousand of them had joined him in Texas.

"First my relatives came," said Juan, "and then my friends came, and then the friends of my relatives and then the relatives of my friends and then the friends of my friends' relatives came. And now those who remained in Totonicapán are sending their children."

He described the chain of immigration with no irony or pride. With a broad, flat face, huge eyes, and a soft, high-pitched voice, Juan always seemed earnest. He could have been reading a phone book or reciting a biblical genealogy. Juan was the first to move, but all it took was one man to establish a link between two worlds. Over time, his haphazard trail north has become a deep, broad channel that carries human traffic steadily in both directions. People come north to work, to visit, to stay. People go south to rest, to open businesses, to retire. After spending more than a thousand years in the Sierra de Totonicapán, fixed and immobile, the Maya of San Cristóbal no longer have a permanent address. They travel the channel comfortably, because at one end they have the mountain towns and villages that sustained them for centuries, and at the other end lies a Mayan immigrant society etched into Houston's urban landscape. The link between them has changed both Houston and Totonicapán, and the travel has changed the people, as well.

When Maya from San Cristóbal arrived in Houston, Juan helped them find work with Randall's, the supermarket chain where he was employed. At the beginning, blacks and Mexican-Americans did most of the janitorial work, but Randall's was expanding rapidly when Juan's people came to Houston. The Maya helped one another capture the new jobs, until about one thousand of them cleaned floors in more than thirty Randall's stores. At those supermarkets, doing maintenance became a Mayan job. Others need not apply.

Floralinda, Juan's wife, began working as a maid and baby-sitter as soon as she joined him in Houston two years after he first arrived. Most of the other Mayan women did the same. They arrived during an epochal change in the U.S. labor market as middle-class American women streamed into the workforce. The short, dark women of San Cristóbal helped raise an entire generation of blond, blue-eyed youngsters, shaping their tastes in food, teaching them a bit of Spanish, and changing the norms of suburban child rearing. The Mayan women changed, too. "Back in San Cristóbal, women work, but only within the family, never outside, never for money," said Floralinda. "Here my life has been very different. I go out every day and I get paid for what I do and I have money in my pocket. For me, this is normal now, just like it is normal for the American women to work."

The Maya of San Cristóbal are devout evangelical Christians who strictly abstain from liquor. They did not like Magnolia and the other old barrios in Houston, which are overwhelmingly Catholic, Mexican, and notoriously rowdy, with their dance halls and numerous cantinas. So the Maya headed for the suburbs, which is where the new jobs were opening up anyway. Out amid the freeways and strip malls, a cluster of faux Georgian low-rise apartment houses became a Mayan village of sorts. The Maya found a welcoming church, filled the pews, and eventually hired their own minister. As their numbers grew, they claimed two more churches. After services on Sundays, they gathered in a nearby park. The men played soccer while the women sat under the trees in tight clusters. Eventually, Juan and his friends organized a team they called San Cristóbal, after their hometown, and began playing against teams put together by other recently arrived Central American immigrants. Ultimately, they formed a league that grew to twenty-six teams, with Juan serving as president for many years. Like many other immigrant groups, the Houston Maya staked out their own territory, defining a space for themselves and erecting their own landmarks in the sprawl.

The landscape also changed back in Totonicapán. Big new houses appeared in San Cristóbal and the hillsides around it as the Houston Maya built homes intended for vacations and eventual retirement. Meanwhile, many of the old adobe houses began to look like miniature Kmarts. Cabinets sagged under the tape recorders, food processors, hair dryers, and other booty brought back from Texas as gifts to those who had remained behind.

Every July for many years, the Maya of Totonicapán have cele-

brated a weeklong fiesta in the narrow streets of San Cristóbal. And
every year, dozens, sometimes hundreds, of the Houston expatriates
have made a point of coming home on vacation at that time of year.
These return trips have become ritualized, a part of the fiesta itself,
and the migration north is commemorated along with the harvests,
the old saints, and timely weather. On the last day of the fiesta,
the entire town gathers to watch a soccer game between a team of
Houston Maya and the hometown all-stars. And each year when the
festivities end, the channel between Texas and Totonicapán has
become busier and more efficient.

"When we go back, people see that our clothes are a little bit
nicer than theirs, that we bring back as presents things that would
be difficult to buy there," Juan said. "They see these things and ask
about life here, and even if you tell them it's hard, they see these
things and they want to come. From there to here is not such a long
trip anymore."

Migration carries risks, of course: the costs of travel, the dangers
of the unknown, fear of failure, the loss of income while looking
for a new job in a new land, and the simple separation from loved
ones. At both ends of the migration channel, kinfolk and hometown
friends can greatly minimize those risks by providing loans, safe
havens, and information. These family networks function as the
brokerage houses of migration. They raise capital, vouchsafe the
investment's legitimacy, and, when it produces a profit, they dis-
tribute dividends in the form of remittances sent home by the
migrant. Not surprisingly, surveys of Mexican communities with
well-established immigration channels show that upward of 90 percent of the people considering a trip north say they are aiming for
destinations in the United States where relatives are already living.
Almost everyone leaving San Cristóbal landed at the home of a relative who could provide room and board for a while. Instead of
struggling alone to learn the ropes in an alien city, newly arrived
Maya were surrounded by compatriots who showed them how to
get around town, where to find work, and how to begin unraveling
the mysteries of American society.

When the human flow through such a channel acquires a certain
momentum, it seems, like a siphon, to defy the laws of nature, or the
laws of the marketplace, lifting people up and over barriers, carrying them into jobs even when unemployment is high. These chan-

nels have also allowed millions of Latino immigrants to defy the laws of the United States by entering the country illegally and working here without proper authorization.

Crossing the Rio Grande was a frightful adventure for Juan the first time, but it soon became a routine voyage for the thousands who followed from San Cristóbal, because they departed knowing exactly where to go on the border, which smugglers to employ for the crossing, and what transportation would carry them most safely to Houston. Juan remembers a scare going through Houston's Latino community in 1986 when Congress enacted sanctions against the employers of illegal immigrants. Even before the law was fully spelled out, the Maya decided they should prepare themselves for whatever was coming, and as usual, they mastered the challenge by working together.

"I saw a Mexican I knew one day and asked him about buying *papeles chuecos* [counterfeit papers], and he told me the price and showed me a sample. That night, several of us met to talk about it, and the next day I told the Mexican I would buy the papers. He thought they were only for me. When I told him we would start by buying twenty Social Security cards and twenty driver's licenses, he almost fell down."

As it turned out, most of the Maya did not need the phony documents because they qualified for the amnesties enacted along with employer sanctions. What had begun as a substantially illegal flow matured into a highly efficient mix of legal and illegal. Among the Houston Maya, and in many other Latino communities, the typical household now includes at least one or two people who are legal immigrants or naturalized U.S. citizens and can sign leases and conduct all other dealings with official bodies. Usually, there are also children who are native-born U.S. citizens and thus entitled to welfare and other government programs. All this makes life much easier for those who are either illegal (usually the most recently arrived) or in various stages of becoming legal. Moreover, the base population of legal immigrants and U.S. citizens provides a means for others to obtain legal status, because U.S. immigration law puts a priority on family visas.

Over time, the net flow of people outward is matched by a steady flow of money coming back from the United States. Both kinds of traffic are necessary to keep the circuit alive. Remittances are more than just a family tithe sent back to the home country as an act of charity or as a means of assuaging guilt among those who bailed out and moved off. The sheer volume of money suggests that more is at stake. By 1992, immigrant remittances worldwide constituted an international monetary flow second in size only to the oil trade, according to World Bank calculations. The money sent home by Mexican workers in the United States totaled between $2.5 and $3.9 billion in 1995, according to estimates by a team of U.S. and Mexican scholars. At those levels, remittances equal about half the value of all foreign direct investment in the country. These remarkable sums offer tangible evidence that an immigration channel forms a bond between sending and receiving communities rather than just a mode of transportation carrying people primarily in one direction. And it is this connection between a person's old home and his new one, between past and future, that gives meaning to the migrant's voyage.

"I remember at first when I was here alone working, it felt very good to get paid, but it felt even better when I went to Western Union to send money home," Juan said. "Then I could say to myself, 'I have done something.'"

The size and importance of remittance flows is an enduring characteristic of immigration. During the second half of the nineteenth century, annual remittances from Irish immigrants in the United States occasionally exceeded $8 million. Considering those sums, the historian Patrick J. Blessing concluded, "large-scale Irish peasant movement to the New World, therefore, was not a mindless flight from intolerable conditions, but, within the limited range of alternatives, a deliberate departure of generally literate individuals who were very much concerned with the survival and well-being of family and friends remaining at home." Typically, individual remittances were largest soon after people emigrated, and if they remained abroad, the money dropped off as they became more preoccupied with new lives. Then families often sent off another emigrant to make up for the loss, and the more experienced voyager acted as host to ensure the newcomer's success.

The same model applies to the Houston Maya and other Latino immigrants. Theirs is not a mindless flight, and they, too, are always looking back to the home country. If anything, the links are stronger today because distances are shorter and the transportation is easier than it was for the Irish and other Europeans. And, as before, there are selfish interests in the migrant's connection to home. The story of Juan and the Houston Maya shows that emigration is not a means of breaking bonds to family and home country but, rather, of transforming them. Juan found satisfaction in going back and forth between two places and using the north to solve the problems of the south. In transforming his relationship to his past, he invented his future.

I first met Juan on a balmy spring evening and soon realized that there are several different ways to measure the distances that an immigrant travels. I was out with Nestor Rodríguez, a friend and valued interlocutor who is a sociologist at the University of Houston. He has been studying the Maya to understand how recent Latino immigrants are breaking well-established patterns, creating new kinds of barrios, taking new kinds of jobs. In a city where the word *Latino* always used to mean Mexican and blue collar, Nestor's was among the first important voices calling attention to the changes occurring in the 1980s. Unlike many academics who write about Latinos purely on the basis of survey data or census counts, Nestor actually got to know his subjects firsthand. He spent so much time with the Maya that he became a kind of unofficial adviser when they set up their soccer league, helping negotiate the use of playing fields with the parks department. One Saturday night, I accompanied Nestor to the league's weekly business meeting.

We drove into the heart of the suburban Central American barrio, past apartment complexes with names like Pelican Pointe, Maple Tree Gardens, and Napoleon Square. Down a side street we reached one that seemed a little more dilapidated than the rest. A sign painted on a sheet of plywood announced that it was called Las Américas, just in case anyone forgot that there was more than one America and that several could coexist in the same place. On a warm evening, apartment doors were open on the exterior hallways of the two-story buildings and adults mingled on the breezeways that overlooked parking lots. Teenagers clustered around cars with booming sound systems, and children played on the sidewalks and the staircases. The architecture was halfhearted faux New Orleans. The ambience resembled the dingiest quarters of that city in ways the builders of Las Américas could never have imagined when it

was new and still had a town-and-country name and rented out to
secretaries and salesmen.

This part of southwest Houston, known generally as Gulfton,
was built up during the 1970s oil boom as a giant dormitory and
playground for young, single office workers. In an area of a little
more than three square miles, there were 90 apartment complexes
with 19,000 units but only 300 detached houses—plenty of bars
and discos but hardly any schools or green spaces. Dozens of the
developments, built by speculators and financed by savings and
loans, crashed along with the oil prices in the 1980s. The yuppie
tenants departed for more prosperous climes. Banks and federal
agencies got stuck with the apartments, but these institutions
proved to be grimly disinterested landlords. They simply lowered
the rents until they found a new clientele. The Central Americans
paid enough to service the loans while bailouts were arranged for
the financier, but the rent did not pay for much maintenance. The
buildings fell apart; the neighborhood duly rotted. By 1990, some
40,000 people inhabited Gulfton, about two-thirds of them Latinos,
mostly immigrants of the 1980s, and among them were more than
11,000 young people with nowhere to go but the streets. Cops and
social workers call it the "Gulfton Gang Factory."

On the Saturday night that Nestor and I went to Las Américas,
there seemed to be noises coming from every direction. A conversation leapt from one iron railing to another. A TV show leaked from a
window. Spanish rap erupted from a boom box; salsa came out of a
car radio. Scattered around the parking lot were a couple of cars and
a pickup truck either being loaded or unloaded with stacks of
cheap suitcases and cardboard boxes. San Salvador, where there is a
big neighborhood called Las Américas, might just as well have been
a few exits down the interstate given all the people who were coming and going.

We walked beyond the main cluster of buildings, back past a
pool drained of water for so long that the pale blue concrete was full
of cracks, as if it were parched mud. There was a small building to
one side that was shedding chunks of stucco. Up on the second
floor, the officers of the soccer league met in an activity room half-
filled with discarded furniture. Over to one side, Juan sat behind a
long folding table. Bright neon lights overhead cast a glow on his
high forehead and accentuated the chiseled flare of his nostrils.
Slowly gesturing with his small hands, Juan patiently explained to

a pair of team managers how they should fill out some forms. They were Salvadorans, men of average height, light-skinned, with curly dark hair. They would certainly call themselves *blancos* (whites), if asked, even though they were probably of a little mixed blood.

Juan, a copper-skinned Maya, sat. The whites stood. That would not have happened in Guatemala. He held pieces of paper in his hand, read from them, and instructed others what to do with them. The Indian spoke. The whites listened. It was a role reversal that revolutionaries and liberation philosophers could only dream about, and it was happening in Las Américas, Houston, Texas. Five centuries after Europeans crossed the Atlantic to claim this hemisphere as their own, an Indian made the rules and whites listened. When Juan finished, he handed the white men his business card, which identified him as the league president.

These things marked the length of Juan's trip far more than the mileage between Totonicapán and Houston. By moving north, Juan did not simply escape a system of caste and class as old as the Spanish conquest. Rather, he brought it with him. And here, on new, more favorable terrain, he surmounted barriers that seem permanent and irreducible in Totonicapán. For Juan and millions of others who have come north in the Latino migration, the United States has been the place to accomplish goals defined in terms of what they meant back home.

After that first encounter, I spent many afternoons and evenings over the next year talking with Juan in his living room. When his wife, Floralinda, was home, she would bring us fruit drinks and sometimes pause to listen, but only rarely did she enter the conversation. Juan never stopped addressing me with the formal pronoun, *usted,* and so I never used the familiar form with him. He was comfortable with silences and spoke only in response to questions. But he willingly looked back at his life and told me what he remembered. After much listening I realized he was disposed to speak of his voyage because he was trying to decide for himself how far he had come.

The trip north to Houston was not Juan's first move. Like so many other migrants from so many other places, Juan's initial move covered much more distance in his psyche than it did on the ground.

"My life was very different from most people's in ways that

always obliged me to open paths. My father died when I was three years of age and my mother left me with my grandparents to go to the capital. She sent me clothes for every holiday, but I did not actually see her again until I was fourteen. I was very alone and I had to dress myself and work from a very young age, and that made me harder and more mature. It prepared me to open paths."

By the time he had reached his early twenties, Juan had a pair of hand looms and some small plots of land that together produced a fair living for him and his family. Then an American corporation opened a factory in the town of Quezaltenango, about ten miles from San Cristóbal. It was a plant employing some three hundred people who assembled and stitched sweaters. One of Juan's uncles went to work there. He told Juan that someone good at handling yarn could make more than the men who worked hard all day outside, fixing roads, building houses, or doing other work for wages.

The factory in Quezaltenango became a meeting place for technologies, capital, raw materials, and design ideas from many different countries. On the work floor, the Maya applied their traditional skills, willingly working for wages that would never be accepted in the United States or Western Europe. The sweaters produced there were shipped back north for sale. It was a glancing blow with another world that would change the mountains forever. The factory had left the United States for the Mayan highlands in search of cheap labor. Like a returning echo, the Maya went from the highlands to Houston in search of better jobs.

"When there is nothing very new around you," said Juan, "it is easy to fear everything that is new. But after the first time you go into a place you have never been before, you begin to lose that fear. Going with my uncle to the factory in Quezaltenango was like that for me."

Juan lost fear of the unknown, and he gained information. He learned how to leave his home to find a job and how to work with others as part of an enterprise. He learned about steady income. At the end of every day, he knew exactly how much he had earned and did not have to worry about the rain, the price of corn, or the cost of yarn. Almost everything at the factory was predictable and regular, which was never the case for Juan as a farmer or a weaver.

Juan also learned about the United States. He had seen American tourists when he went to the old cities of Guatemala to sell his weavings. He had seen pictures of astronauts and big buildings. Images of affluence and order had been laid one upon another, but they had always belonged to a place that was remote and inaccessible. Then at the factory, he heard men talk about people who had gone north, ordinary people like himself, some of whom had become rich doing a poor man's work.

"When I told my in-laws and my mother about what I had heard, they imagined things for themselves very negatively. They said, 'All you will eat there will come out of metal cans and the only job they will give you is sweeping trash.' But I understood already that I was the kind of person who had to learn the truth of things for myself."

About this time, Juan's eldest child, Marco, became sick, and although the diagnosis was indefinite, it pointed to leukemia. Bills for doctors, laboratory exams, and medicine amounted to a financial threat very quickly, and Juan remembered the tempting stories he had heard about the United States. He decided to go, and in the mythology of the Houston Maya, their migration began because Juan needed to buy medicine for Marco.

Illness was as much a part of the Mayan landscape as the steep volcanic hills. Death from illness was something that had always been accepted. Deciding not to accept the unfortunate and the inevitable involved much more than a financial calculus to go live in a land of higher wages.

"It was a sad moment, a hard moment, when I spoke to my wife about what I was thinking of doing," said Juan. "She asked if I had really thought about it seriously and she reminded me that I had never even been as far from home as the border of Guatemala and Mexico, and that it would be a long way to the United States, and that it would be a foreign country. But I told her I was thinking two things. First, I didn't want to fight anymore with this problem of my son's medicine, and to fulfill my obligation to my son, I had to go north to where there was money. Second, I had to do something more with my life than was possible there at home. If I was going to be something different and solve this problem with my boy, I told her, I was going to have to leave the country. Nothing was going to happen if I remained. I told her that if I left, even for just a while, I could try to *sobresalir;* I could try to *superarme.*"

Juan often used those same two words when talking about why he migrated. *Sobresalir* means "to excel; to surpass," and *superarme* means "to improve myself; to surpass myself." They are bold words for anyone who is poor in Latin America, especially anyone who is a full-blooded Indian and whose first language is not Spanish. Juan's unspoken goal was to overcome a social system that sets insuperable barriers in front of people. It is a culture of injustice that has survived political upheavals and economic transformations and that has achieved a hard permanence in Guatemala and in most of Latin America.

When Juan decided to move, there was only one possible destination. The United States broadcasts the ideal of opportunity to Latin America today just as it did to Europe at the turn of the century. This ideal is not simply the Horatio Alger one—virtue and hard work will be rewarded—that native-born Americans hold dear. Instead, ever since Thomas Paine's day, the United States has offered foreigners the opportunity to circumvent social and economic systems that block individual mobility in their homelands.

"I am not ashamed of who I am or of my ancestry, but it is a fact that people come to the United States because those things are less important here," says Juan. "There in San Cristóbal everybody knows everyone else and you cannot hide who you are and you cannot change it. Here, no one knows what family you came from and nobody cares. Here, you can be all new or at least make yourself think you are all new."

By coming to Houston, Juan accomplished something that would have been impossible if he had remained in Totonicapán, but his accomplishment became tangible only when he traveled the channel in reverse and went back home for visits.

"Before, the rich people were the only ones who had nice houses and drove around in cars, and they were very few and very respected. When I went back with a Bronco one summer, no one there had ever had a car like that before. People looked at it and could see that we who were once at a lower level had now come to a higher level. Now all the people who go back from Houston can go around town and know that there is no one superior to them. Now it is us from Houston who are building nice houses and driving big cars."

When Juan spoke of what he had accomplished, he sat on a brown plaid couch in a living room with a vaulted ceiling, fireplace, overhead fan, and entertainment center, and told of overturning a social order five hundred years old from the vantage point of his ranch-style house in a subdivision called Pheasant Run. Juan was no guerrilla fighter or leftist ideologue. He was not driven by a need to attack the system that keeps most Maya poor in Guatemala. Others took up arms in the Mayan highlands and fought Central America's longest, bloodiest civil war. Juan migrated instead, yet his act was no less revolutionary. The difference is that Juan succeeded.

"On the day before I left home, my son was sick, and I had nothing to help him with," Juan continued. "In the afternoon, I told my wife what I had decided, and I asked her to pack this small valise I had in the closet. I told her to pack it with two pairs of pants and two pairs of underwear and a shirt, because I was going to the United States."

That evening, Juan informed his wife's parents that he would be leaving on a bus that departed San Cristóbal at 5:00 a.m. His father-in-law offered to wake him and when he went to Juan's room in the early hours, the older man was crying. Then his brother-in-law came, too, and he also began to cry. They walked in the dark together to the bus station.

"I told them I had no alternative," said Juan. "With little land and little education and little money, I had no chance to *sobresalir* there at home. But the United States was a place where people could work and make their own lives."

He left before dawn, was robbed along the way, and had adventures on the Rio Grande, where the Border Patrol nabbed him a couple of times before he made it through. When he had finished telling the story of that first trip north, I asked Juan whether he had ever worried that in a big, complex country like United States his lack of education and other resources could be more of a handicap than they had been in Guatemala.

"I never thought about it that way," he replied. "Yes, it is a contradiction. It should have been harder for me here than it was in San Cristóbal, but that is not the way it turned out and that's not the way I saw it when I got started." Juan was quiet for a few moments. Then he said, "When you see problems every day, they look very large and you stop in front of them. When you don't know what lies ahead, you walk on because you have hopes."

The sense of the unknown, the unexplored frontier, has always contributed to America's liberating powers. Voyagers like Juan are drawn by the very newness of it all. But as I listened to Juan describe how he and the other Maya made their lives in Houston, I began to see the flip side of this allure. Immigrants are attractive to Americans because as newcomers they seem unsullied by familiar conflicts, especially the conflict between native-born blacks and whites. That apparent freshness helps explain why Latino immigrants prove so appealing to some Americans, who see them as the embodiment of old virtues such as strong families and hard work. Immigrants can be a forever-expanding frontier that defines a re-invented America.

The story of how Juan and the Maya found a place in America and how they came to fill a need here has been told and retold by Juan and his compatriots, and for them it has become the creation myth of the Houston Maya.

According to the legend, Juan left home with no more of a destination than a Houston phone number. He had been told it belonged to two sisters from San Cristóbal who had left town many years earlier and had worked as maids in Guatemala City, where they had been employed by a rich American family who eventually took them to Houston. Neither Juan nor anyone in his family had ever met these women, but he believed they would have heard of his father or grandfather and know them to be good men.

Juan found the women, and they helped him get settled. Eventually, they put him in touch with another Guatemalan, a man who had also lived in the United States for several years and who worked at a supermarket, part of the locally owned Randall's chain. He was not a Maya or particularly friendly, but when Juan went to see him, the man said there was a job opening at his store.

"It was just one of those things of life," said Juan. "Some *morenos* had been working maintenance at the Randall's, and the manager went to them to complain that they were not working hard enough. The *morenos* got angry and debated it, to the point that they wanted to fight with the manager, and then one of them took his mop out of his bucket and threw it at the manager's face, and then the *morenos* took off their aprons and walked away. Soon after this happened, the manager asked the Guatemalan if he knew anyone who could do the work, and I just happened to be around."

At the beginning, Juan worked on a maintenance crew that began its shift before dawn, and then he worked on through another shift, sacking groceries and loading them into cars. His salary was little more than three dollars an hour.

"Maintenance, I have always said, is a matter of being very patient, so that when you clean, you clean everything. With sacking, you can be clever about how you pack the food to get more in the bag and do it quickly, but the most important thing with sacking is that you must treat people in the correct way. That's what makes the difference between the workers who make good tips and those who don't."

Juan sent as much as one hundred dollars a week back to Totonicapán, which was twice as much as most people earned there. The money paid to have the house repainted and the dining room redone. His son went to Guatemala City to see the best doctors.

"It didn't take many dollars from here to make a difference there, and when people noticed, they began to think of what I had done differently."

About nine months after he began working at the supermarket, the manager said there would be openings and asked Juan if he knew anybody looking for a job. Within days, a brother-in-law and an uncle were on their way to Houston.

It was 1979, and the Houston oil boom was nearing its gaudy zenith. The Randall's where Juan worked served the newly rich and the very newly rich, who came to buy groceries in Jaguars and lavishly customized Suburbans. Juan's store became the model as the chain began building huge, high-quality, high-priced food stores. Service became the keynote. Valet-parking attendants greeted the women in Jags, and off-duty Houston police directed traffic on a major thoroughfare so everyone could get in and out of the parking lot hassle-free. All the regular employees wore uniforms that would have passed muster at a prep school. The cilantro was always misted.

During the boom, Randall's expanded along with Houston's suburbs as middle- and upper-class whites moved progressively farther from the city center. Along the way, the chain continually improved the quality of its service. On the one hand, it rode a fundamental demographic trend. On the other, it helped lead a shift toward customer-oriented, upscale retailing. As the chain expanded and perfected its act, Randall's hired more than one thousand Maya from Totonicapán.

"At a certain point, I believe the owners must have decided that they wanted all Guatemalans to do the maintenance and not have any *morenos* doing that work anymore," said Juan. "I believe that because, when they were preparing for a grand opening, they would say to us, 'We need so many people for maintenance to be ready for such and such a date,' and when it came time, we would have everybody ready. We'd have the whole department organized, enough people for all shifts for all twenty-four hours, seven days. From the start, they guaranteed us those jobs, even though they were getting hundreds of applications. Why else would they do this except for the fact that they wanted Guatemalans and nobody else?"

I tried to get Randall's executives to talk about their personnel policies, but they never responded to my requests. I did, however, find a pretty clear statement of those policies in an interview with the chain's founder, namesake, and chief pitchman, Robert Randall Onstead. In 1987, he told the *Houston Business Journal,* "We hire people who are interested in people, people who are cheerful servants." Randall's was by no means alone in seeking that kind of employee.

In his 1991 book, *The Work of Nations,* Robert B. Reich, then still a Harvard professor and soon to become secretary of labor in the Clinton administration, described a category of workers he called "in-person servers," people whose essential qualification is "a pleasant demeanor." By his account, more than 3 million new jobs for such workers were created in the 1980s in fast-food outlets, bars, and restaurants, which was more than the number of routine production jobs still existing by the end of the decade in the automobile, steel, and textile industries combined.

"They must smile and exude confidence and good cheer even when they feel morose," Reich said. "They must be courteous and helpful even to the most obnoxious of patrons. Above all, they must make others feel happy and at ease."

Even a casual survey of the people busing tables, making hotel beds, and unpacking produce in any large American city leaves no doubt that huge numbers of recent Latino immigrants are employed in these kinds of service jobs. They were the fastest-growing supply of adult low-wage workers when such were among the fastest-growing segments of the workforce. But simple availability does not explain the extent to which these newcomers ended up in this niche.

As American metropolitan areas expanded relentlessly into the exurbs, spatial segregation of the races became ever more profound, and the greatest distances developed between affluent whites, who generated low-wage service jobs in their new towns, and poverty-level blacks, who in the absence of immigration might have been candidates for those jobs. Latino immigrants, however, found residential niches in suburbs. In places like Pacoima, in the San Fernando Valley, or Rockville, in Montgomery County, Maryland, or in Houston's Gulfton neighborhood, they took over older, cheaper, less attractive housing by crowding three or four wage earners into every dwelling.

In the new towns, Latinos were neither rejected nor feared, the way poor blacks would have been. The whites, who fled the cities to escape their dread of crime and racial confrontation, generally accepted Latino immigrants as an unobtrusive appendage to their new suburban culture throughout most of the 1980s and early 1990s. Resentment against the newcomers has developed only where Latinos have become a conspicuously large presence.

Juan is convinced that the Guatemalans' behavior was a major factor in their winning acceptance; not their behavior alone, but how it compared to the African-Americans' and Mexican-Americans' who were their prime competitors for the bottom-rung jobs at Randall's.

"I think the managers had seen from their own experience that there are other nationalities that are a little more aggressive than we are, and that has recommended us to them," he said. "This is not to say we are better than others. No, far from it. In fact, we come with real weaknesses, like lack of education and lack of language, but the managers have been able to see in the way we comport ourselves that we do not argue with people, we do not fight even among ourselves, and we do not make demands. It was the only thing we had to offer."

But the Maya had more to offer as well. They had the workings of a migratory channel that not only ensured a supply of ready workers but also guaranteed their performance as cheerful servants.

"Several of us would have long talks with anyone starting at Randall's. We told them the only reason for leaving home was to work, and so there would be no skipping days or arriving late because you felt lazy. Second, we said that even though none of us had much schooling, our parents had educated us to respect others and behave correctly. So at work, there would never be any yelling or name-calling and you would always have good manners and show the Americans you were not a ruffian."

Over time, as more and more workers learned enough English to get along, this coaching became less necessary. Like Juan, many of the Maya became department managers or assistant managers, and they were able to supervise the newcomers directly.

"When they hired somebody new for maintenance, they would spend two weeks with me at my store learning how to run the cleaning machines and how to do the work, and when they were ready, I would send them on. And we always made sure that our new people went to work for our own foremen. That way, if there was any problem, if a man was sick or had to leave work early or anything, we would solve it among ourselves. We would tell the new men, 'If any of the Americans has a complaint or gives you an order, just listen carefully and nod your head and then come to one of us and we'll tell you what to do.'"

Getting jobs at Randall's has become more difficult in recent years because the company has become strict about demanding proof of legal work status. Juan insists he would not send anyone to the corporate personnel office to apply unless the person had valid documents, because otherwise it would damage Juan's reputation.

"Two or three times in the last few years, managers have come to me and said they needed workers, and I had to tell them that we did not have any who were ready."

Now, the newly arrived typically spend a couple of years or so working as busboys or day laborers while they try to get legal status one way or another. Many are disappointed. "We have young boys, seventeen, eighteen year olds, coming now with the idea that they are going to get rich, and no matter how much you tell them that it will be hard for them here, they still come."

Since Juan first pushed a mop, the Mayan workforce has participated in the creation of a new culture out along the freeways. Like other immigrants who deliver pizzas, wash dishes, clean houses, do construction work, or take care of children and old people, the Guatemalans are among the great unseen facilitators of the two-income, cul-de-sac lifestyle so favored by white baby boomers with children.

In Houston, the availability of a low-wage workforce helped speed the growth of a new suburban economy of service and convenience and that, in turn, created greater demand for immigrant workers. In Totonicapán, emigration also became part of a process of change. Remittances and displays of affluence by returning expatriates created new expectations that could only be fulfilled by leaving. The changes at both ends of the migrant channel ensure that the movement between them will be self-perpetuating, unless events intervene to break the momentum.

"When I came, the path was unknown and difficult," said Juan. "Now I see young people coming who were just little children when I left. They have grown up with the idea that coming to Houston is the way to improve your life. To them, it seems natural and easy. So now a whole new generation is coming, and that is why I think we are not yet at the middle of what is going to happen."

When Juan was born in 1956 in the village of Xesuc, just outside San Cristóbal, most everybody spoke to one another in Quiché, the indigenous language of the Maya. By the time Juan married, when he was twenty years old, it seemed natural for him and Floralinda to speak Spanish to each other. Now, Juan's two daughters, one a native-born American and the elder having left Totonicapán as a toddler, speak English to each other and to their friends, and when they became teenagers, they increasingly used the new language with their parents, who understand a good deal but are uncomfortable speaking it.

In just three decades, Juan's household went from Xesuc to Houston, from dirt paths worn smooth to concrete cloverleafs, from his parents' Quiché to his children's English. Juan's Spanish turned out to be no more than a vehicle necessary for the journey. So too, Juan proved to be a transitional figure.

One recent evening, I went to see Juan and found him sleepy-eyed, just getting up from a nap. He was putting in as much overtime as he could get, even if it meant cleaning floors and putting in sixteen-hour days. All of the money he could muster was going back to Totonicapán, where he was accelerating construction on the house he was building in San Cristóbal. It had gotten to be an ever-bigger project. "Now it has three bathrooms, more than we have here, and I want to see it finished soon," Juan told me.

But there was more bothering him, as well. Griselda Soledad, his eldest daughter, had been running with the wrong crowd at school, gang kids. Her high school was a prime recruiting ground for the Southwest Cholos, a street gang that rapidly graduated from graffiti to drive-by shootings. It appeared that Central American youths in Houston had learned how to become gang bangers from their Mexican and Mexican-American neighbors who had been at it for a long time, but the newcomers had developed an exceptionally predatory and self-destructive form of gang culture. It was evident in the violence they inflicted on their own communities and in the name they chose for themselves. *Cholo* (half-breed) is a derogatory term, almost as ugly as the word *nigger* in English. It is often thrown at poor, dark-skinned people in Latin America by those who feel superior to them. In Houston, Juan was baffled that Latino teenagers spray-painted it everywhere as a sign of pride.

My friend Nestor, the sociologist, was busy doing what he could with community groups to help stem what seemed an insanely fast escalation of gang membership and violence. It struck particularly hard among the Salvadorans in Houston. They were the largest Central American community, and since most came after the cutoff dates for the 1986 amnesty, a greater number of them were still illegal and working in the worst-paying jobs. "They came here to escape death squads, and now they live in fear of death squads made up of their own children," Nestor said.

Seeing the amazing things that Juan and his colleagues had accomplished, and seeing what was happening to their children, I had to wonder whether the energy generated by the first wave of migrants was necessarily finite and not transferable to their children. It was as if some tragic laws of thermodynamics applied to immigration. Perpetual motion is disallowed, and entropy is inevitable. It seems so often that the resolute striving, the creativity, and hard work so evident among the immigrant generation dissipate among its children.

Studies of European immigrants and their children in the first half of this century produced the conventional wisdom that assimilation proceeded on a straight line. The second generation picked up where the first left off, producing a continuity of adaptation and a steadily increasing prosperity. Some prominent social scientists recently have argued that a different process—some call it "bumpy-line" assimilation—is developing among current immigrants. Some children are now racing ahead of their parents in absorbing American ways but are turning into unemployable delinquents as a result. In a 1992 article entitled "Second Generation Decline," Herbert J. Gans argued that immigrant children who hold fast to their parents' ethnic communities may do better than those who assimilate rapidly and adopt the American culture that they see all around them, including cynical attitudes toward school and a rejection of low-wage labor.

The leading theoretician of the sociology of contemporary immigration, Johns Hopkins professor Alejandro Portes, reached similar conclusions after working with a variety of collaborators on extensive surveys of immigrant communities around the country. He finds that the chances for downward mobility are greatest for second-generation youth who live in close proximity to American minorities, who are poor to start with, and who are themselves victims of racial or ethnic discrimination. Portes also worries that these youth adopt the thinking of American minority groups in a way that becomes "a ticket to permanent subordination and disadvantage." When "children's acculturation leaps ahead of their parents'," he warns, there is "more a danger signal than a first step toward successful adaptation."

The new patterns of assimilation identified by Gans, Portes, and others point to another important distinction: Building a successful immigrant channel involves different skills and motivations than building a permanent community. The first to arrive are consumed with the logistics of creating a beachhead in the new land. Then, they find fulfillment by sending remittances home and achieving a better standard of living compared to that of those who remained behind. None of that necessarily requires enabling their children to enter the most stable and upwardly mobile sectors of American society. Many current immigrants, especially among some Asian nationalities, emphasize education as a surefire way to launch the second generation, but most of those newcomers, as I've said, arrive with much more education themselves than is common among Latinos. In the barrios, it is easy to find people who are successful immigrants but failures as the parents of American children. This distinction seems more significant among poor Latinos today than among Asians or the European immigrants of an earlier era. People who have traveled most of the way around the world set different goals for themselves than do Latinos who have not traveled very far and are constantly going home. Juan was driven to overcome the limits he faced in Guatemala, but until there was a crisis with his daughter, he paid little attention to the limits his children faced in the United States.

The mere hint of delinquency in their teenage daughter caught Juan and Floralinda as a devastating surprise. Their son, their eldest child, the one whose illness gave Juan the immediate impetus to migrate, had died of leukemia in Houston several years earlier, despite the best efforts of American medicine. Like any parents who have lost a child, they were exceptionally protective of the ones who remained.

Floralinda seemed remorseful: "What we realized is that we did not have much communication with the children because we are both so concentrated on work. We do that work so that we can give them what they want, but the result was that we let them get too far away from us. This would never have happened back home; it would never have happened."

Juan, ever the organizer, was more resolute. "We are dealing with this like it was a war, being constantly alert and attacking from several directions. We went to her schoolteachers, to the parents of her friends, to the people in her church group. It is not nice to say to your child that she can only see these people and not these others. It is not nice to listen in on other people's phone conversations, but those are the things you have to do."

A few weeks later on a Sunday afternoon, I went to see Juan's soccer-league matches. It was late October and the Houston summer heat was finally fading. Hundreds of people had come out to cheer games being played on four adjoining soccer fields. Hard by the sidelines, young men in tight jeans and long curly hair cheered their pals. A bit away from the action, families sat on the grass with coolers and picnics. Little boys in matching short and shirts were just starting to get rumpled as they played with their own little soccer balls. Girls in church clothes were kept close to their mothers.

Five young men strode through the middle of the crowd, heading in my direction and they immediately stood out from the rest: big black sneakers, laces untied; baggy shorts; large, untucked T-shirts; hair cut short on the sides and worn in long ponytails down the back. They sported the uniform of the Southwest Cholos. Three in the back, two in the front, they marched through the crowd, wearing aviator sunglasses. They didn't move in that big-strided walk most common among black gangs. But there was still something familiar about the way they moved. It was an imperious kind of walk. They exuded a particular subspecies of macho that has a very sharp edge to it. It conveys a kind of meanness that isn't there with the Latin men who think themselves peacocks or the sullen ones who drink too much and then explode. When they got closer, I looked a little too hard and the two in front focused their aviators on me as if they were taking aim. It occurred to me that they were just in the wrong uniforms. I had seen that same look and the same walk on men who carried guns and wore uniforms all over Latin America. Even the sunglasses were the same. It was the look of soldiers and policemen who know they can't be touched, of men who hit people they know will not fight back.

A while later, Juan arrived. He had been working since before dawn, had missed church, but now he was talking with team managers, clipboard in hand, supervising, giving instructions. We watched part of a match together, and after we had talked for a while, he confided that things were better at home. He felt that they had intervened early enough with his daughter to head off any serious problems and that she was accepting close supervision. I kept my doubts about his optimistic assessment to myself. Things were fine at his house, Juan insisted, but among other Mayan families, the gang problems were getting worse.

"Some people say there are no problems, that everything is fine with their children, but they are the very ones that are getting into the worst trouble. It is not something anyone wants to talk about outside their own homes. If you have a child who gets in trouble with the police, it is a disgrace for the family, and if you talk about it, people get on the phone and the whole community knows in three or four hours."

The Mayan channel that had carried two thousand people from Totonicapán to Texas was finally confronted with a challenge it was ill-equipped to handle. Crossing the border illegally, finding jobs and housing, dealing with changes in immigration laws, organizing a soccer league—all these things had been done expeditiously. But confronted with the Southwest Cholos, the Maya were giving up.

"I have three friends," said Juan, "men who came here at the beginning, who have sent their wives and children back to San Cristóbal in the past few weeks. They have some kids in trouble already and they have other younger ones and they worry what will happen to them. One of them said to me, 'It would have been better if we had never brought our families to Houston. My boys have been ruined here.' There is a lot of talk now about going back and people are speaking of their regrets."

Before, whenever Juan had talked about going back himself, it was always in the distant future, "when the girls are young ladies and ready to be on their own," and the youngest was only eleven years old then. I asked him if he was thinking of changing his plans and whether that was why he was speeding up construction on his house in San Cristóbal.

"Now it has come to a moment of thinking that things are changing very much and that all of us have to go back to where we came from. It is in the minds of many of us, especially those of us who came when I did and brought our families here."

It was getting to be dusk and most of the matches had ended, but on one field, teams were just warming up. A crude set of lights atop telephone poles began to glow and steadily grew brighter. A little cheer went up from the players. Being able to play beyond the blaze of the Houston sun was no small thing. The lights were one of Juan's proudest achievements, the result of long negotiations with the parks department and a rugby club that had the original rights to the field.

Juan watched impassively from a distance.

"I don't know if I ever told you," he said, "but I feel that the central reason for doing all this, the whole purpose that started it . . . that I failed. I came here to save my little boy and I wasn't able to do that, and for me that means that everything that has happened since I came, that all of it, will always be a failure in some way."

Juan seemed to settle on the image of his son's death because he was trying to find a frame of reference. After almost two decades in the United States, it was no longer so easy to measure the success of his migration by looking back to Guatemala and priding himself on how much more he had become than if he had never left. His daughter's crisis and the ongoing problems among the other Mayan children demanded that he look at his life in the United States from a different perspective. Juan had made the channel his home, allowing his psyche to transit perpetually back and forth between Texas and Totonicapán. Now events obliged him to root himself in his new life and judge its worth solely in terms of what he had accomplished here. The shift did not come easily for Juan. He resisted it, preferring to fix his gaze on the past and assess the value of his enterprise in terms of the child who had died rather than the one with an uncertain future.

Some Latinos come to the United States and resolutely address themselves to making a new life here. Juan represents the more typical case, especially among those who arrive poor and with little education: For them, everything earned by hard work here acquires a greater value when it is held up to old-country comparisons. For them, the barrios are the irresistible links to the south, not just convenient havens from English-speaking America. Their channels are highly efficient and self-perpetuating but are designed for limited goals. These Latinos do not measure success in terms of how well they have adapted to the United States, how much of the language and the culture they have assimilated, or whether they have built communities that can withstand the dangers presented by life in American cities. Often, when they seem to be doing well—bringing ever larger numbers of family and friends into the country, getting jobs, and taking over neighborhoods—they are at a crossroads and deeply vulnerable.

PART II

◈·◈·◈·◈·◈·◈·◈·◈·◈·◈·◈·◈·◈·◈·◈·◈·

CHALLENGING THE HOST

I've spoken of the shining city all my political life, but I don't know if I ever quite
communicated what I saw when I said it.
But in my mind was a tall, proud city built
on rocks, stronger than oceans. . . . And if
there had to be city walls, the walls had
doors and the doors were open to anyone
with the will and the heart to get there.
That's how I saw it, and see it still. . . .
After two hundred years, two centuries,
she still stands strong and true on the gran-
ite ridge, and her glow has held steady no
matter what the storm. And she's still a
beacon, still a magnet for all who must
have freedom, for all pilgrims from all the
lost places who are hurtling through the
darkness, towards home.
    —RONALD REAGAN, *farewell address*
    to the nation, January 11, 1989

✧•✧•✧•✧•✧•✧•✧•✧•✧•✧•✧•✧•✧•✧•✧•

CHAPTER 4

Day People, Night People, Madres

✧•✧•✧•✧•✧•✧•✧• Down in the Flats east of the L.A.
River when the summer sky turns orange
behind the palm trees, the day people and the night people share
the twilight for about an hour. It is the only time they see one
another, but they hardly exchange a glance. No one wants a fight.

The day people wear cheap sneakers or battered work boots,
paint-splattered jeans or dusty chinos, old plaid flannels or T-shirts
yellowed with sweat stains. They have been up since before dawn
doing any work for any wage. They have unpacked trucks, cleaned
apartment complexes, painted restaurants, collected their pay in
cash, and some have already wired it back home. At the end of a
summer day, they are tired and quiet. In about an hour, not long
after it is dark, they will file in the side door of the Dolores Mission
and stretch out for the night on the pews and in the aisles of the old
Jesuit church.

The night people dress precisely in black cross-trainers, thin white socks pulled up above the knees, baggy black shorts hemmed just below the knees, and plain white T-shirts freshly pressed. No leg must show between the shorts and the socks because in the Flats this summer, that is deemed a sign of weakness and the uniform is a sign of strength. They arrive in front of the mission, heralded by screeching tires, and then they lope from one vehicle to another conducting consultations. They are just meeting up and getting started for the night. Rumors about rival gangs must be exchanged, drug sales have to be planned, and sometimes there is a killing that must be discussed.

They are two different sets of people, inhabiting different worlds, even living by different clocks, yet sharing a block of Gless Street. And they share more than the street. The day people came from Mexico, almost all of them illegally. The night people came from Mexico, too, or their parents or grandparents made the trip, and many of them also first crossed without papers. Some of the day people and some of the night people even have their roots in the same little towns in central Mexico, the towns that have been sending people north for generations. On one side of Gless Street, the night people speak of famous homeboys, of battles fought, of alliances made and broken. On the other side, the day people speak of border crossings, of riding freight cars to the cold Midwest, of finding work in unlikely ways. The language and the exploits change, but on either side it is like hearing *corridos* (Mexican folk ballads), so much bravado, so many injustices to lament.

The night people call the laborers *mojados* (wetbacks) and the day people call the gang-bangers *cholos*. There have been fights, even a shooting or two, when the name-calling gets a little too loud. But everyone in the Flats is making up names for themselves. The transformation into a real gang banger cannot be completed until people forget about your real name and instead call you something like Gato, Gumby, or Loco. The day laborers have made up names, too. They buy names with the counterfeit documents that allow them to pass as legitimate immigrants or as native Latinos.

Standing between them one night, I began to realize that they were all in the process of creating new identities for themselves and that the only real difference between the day people and the night people was how long they had been in the United States. Technically, they were all Hispanics in the official listing of ethnic and racial groups. Some prefer the term *Latino*. Regardless of the label, it seemed useless to categorize them according to a set of ethnic or racial characteristics; that only confuses the similarities among them and erases the differences. Such labels focus on what is supposedly unchanging about people, but immigrant identities are in a process of evolution. In the United States, a glance is supposed to reveal everything, and people who are not white are immediately assigned to a minority group. Seeing immigrants that way is a form of blindness. Latinos challenge their hosts to cure the malady.

Down in the Flats and in all the barrios, change can come fast. Even immigrants from the most traditional, closed, conservative rural societies can open themselves up when they hit the road. By the time they get to a place like L.A., they are wide-open. If they stay awhile, the United States changes them a lot and their children become Americans of one sort or another.

There was one baby-faced felon among the gang bangers whom I could readily picture as a seven-year-old making his First Communion. I could see him walking down the aisle of a small-town Mexican church, wearing a white open-collar shirt, his hair neatly parted and slicked down, holding a rosary in his folded hands. He could have remained in Mexico and become a very different person, but now, like the rest of the night people, he walked a walk and talked a talk that had been largely plagiarized from the black ghetto. He and his buddies had done some customizing with East Los Angeles bilingual slang. But no matter where they had started out, no matter how Mexican they might once have been, the gang bangers had become Californians.

By contrast, the laborers had just arrived. They had not been in the United States long enough to be changed by it. They were still fresh and carried with them the energy of the newcomer. The day people and the night people are just different chapters in a single story. It is an American story as old as the nation itself. In extensive studies of the psychosocial adaptation that young immigrants must undergo, Rubén G. Rumbaut, a Michigan State University sociologist, concludes that the process of becoming American is profoundly shaped by the surrounding context in ways that the immigrant may be no more conscious of than fish are of water. "In the final analysis," Rumbaut argues, "it is the crucible without that shapes the crucible within."

·   ·   ·

In the nineteenth century, when the Los Angeles River was still a river instead of a giant concrete conduit with just enough water in it for good splash effects during Hollywood chase scenes, the Flats was pretty good bottomland sitting between the river and the escarpment now known as Boyle Heights. People of different sorts—Indians (*mestizos*), then, after the gold rush, Chinese, blacks, and Jews—lived in the Flats, while the Californios, the ranchers and merchants whose roots predated the Mexican-American War, kept their houses near the old Plaza across the river, not far from where downtown would later be built.

When the railroads came in the 1880s, thousands migrated from the East. European immigrants could book the journey before leaving Ellis Island, condensing manifest destiny into a single ticket. Mexicans quickly became a minority in Los Angeles. By the time the Mexican Revolution began driving people north in 1910, the city was beginning to grow and industrialize, a process that would continue for the next twenty years, thanks largely to World War I and the Panama Canal. The demand for labor was such that the Mexican population of the city grew almost twentyfold in those years. The Flats and Boyle Heights and the rest of East Los Angeles, the place across the river, became one giant barrio, a community where many people spoke Spanish, worked hard, and lived poor.

Those Latino immigrants early in the century experienced a backlash of their own, and once it began, it kept reappearing in different manifestations for twenty years. When the Depression hit, the Mexicans became expendable. Faced with high unemployment and skyrocketing social-welfare costs, many local governments encouraged the immigrants to return home, sometimes offering them cash inducements, sometimes forcibly removing them and their U.S.-born children. About half a million Mexicans went back during the Depression, according to the commonly accepted estimates, but the flow reversed itself again as soon as World War II created manpower shortages.

Copying their look from black jitterbuggers back East, the Mexican youth of L.A. in the 1940s wore big broad-brimmed felt hats, long coats, and baggy pants. They added ducktail haircuts as their own grace note. The strutting zoot-suiters called attention to the barrio and to the resurgent immigrant influx. That proved threatening in the 1940s, just as it did in the 1990s. The Anglos of L.A. became profoundly anxious at the sight of a rapidly growing minority whose young men were mimicking African-Americans. Then and now, Anglos can accommodate themselves to the idea that Latino immigrants come in large numbers to take low-wage jobs, but white people get upset when Latino youth develop an attitude, get sassy, and begin making demands.

The mysterious death of a Mexican boy in August 1942 provided an occasion for the local newspapers to print screaming headlines warning of rampant gang violence by zoot-suiters. The local authorities, goaded on by hysterical town fathers, rounded up no fewer than twenty-three Mexican youths and charged them with murder in the tabloid frenzy that came to be known as the Sleepy Lagoon Case. In the spring of 1943, a few months after the first batch of convictions in the Sleepy Lagoon trials, hordes of off-duty sailors began routinely attacking zoot-suiters while the authorities looked on. Any Latino young man who wandered out of the barrio was liable to be dragged off streetcars or out of theaters, beaten, robbed, and subjected to a forced haircut. During the summer, full-fledged rioting broke out when the servicemen formed caravans of taxicabs, came across the river, and attacked the East L.A. barrio. The zoot-suit riots ended only after the German and Japanese began exploiting the disturbances as fodder for anti-American propaganda in Latin America. At that point, the navy felt obliged to restrain its young men.

Fifty years later, another generation of young people and another wave of immigrants fill the streets, and the city is again uneasy with the changes overcoming it. Now the Flats is urban bottomland with a history. Several freeways converge on the convenient landscape to make a north-south channel. Giant overpasses loom above backyards filled with thick stands of bougainvillea. A chain of whitewashed public housing complexes looks like it was rammed into the neighborhood.

Still convenient to the railroad yards, factories, and warehouses just across the river, the Flats again lures immigrants with jobs. But the Flats also serves as home to third-generation gang bangers and plenty of law-abiding Mexican-Americans who tell the story of the Sleepy Lagoon and can remember the hot nights when the sailors came angrily across the bridges. Young people grow up with those stories and stories of people who braved the border, came north, and always found work.

· · ·

In the evening twilight, some of the day people at the Dolores Mission sit around an old carport hunched atop plastic milk crates, cardboard boxes, or whatever else is available. A little TV perched on a high shelf holds their attention with a Mexican variety show. While some watch plumed dancers shimmy, others wait their turn for the bathroom or tend the few possessions they keep in the little lockers that are the only storage allowed them. The old church serves as a mission more in the Salvation Army sense than what the Spaniards envisioned when they came to California. The men get a blanket and a spot to sleep amid the pews. They have to be out looking for work by 6:30 a.m. and cannot come back until 7:00 p.m. Then they get something as simple as a bologna sandwich for dinner. After dinner, they have some time for entertainment and even then it is very quiet.

Work is what they have come for.

Esteban Espinoza, a small, lightly built man, twenty-five years old, said he is able to send $150 to $200 a week back to his family— eleven adults and children—who live on a *rancho* in the state of Guerrero.

"On Saturday, I send back whatever I have and just keep five dollars for myself, and that is always enough until Monday or Tuesday, and by then I've made some more."

One of Esteban's grandfathers picked chilies and did railroad work in the United States many years back, and his father had gone north for a time, as well. More recently, his elder brother was assigned to be the *rancho's* cash cow, but he met a girl in Los Angeles, a Mexican-American, got married, and stopped sending money. The task then fell to Esteban, who made several short trips to learn how to cross the border and find work. Feeling comfortable, he is now planning to stay a year, until someone else from the household can take his place.

"We raise different kinds of food and usually we have enough to eat, but there is never much money. With someone up here working, there is money every week."

Like most of the men at the mission, he goes out in the mornings to stand at one of several street corners on the fringes of downtown that have become well-known labor markets. Employers come by in cars and pickup trucks to select as many able-bodied hands as they need. No rules apply. The pay is usually the minimum wage, and the work can be anything.

Standing around in the twilight, the day people are full of stories about finding work.

"Me and this other guy spent three days redoing a whole restaurant in Beverly Hills with a pair of Anglos who picked us up and said they wanted us to do the whole job. They did the drywall and we did the painting, but we had to do it all in sign language because they did not speak one word of Spanish. By the end, we were like those deaf-mutes talking with their hands."

Another chimed in, "I waited until four o'clock one day this week. From seven in the morning, I stood on that corner and nothing, nothing, nothing. Then this *chino* [an Asian] comes along and says he needs four people to unload a truck for him in a big hurry. So he takes us to this warehouse, and it is like we start a race to see who can unload these big rolls of cloth the fastest, and he is sitting there laughing, clapping his hands. We finish and he gives us twenty dollars each, and it was less than an hour we worked."

And they also had stories of being cheated.

For Esteban, finding work and collecting dollars to send south is just as routine as planting and harvesting corn back home. He spoke about it matter-of-factly, without a hint of humor or sadness. He clearly understood the possibility of failure. But on this side of the border, he considered it more a matter of choice than of fate or bad luck or bad weather.

"There is always work here," he said, "at least for those who have come to improve themselves. In summer, the only ones who go without work are the ones who surrender themselves to their vices."

On the other side of the street, I asked a gang banger leaning up against a lamppost whether he found work readily available.

He nodded. "There's work, but it sucks."

With just the slightest prompt, he elaborated.

"I'll tell you what sucks," said the gang banger. "What sucks is busting your damn ass for seven dollars an hour. Shit, that won't even hardly cover my expenses."

I asked what his parents did for a living.

"They work. They both work. All they do is work, and, like I told you, it sucks. They been working for years and they got no money. All they got out of all that work is a *chingada* [a fucking], and that's one good reason that it don't interest me much."

At the moment, work didn't matter anyway, he explained, because he was "on disability." And, to make the point as vividly as possible, he pulled down his black pantaloons and his flowered boxer shorts so he could show off two dark red scabby scars the size of quarters on either side of his thigh. Entry and exit: The scars marked a bullet's relatively harmless trajectory.

"That was before the truce," he said.

This mention of a truce so obviously tickled my interest that he and his sidekick knowledgeably led me away from the crowded street corner so they could explain.

In the late spring, word came down that a sister or a niece or some close female relative of someone high up in La Eme—the M, the thirteenth letter, the Mexican Mafia—had been killed by accident in a drive-by. A little while later, a meeting was called at a playground. Two representatives of each gang in the Flats and Boyle Heights were ordered to attend unarmed. Three prominent spokesmen for La Eme stood before them and announced new rules: no drive-bys, no shooting at houses, or else.

The two gang bangers seemed to think they had said too much and said they would proceed only if I promised not to identify them. After I agreed to the ground rules, the wounded one proceeded to pull a small nickel-plated revolver from his pants pocket.

"See, everybody is still carrying. La Eme didn't say put the guns away. They just say if you are going to do somebody, you got to do 'im the right way."

His little sidekick chimed in, "Do it the right way. You want to do some *vato* [dude], it's okay, but you got to do 'im the man's [manly] way."

"The right way." "The man's way." These words were drawn out as they were spoken, rhetorically underlined with awe and reverence.

The wounded one continued: "The right way is that if you are going to do some fucking *vato,* you have to go right up to his face and blow him away and watch him bleed and spill his guts out on the street and watch him die. Then you got to walk away. That is the right way."

Nodding and spitting, the little one said, "That is the man's way."

This prescription was recited with obvious pride. So much so that they did not exhibit even a touch of irony when they admitted that no one so far had achieved these great new levels of masculine heroism.

After the 1992 Rodney King riots, the black gangs in Los Angeles had organized an elaborate and highly publicized truce. It spawned self-proclaimed mediators eager for network news exposure and a new generation of social-welfare organizations, such as Hands Across Watts, that quickly began pumping foundations for grants based on their ability to work out disputes before they led to senseless murders. The East L.A. truce was known only within the barrio, and it had a very simple enforcement mechanism.

"Say I do a drive-by," the wounded one explained. "Either my homeboys take me out or La Eme will kill one of my homeboys on the inside [in prison]."

The sidekick added, "You got to understand, your gang is nothing on the inside. La Eme rules on the inside. They get everyone from every barrio together because on the inside everybody is *raza* [of the same Mexican race], because on the inside it is all *raza* against the *mayates* [niggers]. It's like a war. You follow orders. If they say to waste your best homeboy, you better do it. You kill him when they tell you even if you love the *vato* like a brother, because if you don't do what they say, you and your home are both dead. That's the way La Eme runs things on the inside."

The wounded one said, "Yeah, outside you can run risks, but inside there is nowhere to run. You don't break the law inside because La Eme makes the laws inside."

The two homeboys, identically dressed in black and white like a pair of soccer referees, sat on the curb, smoked cigarettes, and drank malt liquor. It was strange to hear them invoke *la raza* (the race). In the late 1960s and early 1970s, it was a hallowed term in East Los Angeles, but these kids had not been born then. *La raza* expressed the idea that all people of Mexican descent in the United States and in Mexico shared a spiritual union. They had a racial identity that predated the Spanish conquest and that surpassed today's national borders. But even though this ethnic concept served as a symbolic bridge back to Mexico, it was very much a product of the civil rights era in the United States.

During that time some Latinos and blacks asserted distinct group identities as a means of battling the discrimination they suffered. Mexican-Americans in California declared themselves proud members of *la raza,* called themselves Chicanos, and marched behind César Chávez under a red-and-black banner emblazoned with an

Aztec eagle. Having been subject to discrimination under a group identity, Latinos, like blacks, sought remedies as a group. As a political concept, *la raza* energized and informed voting rights lawsuits, school desegregation battles, antiwar protests, and an explosion of ethnic expression in the theater and in murals and other art forms. Like many blacks, these Mexican-Americans shaped a group identity out of a confrontation with American society. Both historical memory and contemporary goals found expression in the vision of perpetual struggle between the white mainstream and a dark-skinned Spanish-speaking tribe with roots in Mexico.

Neither the day people nor the night people embrace that vision of ethnicity. Young gang bangers invoke the concept of *la raza* to explain their blood sport with black gangs. They do not relate their ethnic identity to either a thirst for justice or any sense of Mexican heritage. Meanwhile immigrant workers are anxiously trying to modify their Mexican identity by coming to the United States and certainly do not assert any special claims based on that identity.

Moreover, neither day people nor night people readily fit the framework of racial and ethnic identity that most Americans apply to their fellow citizens and that shapes public policy. That framework evolved when sharp distinctions between whites and minorities were all that mattered. Although native Latino groups— Mexican-Americans and Puerto Ricans—made successful use of civil rights measures as a matter of necessity, the perspectives so important during that time are far too narrow to be of much use in an era of mass immigration, especially when the newcomers are not white but are not black, either. Regardless of whether they are used to impose prejudice, defeat discrimination, or exact privilege, minority-group identities are based on fixed characteristics. The goals may be worthy or not, but the method is always to put as many people as possible under a single label. Making sense of Latino immigration, and making public policy for this era, requires a perspective that illuminates the interaction of newcomers with the new land and the dynamic identities that result.

Looking back to the last great era of immigration for such a perspective is not much help because it is obscured by the myth of the melting pot, which tells us how happily and successfully European immigrants assimilated to American ways. All but forgotten are the settlement houses and the skid rows, the murderous coal mines and the children at the looms. The glories of the melting pot ignore the anti-Semitism, the nativism, the restrictive covenants on housing, and the many less explicit forms of prejudice that circumscribed America for many immigrants and their children. Looking back past the myths should dispel the idea that there is some inexorable force drawing newcomers into the mainstream, and it should be a reminder that ethnic identities are reinforced as a response to adversity. The truth of the European era is that immigrant identities did not weaken but were transformed by confrontation with American prejudice. Sicilians became Italians in New York and Bavarians became Germans in Chicago before their brethren back home developed strong national identities. The immigrants had no choice but to find common cause with like-minded souls, and that produced a sense of ethnic identity that was novel, though rooted in the past, and remarkably enduring.

Examining the lives of European ethnics in New York City in the early 1960s, Nathan Glazer and Daniel P. Moynihan concluded in a book about New York City, *Beyond the Melting Pot,* that "the American ethos is nowhere better perceived than in the disinclination of the third and fourth generation of newcomers to blend into a standard, uniform national type." The point "about the melting pot," they concluded, "is that it did not happen." If the yardstick of European immigration is accurately applied to today's newcomers and they behave similarly to the Italians and Irish described by Glazer and Moynihan, one could expect that in the middle of the next century Latinos will still be living in barrios, remaining within established labor force niches, voting as a bloc, and holding on to Latino culture in cuisine, religion, and sexual mores.

In fact, many Latinos appear to be adapting to this country at a faster pace. There is a substantial and growing Mexican-American middle class in Texas and California that is entirely English-speaking and substantially suburbanized. A prosperous tier of Puerto Ricans and of well-educated South American immigrants has blended into the white mainstream so successfully that it is virtually invisible in New York, Chicago, and other major cities. But these signs of adaptation, no less than the diversity on Gless Street, are further proof that identities are fluid during an era of immigration. The final result of assimilation is substantially determined by the newcomers' experience of the United States, and the ultimate determinant may be money.

In describing the wide range of ethnic identities apparent among

Latinos of differing economic status, Frank D. Bean and Marta Tienda argued in their landmark 1987 study for the Russell Sage Foundation, *The Hispanic Population of the United States*, that middle-class Latinos often "maintained a symbolic connection to their ethnic heritage, as manifested by the continued observance of holidays, the revival of ethnic foods, the practice of cultural rituals and so on," while in many other areas, such as education, language, and residence, "they have increasingly modeled Anglos." But in a country that divides people according to race, language, and economic status, the success of some, even many Latinos, has only a limited impact beyond those individuals. "In a stratified society," Bean and Tienda argued, "it is possible for some members of a group to be socioeconomically successful while the group as a whole occupies a disadvantaged position vis-à-vis the dominant majority."

The character of those who do not make it economically is very different. Bean and Tienda describe a nexus of immigrant ethnicity, discrimination, and civil rights politics. That intersection is the key to understanding the most visible, although not necessarily the most numerous, Latinos—the urban poor. For Hispanics relegated to life in urban barrios, Bean and Tienda found that "ethnicity becomes synonymous with minority status." As such, ethnicity is more than an expression of cultural heritage or a reflection of an economic condition. Among poor Latinos, ethnic identity is a powerful defense mechanism that, according to Bean and Tienda, "offers refuge to its adherents against the very system that produces stratification and oppression."

Latinos are not on a straight track to becoming whites, but they are not indelibly marked as nonwhite outsiders, either. They challenge the schematic of racial identity that Americans use for a wealth of activities, from the appointment of political power to the design of marketing campaigns. But this challenge requires more than devising another category or label. Latino immigration demands a new perspective on ethnic identity, and it is a perspective that first of all must take into account what is happening in the barrios, because they are the scenes of the most complex and most dangerous interactions between America and its newest residents.

The people on Gless Street are not American, at least not in the way most Americans think of themselves, but they are American enough that they are not simply Mexican anymore. Like all immigrants, they cut themselves loose from the places and things that have helped define them all their lives, and by going to a new place, they open themselves up to many new defining influences. Any new concept of identity has to account for the fact that Latino immigrants can and do go home for weekends or for short holidays, and up until the early 1990s they could do it easily, even if they were entering the United States on the sly. Or, they can come to the United States for a month, a summer, or a year, make the money they need and go back home, and then return again whenever they feel the urge. This travel back south constantly refreshes that part of their identity rooted in their homelands. Even for those who remain permanently in the United States, Spanish and Spanish-speaking ways are kept alive in the barrios by the continual stream of newcomers. In most Mexican communities and some other Latino enclaves—like the Dominican barrios of Washington Heights—immigration has constantly replenished the stock of new arrivals for twenty years or more. Few individual communities of European ethnics ever underwent anything of the sort.

Latinos are also the only major group of immigrants who arrive so deeply imbued with American ways. Anyone growing up in Latin America, especially in the nearby countries that send most immigrants, has been saturated with images and information about the United States from birth. Many arrive knowing how to play baseball or just wearing baseball caps backward. They can easily feel American without shucking any of their Latino sensibilities.

While immigration explodes the assumptions behind the old racial categories that have caused so much grief, the United States cannot simply hope to wipe the slate clean and start over. For years, many Americans have viewed Latinos as less than white and have enforced this perspective to exclude them from education, employment, political representation, and much else. This is history and it is inescapable, and every new Latino immigrant becomes a part of this history.

Americans value immigrants according to their ability to assimilate into the white mainstream. The European ethnics gained acceptance only after the melting pot became an article of faith. Latinos now challenge this country to develop a perspective on assimilation and ethnic identity that can embrace the paradoxes so apparent in places like Gless Street. By the standards of the melting pot, who are more American, the day people or the night people? Through their dedication to work and their absolute belief that the United States offers opportunities to the self-reliant, the day people have clearly absorbed something quintessentially American, yet they remain Spanish-speaking illegal aliens. The gang bangers are steeped in the American consumer culture as well as the folkways and the maladies of the American inner city. And yet in their most bitter battles, they call themselves *raza* and march forward as ethnic Mexicans to do battle against American blacks.

Finally, in trying to understand how Latino immigration will change America's urban landscape, it is important to remember that the day people and the night people are not the only people who live in the barrio.

Down in the Flats in the evenings, a third group roams the street, moving through the shadows between the day people and the night people. They are *las madres* (the mothers). Dressed in blue jeans or simple cotton dresses, they make sandwiches for the laborers, and then many nights, especially on weekends, they set out to street corners where there might be trouble among the thirteen street gangs that inhabit the Flats. The mothers are immigrants and natives, Spanish speakers, English speakers, and bilinguals. Most have big families in poor households, and most of them work— sewing in sweatshops, cleaning other people's homes and offices. *"Caminadas de amor"* (strolls for love) are what they call their forays. Carrying snacks and soft drinks, they go to the corners, sometimes as many as twenty of them at a time, and encircle their heavily armed progeny.

"They wait for us. They know we are coming and they wait for us because they like it," said Paula Hernández, one of the stalwarts of the group. "All we ever ask of them is to show respect for others. That, and we pray for them and listen to them. They are always having problems with other gangs and the police, and if we listen to them and treat them in a serious way, we can tell them they cannot solve their problems without showing respect for others."

The mothers deal with the police through a neighborhood watch organization, run clothing drives, operate a day-care center, and help support an alternative school for dropouts. With the Jesuits at the Dolores Mission, they also help run a shelter for battered women and a bakery to provide jobs for neighborhood boys. Considering how bad things are, *las madres* are not going to redeem the Flats anytime soon. But, amid the bougainvillea and the bungalows, beneath the freeway overpasses, they try to maintain order. At the heart of a sophisticated metropolis and within sight of office towers housing international banks, the mothers are the most coherent civilizing force in their community, more potent than the police, more consistent than any government agency, more respected than the schools. They represent yet another form of identity that is growing in the barrios. The mothers are a voice of resistance against life at the bottom of a stratified society. They echo the protests of the civil rights era, but in immigrant tones. They use Spanish words to master the downtown bureaucracies of public housing and Medicaid. *Las madres* represent a form of Latino identity that is as pragmatic as it is cultural and that remains proudly ethnic even as it seeks to engage America.

"Of course we are scared, and we get tired because we work all day and then come back to this," said Mrs. Hernandez, gesturing down a dark alley where young male voices could be heard cackling.

Sheltered in the orange glare of a streetlight, the mothers formed a tight circle. They are bound together by more than civic spirit. Like most Latinos, *las madres* emerge from a culture that places little stock in institutions. They are at most a generation or two removed from countries where governments are more feared than trusted.

They've grown up believing that *compadrazgo* is the strongest bond outside the family. When the parents of a newborn child ask another couple to serve as the baby's godparents, the four become *compadres,* and it is understood that thenceforth their friendship is a bond for life that can be relied on for practical and emotional support even when relatives fail to heed the call. The baptism ceremony celebrates the ties among the adults as much as the arrival of an infant. And *compadrazgo* is just a formal expression of the kind of networking that begins with kinship and that usually goes much further in Latino cultures, especially in small towns and rural areas.

So there is something very Mexican about six women standing under a streetlight, looking out for their families and for one another, just as there was something very Mayan about how Juan Chanax and his *compadres* helped one another find work. But in places like the Flats, those linkages are finding new expressions and are being put to new purposes as these communities contend with the twin challenges of urban decay and steady immigration.

The mothers of the Dolores Mission are allied with an umbrella group called Las Madres de East L.A. It became one of the best-known community organizations in the city after it won a long battle to keep a prison out of the barrio, and then it won national fame by enlisting middle-class Anglo environmental groups to help it defeat plans to build a toxic-waste incinerator nearby. These battles in the 1980s helped promote a new civil rights cause, environmental racism, which alleges that environmental hazards have been inordinately, even intentionally, concentrated in poor and minority communities.

With little coordination or hierarchy, the mothers in the Flats and all across East L.A. also form a powerful grassroots political force. They helped elect Gloria Molina as the first Hispanic on the Los Angeles County Commission, and they have given important backing to several other insurgent political campaigns. When Proposition 187, the anti–illegal immigration initiative, held a huge lead in the polls, they went door-to-door to make sure that at least barrio voters would reject it.

And this is not just a Los Angeles phenomenon. In the late 1980s and during the 1990s, barrio community organizations helped elect candidates, most of them women, to top offices in El Paso, Houston, Miami, and New York. In defiance of well-established Latino political bosses, many of these *madres* became the fresh faces and surprise winners when the ballots were counted.

"Sometimes someone says they wish things could be like they are in Mexico," Paula Hernández said. "They think women don't have to worry about their families so much there. Well, it is true women have to do more here. We are away from the children more because we work more, and that makes problems. But it is here that we have learned to get over our fear of saying what we think. It is here we have learned to work together as mothers. That happened because we were here."

Whether they are in Congress or out in the streets pacifying gang bangers, all this activism by Hispanic women reflects two political developments that are fundamentally American: the increasing prominence of women in electoral politics and the growing dynamism of community-action groups that coalesce on specific issues at the neighborhood level. These are national trends that cut across regions, economic classes, and racial or ethnic groups, and there is nothing distinctly Latino or immigrant about them. Indeed, outside the United States, Latino political culture remains male-dominated despite significant changes in the status of women over the past thirty years.

Using minority-group status to get leverage on institutions, electing female politicians, creating community-based organizations to funnel government funds into their neighborhoods—on all these many fronts Latino immigrants are adapting to the United States and learning to use American tools to fix their problems. But at the end of the day as they walk in the dark, traveling between the day people and the night people, making a community out of both, they are *comadres,* creating a sisterhood just as their mothers and grandmothers and generations of Latinas did before them in places far away. The *madres* are neither American nor Mexican. They are creating something new in the barrios out of the old ways they brought from the south and the tools they discovered on American terrain.

Down in the Flats when it started getting late, the mothers had gone home, and the night people dispersed to make their rounds. Cars screeched away. As one big black-and-red sedan pulled out, four or five firecrackers flew from the windows in a kind of mock drive-by. Some of the remaining lads flinched, their hands reaching to their pockets.

At the mission door, the day people started filing in, giving their number to a man with a clipboard. They rolled themselves in olive drab blankets, propped bundled clothes under their heads, and read *fotonovelas,* which are comic books with photos of actors instead of drawings and with soap-opera plots instead of superhero fantasies.

"*Los Angeles ya es Latino,*" Los Angeles is already Latino. The sentence was spoken by a man in white painter pants and a faded work shirt as he smoked a last cigarette before going in to stretch out on his pew. Earlier, he had entertained me and several other of the laborers with stories of how he had crossed the border so many times that he no longer used a *coyote,* a guide. He told tales of escaping from police who pursued him unjustly in Mexico and of eluding immigration agents in the United States. It was a migrant's *corrido* sung by a nicotine campfire. The mission door was about to close, and now the man was talking about California's governor, Pete Wilson, who had been much in the news those days with his plans to balance the state government's budget by shutting down the border.

"Los Angeles is already Latino. It is too late for Wilson. What is he going to do? Deport us and all the Chicanos, too? If he wants to send two million people to Mexico, okay, let him do it; Mexico will send six million back. Then all of California will be Latino."

Two young laborers, teenagers by their looks, were terribly amused by this and so the older man indulged them. He was a natural-born ham, and before he had finished his cigarette, he had them in stitches.

"If he tries to send all the Latinos out of Los Angeles, all the *blancos* will go crazy in their dirty houses and all the *koreanos* with no one to work for them will go crazy, too. And so they will invite us— yes, *invite* us—to build a subway from Tijuana to Los Angeles that goes right under the border and under the noses of *la migra* [the immigration authorities]."

One of the boys tried to put icing on the joke as they walked into the church. "Yeah, we will get on the subway in Tijuana and they will serve us steaks at tables with napkins, and by the time we are finished eating, we will be here at Union Station."

"Los Angeles ya es Latino."

❖·❖·❖·❖·❖·❖·❖·❖·❖·❖·❖·❖·❖·❖·❖·❖·❖·

CHAPTER 5

Living by American Rules

❖·❖·❖·❖·❖·❖·❖·❖·❖·   Long before any of today's Latino immigrants were born, their destiny began to
take shape in South Texas. It happened when signs reading NO
MEXICANS blocked entry to cafés and theaters. It happened when
brown-skinned men were horsewhipped on dusty streets. It happened whenever an all-white jury sat to hand out justice.

It happened in the border towns from El Paso to Brownsville, and
up through the scrublands, in the little towns and big ranches, and
up to the cities—San Antonio, Corpus Christi, Houston. These are
the places where Mexicans remained after Texas won its indepen-
dence in 1836. Over time, they became as American as anybody else
born on the U.S. side of the border, and eventually South Texas
became the ethnic and demographic heartland for the largest group
of native Latinos, the Mexican-Americans.

South Texas is where you find the roots of city barrios all the way west to L.A. and north to Chicago. It is where much of the music, the language, and the food comes from and where many of the family trees begin. But most of all, this is where Latinos experienced discrimination most brutally and where they first fought back. Before the Civil War Texas was the only slave state well-populated by Latinos, and in the first half of this century it had its own version of Jim Crow segregation, which it imposed to differing degrees on both blacks and Latinos. In South Texas in the 1950s, Mexican-Americans became the first Latinos to use civil rights laws to demand and win recognition as a minority group. This experience eventually shaped the way that Latino immigrants would establish their own identities even though they shared none of the Mexican-Americans' history. South Texas is where Latino ethnic politics took shape, where the tools and strategies and goals evolved. South Texas in the 1950s was a mean place, and it had been mean for a long time.

In South Texas, there is a bogeymen who emerges from memory, not imagination. He represents government authority, not a fairy-tale villain. Latino children there are told they better behave or else *los rinches* (the rangers) will come get them. At the turn of the century, the Texas Rangers exercised instant and total justice, lynching Mexican-Americans virtually at will. The worst of it came during World War I, after the discovery of the so-called Zimmermann telegram, in which the Mexican government allegedly plotted with Germany to enter the war and retake Texas and the Southwest. During the following wave of paranoia, hundreds, perhaps thousands, of Mexican-Americans were summarily executed by *los rinches*. After a state investigation in 1919, the legislature cut the Rangers down to a few dozen officers and deposed them as the state's most powerful police agency. The Rangers passed into Texas myth and were glorified. *Los rinches* remained alive in Mexican-American minds differently, and now, generations later, they are part of the terrain that shapes life for Latino immigrants.

As in the rest of the United States, traditional ways began to change in South Texas when the veterans came back from World War II and claimed their due. Mexican-Americans had served in proportionally high numbers. They were part of a generation that had begun to move off the land into the towns and cities of Texas during the Depression. Going off to war and moving to the cities created expectations, and when those expectations ran into the old Texas, there was a certain restiveness.

In South Texas, returning Mexican-American servicemen organized themselves to get what they had been promised. These Latinos expected that their sacrifices would be recognized the same as everyone else's. They quickly became a significant force on the Texas political landscape, but there was no hint of ethnic ambition in their goals or tactics. Consider the name they chose: the American GI Forum. Like most Latino activists up until that time, they wanted to jump across the racial and ethnic barriers in American life rather than fight to have them lifted. As had happened before in controversies over schools and other segregated facilities, Mexican-Americans did not protest against racial separation as long as they were treated as whites were. But in South Texas, they were still outsiders, even though they had spilled their blood in America's defense.

When duty called, Macario García left Sugarland, Texas, a farm town just south of Houston where Latinos and blacks worked the fields and whites owned the land. An army staff sergeant, he won a Congressional Medal of Honor. Returning home after White House ceremonies, he was refused service at a diner that did not feed Mexicans or blacks. Before the war, such an affront would have been swallowed. But García became a cause. In the barrios, people named their children after him, though they did not take to the streets. Now there are streets named after him.

James DeAnda was among those who tried to change Texas when he took his brand-new law degree to Houston in 1951 and looked for a government job.

"I remember filling out job applications that asked not only race but also nationality, and in those days we were all just considered Mexicans, no matter what we looked like, where we were born, or what language we spoke."

DeAnda is a red-blooded Texan in every way. He attended Texas A&M when it was still an all-male, all-military institution. Graduating as a member of the Corps of Cadets offered a kind of validation as important in Texas as making it through the Citadel was in South Carolina or VMI in Virginia. DeAnda drawled out his vowels and wore his boots as well as any of his blond-haired classmates. In most every way, he has always been more American than Mexican, but fine distinctions on matters of race and ethnicity were not a habit in Texas or anywhere else in the United States in 1951.

DeAnda remembered, "At the time, there were no Hispanics or blacks working as lawyers for any federal agency or for any state agency or for any county agency that I know of, and I applied for jobs at many of those places. About the only Mexicans employed in any of these offices were doing maintenance or the low-level clerical work. I even applied at the FBI. . . ."

DeAnda's voice trailed off. He was laughing so hard at himself that he couldn't keep talking. It is funny to him now because much has changed. Jimmy Carter made him a judge on the U.S. District Court for South Texas, and during nearly twenty years on the bench he had ample opportunities to decide matters of law for the agencies that had once turned him away. But in the early 1950s, DeAnda worked for small law firms and made his mark by filing suits that challenged the old culture of segregation. Practicing in Corpus Christi, he fought deed restrictions that prohibited Mexicans from living in whole sections of the city unless they were employed as maids or gardeners. He sued a school district that systematically kept Latino students in first grade for at least three years; education officials claimed the children didn't speak English, and then refused to promote them.

"These children were nine years old by the time they got out of first grade. It was a disaster. They were teenagers quitting school before they got to fifth grade. Then it all came to a head with this one couple who prohibited their daughter from speaking Spanish, didn't teach her a word of it, because they thought that was the way to get her an education. Well, the school superintendent put her in the Mexican school anyway, and then we had our case."

Sometimes he tried to negotiate. There was a small town that allowed Latino kids to swim in the public pool one day a week and blacks not at all. DeAnda sought a settlement with the town council.

"First, they tried to lease out the pool and claim it wasn't a public facility, but that dog wouldn't hunt," he recalled forty years later, guffawing at some memories, wincing about others. "So I went back out to talk to these good old boys again, and one of the councilmen says to me with all sorts of savvy, like he figured he had outsmarted me, he says, 'Well, what about if we fix it so the Negroes swim with your people?' He figured I'd settle for anything but that, and so I said to him, 'Well, I'd like that fine, because eventually we are all going to be swimming together anyway.' I thought they were going to kill me right then and there, and I got myself out of town."

A few weeks later, he returned to resume the discussions, but no discussion was necessary. The pool was closed—permanently. The town fathers had taken a bulldozer to it and filled it in with dirt.

"I guess I didn't accomplish much except keeping everyone from swimming. Those kind of things tend to stick with you."

Sitting beneath sleek decorator lights in the conference room of a downtown Houston law firm, DeAnda, now retired from the federal bench, occasionally paused. His eyes squint tight—perhaps he shut them—as he paused and went back to a different world and remembered.

"Back then, Jim Crow was the law of the land when it came to blacks, and it was a matter of custom and culture when it came to Hispanics. That didn't make it any easier to live with. In fact, that meant it was harder to fight sometimes."

In Texas and throughout the South, blacks as a group suffered official segregation. Public institutions backed by law designated people as unworthy based on the color of their skin, and there was nothing subtle about it. When blacks battled discrimination, they did so as a group fighting laws that existed on paper. In South Texas in the 1950s, discrimination against Latinos was different because it was not based on the single immutable characteristic of skin color and because it was not primarily a matter of law. Culture and convenience dictated that poor, dark-skinned Mexicans should not mix with whites, that they should go to inferior schools, and that they would always work at the bottom of the labor force. And while segregation applied to all blacks, the discriminatory culture of South Texas distinguished among Latinos, treating some like Mexicans and others not.

From the time of the conquistadors, there have always been rich Latinos north of the Rio Grande. And from the time of the Texas republic, they have been tolerated by Anglos as long as they abandoned any allegiance to Mexico. Whether they were downtown merchants in San Antonio or ranchers in the Rio Grande valley who traced their deeds back to the royal court of Spain, these Latinos were accepted as white—especially the daughters of the rich. Intermarriage with light-skinned, upper-class Hispanic females was allowed for white Texans. However, only a tiny fraction of the Latino population fit into this elite category.

The vast majority of Latinos were poor and dark-skinned, and they were labeled "Mexicans," a designation that undermined their legitimacy at the onset. This was a mixed population in terms of its legal status, just as the Latino population nationwide today is a mixture of citizens, legal immigrants, visitors, and illegal aliens. By painting them as foreigners, they could be relegated to second-class status more readily, and the poor especially were tainted with the specter of illegality.

The pejorative epithet applied to African-Americans, "niggers," referred to their skin color and was meant to mark them as inferior, even evil, as a consequence of their race. "Wetbacks" was the epithet used to insult Latinos in South Texas. It marked a group that had no civic standing, that did not belong to the body politic. As a group, they were thought of as "illegal" and that meant they were treated as if they did not merit protection of the law. Both epithets denoted people who could be abused casually. In the Deep South, sharecropping and Jim Crow went hand in hand as the economic and political elements of the system that kept blacks enthralled after the abolition of slavery. In Texas, as well as in the agricultural areas of California and the Southwest, the culture of discrimination against Latinos facilitated the use of Mexicans as a pool of cheap labor. It is easy to deny decent wages and working conditions to people who lack political standing and who have been marked as inferior creatures. In both cases, the systems of economic exploitation and political discrimination operated with the tacit cooperation of the federal government.

White landowners used the *bracero* program for four decades to ensure an excessive supply of labor and the low wages that went with it. Even the ready availability of more than 300,000 seasonal workers a year did not satisfy them. In 1952, the growers and businessmen of Texas, California, and the Southwest persuaded Congress to adopt the so-called Texas Proviso, which specifically exempted the employers of illegal aliens from any penalty. It remained the law until 1986.

A heavy strain of economic bias has always pervaded the discrimination inflicted on blacks and Latinos in the United States. They are disparaged and disliked in part because they are poor, and some would say are meant to stay poor. The fact that they were field hands, whether as sharecroppers or *braceros,* helped define their place as a people excluded from full participation in American society. And this economic element of discrimination has had a greater salience for Latinos than for blacks, if only because the bias against blacks is so elaborate.

In the Deep South, white society went to extraordinary lengths to justify Jim Crow, fabricating a group identity for blacks by corrupting science, history, and law. None of that was necessary in the land of mesquite and prickly pear. Poor Latinos were "Mexicans" and as such were part of the landscape. They were not threatening or dangerous. No one was going to fight a civil war over them. An elaborate system of segregation laws was not required to ensure their subjugation.

The law only recognized two races, white and black, and that made it easier to keep lower class Mexicans in their place. The law officially categorized Mexicans as whites. It did not grant them status as a separate group, nor did it recognize that they were subject to discrimination. That meant that when Latinos began to rebel against Texas racism in the 1950s, the first thing they had to do was to prove they were a distinct category of the population. They had to become like blacks in the eyes of the law. Only then could they proceed to show that they were victims of discrimination.

When DeAnda and his colleagues decided to fight discrimination in South Texas in the 1950s, they found a ready target in jury-selection practices. For decades, federal and state courts had ruled that it was a violation of equal protection rights for juries to issue indictments or verdicts when persons of the defendant's race had been deliberately excluded from serving on those juries. This interpretation of the Fourteenth Amendment typically applied when local authorities took overt steps to keep African-Americans out of jury pools.

In the infamous Scottsboro Case, nine young black men, ages thirteen to twenty-one, were indicted in Alabama in 1931 on charges of having raped two white girls. Eight of them faced an all-white jury and were quickly tried, convicted, and sentenced to death. With backing from the International Labor Defense, Clarence Darrow, and the NAACP, the case became a cause célèbre. Four years after the verdict, the U.S. Supreme Court, in *Norris v. Alabama,* reversed the convictions on the grounds that no blacks served on Alabama juries. The mere absence of blacks from juries was found to

be evidence of discrimination, with no need to prove that local officials had systematically set out to block their participation. Under
what came to be known as the Negro Exclusion Rule, de facto discrimination could be proven without showing discriminatory
intent.

When a man named Pete Hernández was indicted, convicted, and
sentenced to life imprisonment for the murder of one Pete Espinoza
in Jackson County, Texas, DeAnda saw a chance to invoke the
Scottsboro decision. The details of the crime and the eventual fate of
the defendant have long been forgotten, but the case of *Hernández
v. Texas* made it to the U.S. Supreme Court in 1954 and its outcome
changed the course of American history. At the time of Hernández's
indictment and trial, no person of Mexican descent had sat on any
Jackson County jury for at least twenty-five years, even though
Mexicans made up about 14 percent of the county's population and
were overwhelmingly native-born U.S. citizens.

When DeAnda invoked the Scottsboro case in the state courts, he
lost. The Texas Court of Criminal Appeals, the top state court on
criminal matters, ruled that because the Fourteenth Amendment
had been adopted in the wake of the Civil War, it recognized only
two classes of people as coming under its guarantee of equal protection: the white race and the Negro race. The Texas court designated
Mexicans not a distinct race, but, rather, white people of Spanish
descent, and so it found there was nothing wrong with bringing
them before all-white juries, even if no Mexicans ever served on
those panels. It was just white people judging white people,
although some of the white people, the defendants, were Mexicans,
and others, the white people on the juries, were always Anglos.

DeAnda and his colleagues had watched the NAACP, led by
future Supreme Court justice Thurgood Marshall, win several federal court decisions that transformed the equal protection clause of
the Fourteenth Amendment into a powerful tool for attacking segregation. The Mexican-American attorneys believed that *Hernández*
would get them similar results. They went before the U.S. Supreme
Court during the same term that produced the landmark decision in
Brown v. the Board of Education of Topeka, Kansas, which struck
down the "separate but equal" doctrine in public schooling and
doomed Jim Crow by opening vast areas of state and local policy to
federal intervention. Issued just two weeks before *Brown,* the deci-

sion in *Hernández v. Texas* would have almost as huge an impact on discrimination against Latinos.

DeAnda has no trouble remembering his favorite piece of evidence from the case.

"Right there in the Jackson County Courthouse, where no Hispanic had served on any kind of a jury in living memory because Mexicans were white and so it was okay to bring them before all-white juries, they had two men's rooms. One had a nice sign that just said MEN on it. The other had a sign on it that said COLORED MEN and below that was a hand-scrawled sign that said HOMBRES AQUÍ [men here]. In the jury pool, Mexicans may have been white, but when it came to nature's functions, they were not."

That little bit of Texas lore impressed Chief Justice Earl Warren enough that he cited it in his opinion on behalf of a unanimous court. Warren also noted that "the participation of persons of Mexican descent in business and community groups was shown to be slight. Until very recent times, children of Mexican descent were required to attend a segregated school for the first four grades. At least one restaurant in town prominently displayed a sign announcing NO MEXICANS SERVED."

All of this, the court decided, was ample proof of the Hispanics' claim that they constituted "a separate class in Jackson County, distinct from 'white.'" In reversing the Texas court, Warren concluded, "The Fourteenth Amendment is not directed solely against discrimination due to a 'two-class theory,' that is, based upon differences between 'white' and Negro."

Once the Hispanics of South Texas could be defined as non-whites, it was easy to meet the test of the Negro Exclusion Rule. The lawyers had only to show that no Latino was among the more than six thousand persons who had served on Jackson County juries in the prior twenty-five years.

In the *Hernández* decision, the Latinos of South Texas had been recognized as a discrete group with grievances and with rights that could be ascribed to them collectively and not merely as individuals. This designation constituted a new social and political status that encompassed all Latinos regardless of whether they were rich or poor, whether they owned land or worked it. Moreover, they gained this recognition under the umbrella of the Fourteenth Amendment, which was adopted in 1868 to ensure the enfranchisement of former slaves and which remains a mighty vehicle for the assertion of political equality.

In the *Hernández* decision, Chief Justice Warren wrote: "Throughout our history differences in race and color have defined easily identifiable groups which have at times required the aid of the courts in securing equal treatment under the laws. But community prejudices are not static, and from time to time other differences from the community norm may define other groups which need the same protection."

This idea that prejudice is dynamic rather than static proved to be as potent as the court's finding that separate was not equal. With the *Hernández* ruling, the Supreme Court affirmed that being nonwhite, being a minority, need not emerge from the unique experience of African-Americans as slaves and as victims of de jure segregation. Instead, the justices stated that discrimination could result from differences more difficult to recognize than race and skin color. This decision also found that over time new groups could emerge that deserved special protection because they are victims of newly developed or newly recognized prejudices. *Hernández* opened a door for the Mexicans of South Texas, and eventually all other Latinos would pass through that door. With *Hernández* and several other decisions that expanded the minority-group concept beyond blacks, the court eventually also opened doors for women, Asians, the disabled, and many others who would assert rights on the basis of a group identity.

Mexican-Americans did not initially seek designation as a group, nor did they seek an identity that set them apart. As Earl Warren noted, they were defined as different by the prejudices they suffered. They did not ask to be placed outside the mainstream of society and relegated to an inferior position. Separateness began as a manacle imposed on them in South Texas. Latinos asserted a separate status for themselves only because they had no other choice. If they wanted to fight prejudice, that was the only available strategy. To achieve social justice, Mexican-Americans had to become nonwhites before the law. Like the separateness that results from prejudice, separateness was also imposed on them, albeit in the form of a remedy.

Failure to understand this history of discrimination has caused a variety of commentators across the political spectrum to depict Latinos as opportunists masquerading in a minority-group guise for the perceived advantages it brings. For example, in *The New American Nation* the liberal author Michael Lind erroneously states, "Mexican-Americans were never formally segregated in education and public accommodations, denied the right to vote or serve on juries." He claims that although the law treated them as whites, Mexican-Americans and other Latinos "had to be redefined" as a race resembling blacks "in order to participate in the racial preference spoils system." According to Lind, it was all the work of "entrepreneurial politicians eager to win electoral rewards by making new groups eligible for benefits." Such views, though widely held, underestimate the painful past and greatly overvalue what Latinos have gained.

The logic and the mechanisms of civil rights law developed as a solution to the plight of African-Americans, and it was never particularly well suited to Latinos. As a group, Latinos lack the moral authority invested in African-Americans because of their experience of slavery and formal segregation. As individuals, Latinos do not share a single, immutable, easily recognizable marker like skin color that distinguishes them from all others. Nonetheless, civil rights law provided the only available remedies when native Latinos pressed discrimination claims that were ultimately judged valid. The process of redressing those grievances began in Texas in the 1950s, and it continued with important cases involving Puerto Ricans and bilingual education in the New York City public schools, school desegregation in Houston, bilingual education in Chicago, and voting rights all across Texas, the Southwest, and California. The process has continued into the 1990s, and the basic finding of *Hernández*—that Latinos suffer discrimination as nonwhites and therefore are eligible for civil rights remedies—has been validated and revalidated dozens of times in the federal courts.

As the United States adjusts its means of managing race relations to account for the new era of Latino immigration, there will be no erasing all the ugly things that happened in South Texas and in all the other places where Latinos have suffered discrimination. The pain of rejection and the use of civil rights tools to overcome it are an indelible part of the Latino experience in the United States, and eventually they become part of every immigrant's experience of the United States. South Texas shapes the context into which Latino immigration flows. The newcomers live among Latino natives and learn the rules of the game from them. Moreover, minority-group politics and the application of civil rights law are still the only game

available to Latinos when they seek redress of contemporary grievances. South Texas is history, and it is impossible to forget history
and pretend that Latino immigrants can be white. But it is equally
impossible to pretend that Anglos and African-Americans will simply go along as a rapidly expanding Latino immigrant population
asserts the special privileges of an aggrieved minority.

As Chief Justice Warren wrote in the *Hernández* decision, "Community prejudices are not static." At the very time that Latino
immigration was growing, the civil rights era was ending. Much of
white America has now lost its enthusiasm for initiatives to reduce
or remedy discrimination and many people actively oppose such
efforts. That leaves the nation in an ambiguous and evolving position. Civil rights laws remain on the books even as the courts—
especially the Supreme Court of the 1990s—restrict their application.
While most Americans support the idea of racial equality, they have
grown wary of governmental efforts to mandate it. The United
States is increasingly uncertain how to manage ethnic relations in
an era when immigration makes those relations increasingly complex. That is a volatile condition, and it cannot last. The mixture of
unstable elements is bound to produce a reaction, possibly a violent
one.

Some of the battlegrounds—schools and jobs—will remain the
same as whites, blacks, native Latinos, and immigrants, both Latino
and Asian, jockey for advantage and do battle over claims of discrimination. Meanwhile, the anti-immigrant backlash has already
defined new issues such as immigrants' eligibility for welfare and
affirmative-action programs. Instead of primal issues like the separation of the races, the conflicts will produce thickets of competing
rights, and the new mechanisms for managing ethnic relations will
have to detach the claims of immigrant nonwhites from those of
native minorities. Even as society defines a place for the newcomers,
it will still be resolving voting rights claims brought by African-
Americans and other unfinished items on the nation's civil rights
agenda. And all the while, this country will need to address new
forms of prejudice without relying on historical grievances as a
ready guide to right and wrong. Every one of these steps will be
made more difficult by the fact that the United States has squandered its best opportunities to establish effective immigration controls and must now contend with both an unmanageable flow and
the resentment it breeds.

CHAPTER 6

❖•❖•❖•❖•❖•❖•❖•❖•❖•❖•❖•❖•❖•❖•❖•❖•❖•❖•❖•

Branding the Babies

❖•❖•❖•❖•❖•❖•❖•❖•❖• In his memoir of the Reagan administration, *Revolution,* former domestic policy
adviser Martin Anderson recalls a cabinet meeting on July 16, 1981,
that dealt with proposals to combat illegal immigration. A congressional commission headed by the Reverend Theodore Hesburgh,
president of Notre Dame, had recently recommended legislation to
outlaw the employment of illegal aliens. An interagency task force
headed by Attorney General William French Smith had decided
that to enforce such a ban the administration ought to propose the
creation of an upgraded, counterfeitproof Social Security card that
everyone—native-born Americans and immigrants alike—would
have to present when seeking work.

These were not new ideas and the ID card suggestion in particular set off conservatives, like Anderson, who wrote, "Such a card is
an indispensable tool of a totalitarian state." At the cabinet meeting,
he raised his objections with the President, and Interior Secretary

James Watt, who often spoke for the Republican right, then joined in the criticism. Comparisons to concentration camp tattoos were bandied about. That set off the attorney general and others who believed a worker identity system was the only way to control illegal immigration. Voices got louder.

When it seemed an all-out argument was about to erupt, Reagan intervened. Anderson reports:

> The president spread his hands forward across the polished surface of the table, leaned back and looked directly at the attorney general. Smiling broadly he joked, "Maybe we should just brand all the babies."
> For about ten seconds everyone laughed and smiled, and that was the end of the national identification card for 1981.

Anderson drew the lesson that it was dangerous to let an ad hoc group, like a select commission, develop major proposals outside the normal flow of policymaking because a President could end up facing options that his administration did not like but could not easily reject. It happened to Reagan in 1981, and it happened again to Bill Clinton in 1994 when he had to contend with a congressional commission headed by the late Barbara Jordan, the former U.S. representative from Texas. Her commission saddled Clinton with a high-tech plan for a computerized government registry of the nation's entire workforce that employers would have to consult before they could make a hire. Jordan even went public with an admonishment that Clinton could get it all started immediately by executive order. The administration graciously welcomed the commission's ideas, thanked Jordan, and then quietly buried the plan.

But there is another truth underlying the episode Anderson recounts: Although everyone at that cabinet table held the same public position on the evils of illegal immigration and the need for a crackdown, they could not agree on any course of action to control it. Every option fostered harsh disagreements because illegal immigration is that rare kind of issue that breaks up traditional coalitions, zigzags across the ideological landscape, and yet still manages to arouse powerful emotions. In the end, President Reagan, like many other policymakers confronting this issue, found it easier to punt than to make a hard decision.

For thirty years, the hallmark of U.S. policies on both legal and illegal immigration has been a paralyzing bipartisan ambivalence. Everyone in Washington has long agreed that immigration needs to be regulated, but no effective or lasting agreements have been reached when it comes to spending government money, risking economic disorder, or taking political heat in order to control the flow. When policies were enacted, they emerged from compromises that sank resolutely to the lowest common denominator. But Washington should not get all the blame. Although every citizen had a great deal at stake, the public never paid much attention to immigration-policy debates.

The arcane lexicon of visa numbers, immigrant categories, and work authorizations shapes the content of the American population. Immigration policies help determine the qualifications of the workforce, the language of the cities, and the texture of civic life. From the mid-1960s to the mid-1990s, U.S. policies permitted, even encouraged, a massive flow of people northward from Latin America, especially from Mexico. This demographic watershed occurred without any consensus as to its values or its costs. The ambivalence at the heart of U.S. immigration policies throughout this period has deeply colored the experience of every Latino newcomer because immigrants were allowed into the country but were not necessarily welcomed. Meanwhile, the lack of public purpose has added greatly to the uneasiness of the native population, the whites and blacks, who feel beset by an event they do not understand and cannot control. All of this is most evident in the failure to develop adequate policies to control *illegal* immigration, and on that point the challenges pressed by Latino immigration have grown more serious and more complex with every half step and lost opportunity.

In 1974, Watergate still pounded the national psyche, the Vietnam War had entered its humiliating endgame, the Arab oil embargo had caused long lines at gas pumps, and the economy was suffering a vicious combination of recession and inflation that came to be known as "stagflation." Under those conditions, for the first time during the current wave of Latino immigration, illegal aliens became a cause of trepidation. Immigration Commissioner Leonard F. Chapman, Jr., a retired Marine Corps general, traveled the country in 1974 and 1975, promising that he could open up a million jobs for American workers "virtually overnight" if Congress would just give him enough men and money to seal the border and carry out mass deportations.

In the dark days of the mid-1970s, illegal immigration did not get nearly as much attention as inflation, but it looked much easier to solve. That turned out to be wrong. Inflation went away. Illegal immigration didn't.

In the 1930s and 1950s, there was an easy solution at hand when economic conditions soured and illegal aliens came to be scorned as excess labor: Washington conducted mass roundups and deportations and pushed the unwanted back across the border. But that option faded after native Latinos successfully asserted their civil rights claims. No law-enforcement agency could grab people out of barrios without producing a storm of demonstrations and lawsuits. As a result, General Chapman's hard-charging proposals never got a serious hearing in Washington.

But another strategy developed support very quickly. By widespread agreement, illegal aliens, most of them young single males, came north to take advantage of the job opportunities and higher wages in the United States. If government could eliminate the "jobs magnet," the illegals would stop coming. Congressman Peter W. Rodino, Jr., the New Jersey Democrat who had gained a national voice as chairman of the Nixon impeachment hearings, promoted legislation to outlaw the employment of illegals, and it quickly drew widespread support in Congress, among immigration and labor experts, and among a variety of interest groups. But almost immediately, two major dilemmas emerged: how to satisfy the employers, especially fruit and vegetable growers, who claimed they were dependent on illegal immigrant labor, and what to do about all the illegals already in the country.

Washington wrestled with these difficulties from 1975, when Attorney General Edward H. Levi convened a cabinet committee to study a proposal for a workers identity document, until the enactment of the Immigration Reform and Control Act of 1986. Along the way, the published proceedings of the select commission headed by Father Hesburgh filled a bookshelf. Two presidential interagency committees issued full-scale reports, and three Congresses considered legislation before the 1986 law was passed.

What emerged from this decade of deliberations was an ambitious balancing act. As originally conceived, the law aimed at stifling future illegal immigration while wiping away the legacies of the past. The jobs magnet would be eliminated by imposing penalties on the employers of illegals and establishing a tough enforcement regime. Meanwhile, illegal aliens already in the country would get an amnesty, allowing them to acquire legal-resident status and eventually citizenship. A broad agreement developed around the idea that an enforcement crackdown had to be paired with an amnesty because maintaining a large population of illegals—no one knew how many; the estimates ranged from two to twelve million—had a corrosive effect on the nation. But as Washington studied, debated, and compromised, narrow interests prevailed over the grand design. The end result of all that effort was that the United States lost its last, best chance to deal effectively with illegal immigration.

First, the amnesty was narrowed at the insistence of some labor unions that feared a flood of newly legalized workers would compete with their memberships, some conservatives who opposed generous dealings with lawbreakers, and some congressmen who simply did not like the idea of letting a large number of Mexicans become legal residents all at once. Instead of a clean sweep, the amnesty was tailored to benefit only those illegals who had already been in the United States for some time; eventually, only those who could produce documentary evidence they had been in the country since before 1982 would qualify.

But this narrower program worried the fruit and vegetable growers in California and the Southwest, who insisted they would lose too much of their workforce. Led by Pete Wilson, then a senator, on the Republican side, and Leon Panetta, then a congressman, later Clinton's chief of staff, on the Democratic side, California legislators argued for a guest-worker program. Eventually, Panetta and others hammered out a plan to satisfy the growers with a second amnesty of their very own. It offered legal status to people claiming to have done seasonal agricultural work in the past. The agricultural program was supposed to produce about 400,000 applicants. Nearly 1.3 million people turned out amid well-documented charges of fraud by thousands who had never soiled their hands but who bought bogus documents allowing them to claim they had worked as vegetable pickers. About 1.7 million people signed up for the general amnesty.

Over time, the amnesties failed to achieve the intended objectives
and laid the groundwork for future crises. The amnesty recipients
represented only about 60 percent of the illegal population at the
time, according to Immigration and Naturalization Service estimates, and the rest of the illegal population remained in the shadows. This meant that the nation's big cities continued to play host to
the social networks and economic structures that facilitated illegal
immigration, and so the illegal population could grow again at will.
The original goal of the amnesty program—to allow the country to
start over again with a clean slate—was critically compromised by
the legislative bargains necessary to get it enacted.

A majority of the amnesty applicants were lone males, especially
among the Mexicans. Once they got their amnesty papers, a new
kind of illegal traffic developed for purposes of family reunification
as men now secure in their position here sent home for their wives
and children. Washington decided it could not break up these families, and so it allowed the relatives of amnesty recipients to live in
the country illegally while their applications for legal status were
processed. As of the end of 1995, some 824,000 such relatives still
awaited visas, creating a backlog that choked the immigration system. Moreover, the homes of amnesty recipients served as a secure
base for newly arrived relatives and friends with no claim on legal
status. The net effect was to stimulate a larger flow of illegals and
to proliferate the phenomenon of mixed households where legal
and illegal immigrants lived together permanently and as complete
families.

The amnesties would never have backfired so badly had it not
been for the fact that the other half of the great legislative bargain—
employer sanctions—had not also been compromised beyond any
hope of effectiveness. During the decade-long debate that preceded
enactment of the 1986 law, employers complained they would bear
the burden of determining whether a new hire was eligible to work
or not and would face penalties if they made a mistake. Several
ideas were put forth to ease that burden. One of the most persistent
suggestions involved the creation of a system that would allow
employers to easily verify the identity and work eligibility of a job
applicant.

The proposals ranged from a national identity card to a computer
registry based on Social Security numbers. At every turn, civil lib-

ertarians objected to the potential for government intrusion. Meanwhile, Latinos and some civil rights advocates complained that only foreign-looking people or people with unusual names would be subject to strict checks by employers, thereby creating a new type of discrimination. Finally, the business community fought any proposals that increased their exposure to legal penalties or that imposed greater administrative costs.

Instead of a new identity system, the 1986 law allowed employers to accept a laundry list of documents, including many that were easily counterfeited, as proof of a worker's legal immigration status. Huge legal loopholes were created for employers who wanted to claim that they had made an honest mistake in hiring an illegal alien. Moreover, Congress failed to create an enforcement mechanism for even these loose rules.

The plan was to rely on voluntary compliance, and for nearly two years INS agents visited workplaces all over the country, explaining the new law and the new forms and procedures, but avoiding almost any enforcement activity during this "education" period, which lasted into 1989. Most diligent employers complied. These were the sort of businessmen who would routinely check the identity of a new hire anyway and who would want to be sure of paying the proper withholding and Social Security taxes. These were the same employers most likely to keep safe workplaces and pay good wages and offer medical insurance. The law shut illegal aliens out of these workplaces unless they could come up with some good false papers and a valid Social Security number. But a huge gray area of the labor market remained open to them among employers who just wanted to observe the letter of the law and would not look too closely at counterfeit documents or get too preoccupied when government computers rejected a bad Social Security number. In a darker sector of real criminality, there were the many businessmen willing to break the law, who not only knew they were hiring illegal aliens but also knowingly violated many other rules designed to keep jobs safe and fair.

The government made no credible effort to seek out and punish employers who continued to hire illegal aliens. Between 1989 and 1994, the number of INS agents assigned to the enforcement of employer sanctions dropped by half, as did the number of fines issued. Despite an illegal population of an estimated 4.5 million people nationwide in 1994, the INS completed only 1,761 cases producing fines against employers. Meanwhile, it had accumulated a backlog of 36,000 leads on possible violations that had never been investigated. And so the illegals kept coming, and kept finding jobs.

For employers, the temptations mounted. The rapid expansion of service industries, intense competition among national chains in areas like food service and retailing, and global competition in many areas of manufacturing, all helped create a growing segment of the economy that employed large numbers of low-wage workers. Most of these enterprises operated on such thin margins that hiring illegals at illegal wages meant the difference between profits and bankruptcy. Employers in these sectors faced intense economic pressures to reduce costs by breaking workplace laws, and the government generated no counterpressure obliging them to follow the rules.

Labor Department inspectors reported that only 47 percent of the workplaces they visited were in full compliance with the rules on verifying the immigration status of new hires in the early 1990s. Most often, these job sites violated many other rules as well. For example, in the California garment industry, which relied heavily on the work of illegal aliens, a 1994 Labor Department survey found that nearly 93 percent of the manufacturers violated health and safety rules, 68 percent failed to pay proper overtime, and 50 percent did not pay their workers the minimum wage. In 1996, the Labor Department estimated that about half of the 22,000 cutting and sewing operations nationwide qualified as sweatshops and admitted that it did not have the manpower to enforce basic wage and safety laws in these establishments.

It was not until 1995, after illegal immigration threatened to become a major issue in presidential politics, that the Clinton administration launched modest efforts to increase work-site enforcement and accompanied each initiative with lavish public relations campaigns. But as before, the government relied on the goodwill of employers who had already demonstrated a penchant for breaking the law. As the Democratic party launched its now-infamous soft-money fund-raising crusade with corporate America, the Clinton administration, under the aegis of Vice President Al Gore's government reengineering program, determined that the best way to regulate business was through "partnerships." For its part, the INS cloyingly proclaimed that it "treats the employer as the client rather than the enemy." In a much-heralded program dubbed Operation Jobs, the INS actually allowed employers to keep illegal alien workers for sixty days after a job site had been raided, so that the business could find replacement workers and avoid any economic losses. In the garment industry, the Labor Department struck a series of voluntary agreements with big-name retailers and designers like Kathie Lee Gifford who wanted to avoid any more of the bad publicity attendant to selling sweatshop products. The big names insisted they never knew that their clothes came from sweatshops, because all the manufacturing was handled by subcontractors. Then they made noble-sounding promises not to purchase from sweatshops again, but they refused to accept legal obligations to guarantee the quality of wages and working conditions at their subcontractors' factories, nor would they agree to pay enough for a garment to ensure that workers received decent pay. Even if all these businesses follow through on their good intentions, the government's voluntary arrangements do nothing to discourage the rogues. Employer sanctions have been meaningless for a full decade, and anyone who sees profit in breaking the law—both unscrupulous employers and the illegal aliens who would work for them—has found all the means necessary to circumvent it, starting with an ever-larger and more sophisticated industry in counterfeit documents.

The 1986 law was supposed to complete its attack on illegal immigration by invigorating the INS with new funds and new programs, including a crackdown at the border. Congress, however, neglected to appropriate the promised dollars. So, in response to the bureaucratic imperatives created by the amnesty and employer sanctions, the INS initially shifted resources from the border to the interior of the country. Meanwhile, the war on drugs had become such a sexy new priority in Washington that the hunt for cocaine shipments also drew attention away from the illegal human traffic. The number of border apprehensions and other data show that the illegal flow dropped off for about a year after the 1986 law went into effect, as immigrant networks waited to see what would happen. Once it became clear that employer sanctions were no deterrent to getting a job, the numbers began to climb again. Soon the relatively unprotected border region became ever more chaotic and even violent. By 1989 crowds of a hundred people or more routinely would gather at twilight on the Mexican side of the most popular illegal crossing points around San Diego. As darkness fell, the crowds would rush north. Border Patrol agents might be able to grab a few people at a time but would have to watch dozens running by. Agents who got too close to the crowds often found themselves ducking a hail of stones. In 1993 the Clinton administration, under heavy pressure from Congress, responded with the first of several emergency plans to boost the border force. Adding new agents with better equipment and building miles of fence partially displaced alien smuggling from traditional crossing points into more remote areas, but the new efforts failed to either reduce illegal immigration or quell demands for more action.

After the Republicans took control of Congress in the 1994 elections, a few angry legislators vowed to enact omnibus legislation that would both attack illegal immigration and drastically reduce the level of legal immigration. Speaker of the House Newt Gingrich gave the go-ahead but said that the Contract with America and its revolutionary overhaul of the federal budget would take precedence, and that effort, of course, became mired in government shutdowns and a confrontation with the Clinton administration that lasted right through the 1996 elections. In the meantime the gnarly and inept sponsors of the GOP immigration bill, Senator Alan K. Simpson of Wyoming and Congressman Lamar Smith of Texas, constructed legislation so overreaching that it attracted opponents from every corner. Eventually, divisions in the Republican ranks doomed the effort to cut legal immigration, and what survived to enactment was a disjointed packet of measures on illegal immigration that hewed to the tradition of ambivalent, largely rhetorical policymaking.

As finally enacted, the Illegal Immigration Reform and Immigrant Responsibility Act of 1996 authorized a whopping increase of five thousand Border Patrol agents in five years—doubling the size of the force—plus the addition of fifteen hundred support personnel and the construction of a triple-tier fence on the border south of San Diego. While ordering this warlike mobilization on the border, Congress demurred when it came to more complicated and controversial aspects of the fight against illegal immigration. For example, on the questions of jobs, the law established a small voluntary pilot program whereby employers would have the option of calling the

INS to check a job applicant's eligibility. However, there was no added manpower or money dedicated to the enforcement of employer sanctions. The 1996 law was enacted amid mounting evidence that a large share of the illegal population—the INS estimates 40 percent—enters the country not by sneaking across the border but by legally coming through airports and other entry points. About 125,000 people a year, according to the INS, arrive with temporary visas as tourists or students and then remain illegally. However, Congress declined to appropriate funds to hire three hundred investigators to search out visa overstays, as originally authorized by the 1996 law. In September 1997, a year after the law was enacted, a report by the Inspector General of the Justice Department concluded, "INS has no specific enforcement program to identify, locate, apprehend, and remove overstays."

On another front, the 1996 law increased penalties for alien smuggling and document fraud and authorized use of wiretaps and the seizure of assets when dealing with criminals who traffic in human beings, but just as it failed to address overstays, the law also failed to ensure the creation of an adequate investigative force to find smugglers and counterfeiters. Commenting on the buildup at the border and the neglect elsewhere, INS special agent Robert A. McGraw complained that "Congress and the administration . . . remembered the policemen and forgot the detectives." Writing in the Federal Law Enforcement Officers Association journal, McGraw argued that "Neglect of INS investigations . . . continues, and this means little or nothing is likely to improve."

By 1996, the illegal population was again about as large as it had been when the 1986 law was enacted—5 million people—and was growing at a rate of at least 275,000 people a year, according to the INS. Like an antibiotic administered in an insufficient dose, the 1986 law and the equivocations that followed not only failed to eradicate illegal immigration but allowed the disease to develop a tolerance to the cure.

Another layer of ambiguity and another unauthorized population developed out of the political-asylum system, which was the conduit through which most Central Americans sought legal status after they had entered the country without authorization. A massive backlog developed in the 1980s as a result of administrative chaos, insufficient resources, and court decisions that found that victims of the U.S.-supported military in El Salvador had faced systematic discrimination in the asylum system. By 1994, the asylum backlog covered about a million individuals who were allowed to live and work in the United States even though their cases had never been decided. In addition, half a million Salvadorans, some of them also amnesty applicants, were granted various forms of temporary legal status and were allowed to remain in the United States even after these temporary grants ran out.

As a result of all these failed immigration policies, more than half of the entire Latino foreign-born population of the United States has had some direct experience of illegality. That includes those who have received legal status through the various amnesty and asylum programs as well as those who live here permanently with no claim on legal residence. Making a home in the United States in defiance of the law became a normal occurrence because the law failed, and the most concrete proof of that failure lies in the tacit acceptance of a huge population of illegal aliens by American society at large. The Supreme Court diagnosed this acquiescence when it ruled in 1982 that the children of illegal aliens could not be denied access to public education. Justice William J. Brennan, Jr., wrote that illegals live in the United States, "enjoying an inchoate federal permission to remain." A decade later, Zoë Baird, Clinton's first nominee for attorney general, echoed the same sentiment when she tried to explain to the Senate Judiciary Committee why she had hired an illegal alien as her nanny, saying that she felt that the INS "gave tacit approval to the situation."

Illegal aliens are easy to castigate. Their presence in large numbers encourages abuses in the workplace, weakens sovereign control of the borders, undermines law enforcement, and convolutes the process by which immigrant communities establish their place in American society. But illegal aliens are the wrong target for public rage. The real culprits are the officials of both political parties who have refused to make hard choices. This inutile ambivalence is also apparent in the way policies on *legal* immigration have developed.

One morning in late October 1990, Senator Ted Kennedy went over to the House side of the Capitol with a big manila envelope under his arm. Walking down an isolated corridor, he entered a hideaway meeting room, where he was met by Congressman Jack Brooks, the Texas Democrat who chaired the House Judiciary Committee. Their task was to reconcile the differences between the House and Senate versions of legislation that would overhaul the legal immigration system for the first time in twenty-five years.

Most of the important provisions had been debated, compromised, and voted on several times already, but a few big disputes remained unresolved. Congress was due to adjourn in three days. The two Democratic leaders knew that if they did not get the bill passed right away, it was going to die. Like the 1986 reform aimed at illegal immigration and many other laws passed in the later years of the Democrats' reign in Congress, the Immigration Act of 1990 was born of a marriage between good intentions and rank expediency.

As they stood on opposite sides of an antique table, preparing to sit down, Kennedy lifted the broad flap of the manila envelope and, with a grin, showed Brooks what was inside: a big box of Davidoff cigars. Kennedy had recently quit smoking them, but Brooks still consumed the stogies with relish. Kennedy closed the flap and set the box down in the middle of the table.

In a negotiation that lasted most of the day, Kennedy would slide the box a little toward Brooks when the House side compromised on a point, and he would pull it back toward himself whenever he thought the Senate was getting a raw deal. As the cigar box slid back and forth and the two powerful chairmen chuckled at their private joke, the fates of millions of people and the future face of America got kicked around.

Under Democratic leadership, both houses of Congress had decided to brush aside Republican demands for lower limits on legal immigration, and instead the Democrats proceeded to increase the numbers, which had already grown steadily for more than a decade. The House and Senate Democrats differed mainly on the size and some of the content of the increase. In order to make everybody happy, Brooks and Kennedy came up with a bit of legislative hocus-pocus and created a "pierceable cap" for legal immigration, a limit designed to be broken.

The bill had already become a "Christmas tree" in congressional parlance, meaning that it was hung with a variety of detailed provisions meant to satisfy special interests, and as the cigar box went back and forth across the table, more ornaments were added. The bill finished with special visa deals for the Hong Kong Chinese employees of U.S. businesses, for the Irish, for Salvadorans, for Filipino war veterans, and for religious workers. There was a new Hollywood visa, the "O visa," for artists and entertainers of "extraordinary ability," and a New York visa, the "P visa," for artists and entertainers who received international recognition.

The cigars ended up with Brooks and both houses approved the bill at the last possible moment before Congress adjourned.

As a result, just as the country slid into a recession that would hit states with the biggest immigration the hardest, the number of legal immigrants increased by about a third, some 200,000 additional people a year. Over the course of a decade, the cigar box deal had the potential to increase the U.S. population by about 2 million newcomers, something like adding a city the size of Seattle or Pittsburgh. These immigrants, in turn, would gain the right to sponsor their relatives for visas, and so each increase in immigration contained the seeds of even larger flows in the future. Even though the law would have a huge impact on the land, no one felt obliged to explain the whys and wherefores to the American people. This became standard practice.

When Simpson and Smith proposed wholesale cuts in legal immigration in 1995, they did not offer much of a rationale, other than to claim that existing policies allowed too many newcomers. With the backlash spreading from California across the country, they simply proclaimed that they spoke for the public, but they never articulated a set of motives and goals that the public might support. They did not even attempt to explain their demonstrably false claim that legal immigration did so much harm that it needed to be slashed from one year to the next. In the circumscribed world of immigration policymaking, the absence of reasoning has never been an impediment to action. When the Republican Congress seemed an unstoppable steamroller in early 1995, Barbara Jordan went to Simpson and Smith to volunteer her services. "We were created by Congress," Jordan told reporters. "We were not created by some act of divine intervention." Choosing to be relevant rather than consistent, Jordan pawned her gravelly-voice respectability to a pair of subcommittee chairmen. Racing to meet legislative deadlines, Jordan had her commission whip out recommendations to cut overall visa numbers by a third, despite the fact that just nine months earlier it had reported to Congress that insufficient time had passed since the implementation of the 1990 act to assess the value of current immigration levels. In her eagerness to exercise influence over her newly adopted métier, Jordan went to the White House on June 7, 1995, and took all of fifteen minutes to convince Clinton that he, too, should reverse his position and back cuts in legal immigration.

The idea of cutting the legal numbers, however, was susceptible to precisely the same kind of lobbying that had produced the cigar box deal. Once again, the American public was not even a bystander, because it could hardly see what was going on. By early 1996, manufacturing companies and high-tech entrepreneurs who wanted a guaranteed supply of foreign technicians joined with Latino and Asian groups and libertarian conservatives to form a powerful coalition against the cuts in legal immigration. The backlash had developed at the grassroots level during a recession, but during an economic expansion, much of corporate America was determined to resist any move that would restrict the growth of the labor force and might thereby induce wage increases. At one point during the debate over the immigration bill, the National Association of Manufacturers and other corporate groups considered launching a multimillion-dollar public relations campaign extolling the virtues of legal immigration in order to rally public opposition to the Simpson-Smith proposals. Instead, they opted for a guerrilla campaign, during which top lawmakers and administration officials were ambushed by corporate executives who controlled troves of campaign donations. One Republican after another withdrew support for wholesale cuts, especially those that would involve highly skilled immigrants, and Clinton, as was his habit, sensed the shifting winds and changed his position again. The deeply flawed Simpson-Smith plan for a radical change in direction died in 1996, but so did the prospect for a measured, gradual reform of the legal immigration system.

Ambivalence—abetted by political cowardice—prevailed yet again with the enactment of a welfare-reform law just before the 1996 campaign began its final stretch. The law barred legal immigrants from many forms of social assistance and government-funded health care, targeting the elderly and the disabled. Supporters of the measure decried foreigners who came to commit fraud on the commonweal and demanded the cutoff in order to halt a great drain on the public treasury. Clinton wrung his hands about the harsh treatment of immigrants but signed the law anyway, because he did not want to face the electorate as an opponent of welfare reform. Behind the rhetoric, legal immigrants merely served as an easy fiscal target because the White House and Congress needed to find budget savings to finance the work programs that replaced traditional welfare. Within a year, once the budget picture looked better and the welfare rolls began to drop, many of the eligibility cuts were restored, but there was no way to erase the widely broadcast and largely false allegation that immigrants were predisposed to welfare dependency.

In 1997 a team of twenty experts from the United States and Mexico announced the results of a three-year study of migration patterns and policies commissioned by the governments of the two nations. Looking back over the past half century, the Binational Study on Migration listed its first major conclusion under the heading "Episodic Nature of U.S. Responses." Its second conclusion was labeled "Unintended Consequences." "The disjunction between policy intentions and actual outcomes has been a perennial feature of immigration history," the report said. Perhaps the clearest evidence of that disjunction lay in the study's demographic estimates. During the 1980s, between 2.1 million and 2.6 million Mexicans took up permanent residence in the United States, counting both legal and illegal arrivals. That was nearly double the number of the prior decade. But in the first half of the 1990s the number doubled again—1.9 million new residents from Mexico between 1990 and 1996—despite the fact that throughout this period the U.S. government was supposed to be implementing measures to reduce the flow, at least the illegal component of it. What is even more remarkable is the composition of this growing influx. According to the binational study, widely regarded as the most authoritative undertaking of its kind, illegal aliens from Mexico outnumbered legal immigrants during the 1990s. It estimated 630,000 unauthorized migrants compared to 510,000 legal immigrants, and this does not include the many thousands of illegals who come for temporary stays. The largest category—760,000 people—was composed of Mexicans who gained legal admission under the amnesty for agricultural workers or as family members of amnesty recipients. In immigration, unintended consequences translate into enormous demographic events.

The final report of the Hesburgh Commission recommended in 1981 that the United States "close the back door" of illegal immigration so that it could "open the front door" of legal immigration. That distinction and the benign trade-off it suggests have defined immigration policy for nearly twenty years, but too many options have been misused and the flows have grown too large for anything so simple to have much meaning now. The issue is no longer illegal versus legal but controlled versus uncontrolled. Advocating controlled immigration does not necessarily imply reduction in the numbers of immigrants, let alone the embrace of an anti-immigrant backlash. The size of the flow and the details of the law are less important than the distinction between immigration that takes place with the conscious acceptance of the hosts and that which appears to happen haphazardly.

Without controls that enjoy the understanding and support of the host society, it is impossible to set priorities and develop strategies designed to ensure that immigrants and their children make the best possible contributions to their new land. As a matter of practical politics, it is impossible to secure public spending for programs to ensure the successful integration of immigrants—whether it be to teach them English or to vaccinate their children—if there is no public confidence in government's ability to control the flows. In the absence of clearly articulated goals and of effective enforcement, the absorption of immigrants proceeds as a matter of social evolution more likely to produce conflict than consensus. That occurred during the later stages of European immigration. From the 1880s until World War I, Washington appointed special commissions and implemented measures—such as a literacy test—that created the impression of control without substantially reducing the flow. The result then was a period of harsh nativism that darkened the experience of all newcomers in the early part of this century and a backlash that eventually forced Congress in 1924 to adopt an almost complete shutoff of immigration. That may not seem like much of a danger today, as the United States enjoys a record-setting economic expansion, but as the binational study concluded, "The debate on immigration into the United States waxes and wanes with the economic cycle. When the U.S. economy falters, restrictionist sentiment grows more intense."

After the economic downturn at the start of the 1990s, restrictionist sentiments blossomed in California. That backlash should be remembered as an example of what a short and shallow recession can induce, and it should be viewed as a small foretaste of what might occur if the United States experiences a serious downturn and people begin to ask how it is possible that Washington let immigration go uncontrolled for so long.

CHAPTER   7

◆·◆·◆·◆·◆·◆·◆·◆·◆·◆·◆·◆·◆·◆·◆·◆·◆·◆·◆·

Save Our State

◆·◆·◆·◆·◆·◆·◆·◆·◆· During a routine visit to an Orange County social service center in 1992, Barbara Coe became frightened by the changes immigration had brought to California.

"I walked into this monstrous room full of people, babies and little children all over the place, and I realized nobody was speaking English," recalls Coe. There is no outrage in her voice. She is a sixty-year-old grandmother quite certain she is describing events that simply defy common sense.

"I was overwhelmed with this feeling: Where am I? What's happened here? Is this still the United States of America?"

By Election Day of 1994, when the Proposition 187 ballot initiative to combat illegal immigration drew more votes than any candidate on any ballot anywhere in the country, Coe had found 4.6 million Californians who shared her fears. More than any other event, the overwhelming passage of Proposition 187 crystallized the backlash. It gave political expression to all the anxieties already produced by the new wave of immigration, and it showed that once fear of immigrants spreads to a sizable portion of the electorate it can have a potent impact on the nation as a whole, even if that fear is not shared everywhere. No other states adopted similar measures, and some prominent political leaders in Texas and New York argued that punitive actions against illegal aliens would do more harm than good. Nonetheless, the California vote provided a dramatic illustration of the anxieties that often lay latent in a host society during a time of large-scale immigration. Fear of the unknown, hostility toward the stranger, resentment toward newcomers who embody change, all these feelings ebb and flow and take different expressions at different times and places. When these anxieties find a political expression, they can define an identity for an immigrant group. Proposition 187 defined the new immigrants, most especially Latino immigrants, and it defined them as a threat.

To understand how Proposition 187 imposed an identity on Latino immigrants, it is important to return to Barbara Coe, who is quick to note that she went to that service center in 1992 just to help secure some public health benefits for an elderly friend, a crippled World War II vet. It is a story she has told often and so the details are all in place.

"I tried to find someone to help me, but there were three windows to serve Spanish-speaking people, two for Asians, and one for English speakers, and it was closed."

A short, slender woman with close-cropped blond, almost white hair and long nails painted a creamy color, Coe says she was "a little aggravated" by the time she got to see a counselor because "I had my toes stepped on and my shins kicked in that mass of humanity."

Advertising the approaching climax of her story with a voice dropping to an exasperated whisper, she says, "And so I asked this woman, this counselor, I asked, 'You tell me what's going on out there—what is it?' When the counselor told me that lots of those people waiting were illegal aliens and they were getting benefits instead of citizens like my friend, I walked out of there outraged. I decided I had to do something."

Coe was either misinformed or has suffered a lapse of memory, because it is highly unlikely that illegal aliens would crowd into a social service center. They are not eligible for most forms of public assistance, and they usually avoid government offices because their identities might be discovered.

What Coe did perceive, and what does seemingly defy common sense, is the breakneck pace of demographic change in Southern California. Once an overwhelmingly white middle-class community, Orange County is now home to the largest population of Vietnamese outside Ho Chi Minh City. As former military allies fleeing after the U.S. defeat in their nation, they arrived as refugees, which means they are specially privileged legal immigrants with full rights to many benefits and services. And like the rest of Southern California, Orange County also experienced a large influx of Latinos that included many citizens and legal immigrants eligible for public assistance, and along with them came illegals, who are not eligible.

Middle-class homeowners who had abandoned Los Angeles in favor of distant white suburbs suddenly found themselves surrounded by people frighteningly like the ones they had tried to escape: poor nonwhites. And worst of all, these foreigners had penetrated the enclave and were living among them. Borders and boundaries had broken down.

Altogether, immigration produced a vast demographic change in Southern California that is easy for outsiders to underestimate because no other part of the nation has ever experienced anything like it since the turn of the century. In the 1990 census, the foreign-born made up 33 percent of the population in Los Angeles County, and within a few years it was getting close to the 40 percent mark reached by New York in 1910 at the peak of the European migration. The change was not limited to the central city. In 1960, Hispanics made up one-tenth of the population in the five-county L.A. region, but by 1990 they represented one-third. It is a big change and it came quickly. Under such circumstances, some kind of reaction by the people who witnessed this change in their community was inevitable. Barbara Coe walked out of that government office building in 1992 outraged. She quickly discovered she was not alone. Lots of people were holding meetings and writing letters to their congressmen all over that swath of coastal plain south of Los Angeles that was once orange groves and ranches and then had been white and affluent and was now polyglot and embattled. Coe checked out some of the citizen groups and decided to form one of her own because she wanted to do more.

"I am not the sort of person to go to meetings, drink tea, and wring my hands."

Looking for a way to get quick results, her group hit upon the idea of using a ballot initiative to combat illegal immigration. They took as their model the angry middle-class whites who fought property tax increases in 1978 by passing Proposition 13, an initiative that froze tax rates for existing homeowners.

Proposition 187 sought equally profound changes. It would prohibit illegal immigrants from receiving social or welfare services, ban them from public schools and universities, and prevent them from receiving publicly funded health care except in emergencies. Anyone seeking these benefits would have to document their immigration or citizenship status, including every child registering for public school. Administrators would be obliged to report "suspected" illegal immigrants to the authorities.

To draft the proposition, Coe's group enlisted two Reagan-era immigration officials, Alan Nelson, who had been commissioner of the Immigration and Naturalization Service, and Harold Ezell, who had been in charge of the INS western region. Both Nelson and Ezell were political appointees with little experience of immigration matters before they took office. Throughout most of the 1980s, they presided over an immense influx of illegal immigration, an almost-complete breakdown of border controls, and a series of bureaucratic and budgetary debacles that filled voluminous reports to Congress. Given that track record, Nelson and Ezell might have seemed a curious choice, but officials charged with enforcing laws rarely get blamed when they fail at their jobs. Instead, they blame it all on the criminals. Some like Nelson and Ezell actually find new careers denouncing the lawlessness. Not surprisingly, they proved no more effective in drafting the proposition than when the federal government was at their disposal. They produced a document so profoundly flawed as an instrument of public policy that both state and federal courts blocked its implementation hours after it was approved on Election Day.

But that didn't matter one Friday evening in 1994 as the September twilight began to settle over the freeways of Orange County. The election campaign had come to Buena Park, an artificial town with a bilingual name just up the Santa Ana Freeway from Disneyland.

A crowd was gathering at a combination health club/bowling

alley/conference center. Everywhere inside there was red-white-and-blue plastic bunting, Styrofoam boaters, and pictures of vengeful eagles. The star attraction that night was H. Ross Perot. His name would not appear on any ballots that November, but rather than be upstaged by the Republican revolution, he had undertaken a campaign tour of the nation to remind people just how right he had always been about everything.

Wearing a royal blue suit and a white turtleneck, Barbara Coe arrived accompanied by Art Jacques, a fullback-sized man with a bushy black mustache, wraparound sunglasses, and an enormous steel belt buckle that had a horseshoe on it. He often accompanied Coe to campaign events and seemed to serve as a bodyguard, though perhaps not in the classic sense. Coe introduced him, saying, "When people accuse me of being a racist, I tell them to talk to Art Jacques. He is of Mexican ancestry and he is behind us one thousand percent." Shaking hands with a powerful grip, Jacques puffed out his chest and said bullishly, "That's right. She ain't no racist and I'm here to prove that." Only a fool would have pursued the subject any further.

Coe was excited. Supporters of 187 had been in touch with Perot's people and the Californians hoped he would endorse the proposition that night. They thought they needed his help urgently. Recent polls had shown voters slipping away from 187 for the first time. Statewide organizations of teachers, school boards, hospital administrators, and sheriffs had all urged rejection of the initiative, arguing that turning children out into the street and denying health care to the sick would do much more harm than good.

"All those people coming out against us are just greedy," Coe said. "The teachers and doctors don't want to lose the billions of dollars they get for taking care of illegals. They are just greedy. But, I'll tell you something: I'm not going to turn tail and betray my country just because someone is paying my bills."

Handing out leaflets to the crowd of middle-aged and elderly whites, she found a willing audience, and she did not pull any punches. Thick-waisted men and women with blue-gray hair listened intently as Coe warned, "People out there, you know, are getting very angry, more every day. And we are working very hard to pass this because we are so frightful that there will be violence unless this problem gets solved by law and order. People have lost houses, they've lost jobs, some people have lost lives because of the illegals, and we are just hopeful that by passing this we can prevent violence. That's what we are about."

Soon it was time for everyone to take a seat and listen to the long series of speakers who would take the podium before Perot. Appearing on behalf of Proposition 187 was Bill King, a thirty-two-year veteran of the INS, now retired, another former cop deploring the failure of the law.

"Our borders today are totally out of control. They are totally out of control and open to anyone; anyone can get into this country."

Almost as soon as he began speaking, it was as if a fuse had been lit, and the crowd began exploding. King seemed taken aback. "You're great, you're great," he said before returning to his litany of horrors. "Our borders are totally open to drug smugglers, alien smugglers, criminals of all types, disease carriers and job seekers. And it's just not right."

The crowd exploded again, jumping to its feet, something it never did when Perot came along later to talk about budget deficits and trade agreements, without making any mention of illegal immigration. Like Perot during his 1992 presidential campaign, King hammered away with visions of economic, social, and cultural decline.

"We once had a proud education system in this state and it is being trashed."

And whatever evil he identified, he always found the same culprit.

"I would ask the medical profession that is so busy trying to defend its Medicare money right now: If there is a resurgence of disease in this country, where is it coming from? Well, the answer we all know is that a large part of the disease proliferation we are experiencing now is coming across the border every night on the backs of illegal aliens who don't belong here."

His voice rising with anger, King said that illegal immigrants are like burglars because "they both trespass with criminal intent. Just as a burglar comes into your home to steal your property, the illegal alien is coming here to take your jobs and deplete your resources."

King predicted victory for the proposition. The crowd rose to its feet. Moments later, Coe, King, and other figures from the 187 campaign were on the stage with the leaders of the California branch of

Perot's United We Stand America. A young woman in a shimmery dress led them in a hymn of patriotic discontent. They all held hands and swayed. The audience joined them.

> *I'm proud to be an American*
> *Where at least I know I'm free . . .*

Supporters of Proposition 187 liked to call it the Save Our State initiative. The name was fitting. An SOS is a distress signal. It is not a cure or a remedy, but an expression of fear. The people in Buena Park that night dreaded immigrants more than they disliked them. Many, like Coe, insisted that they got along fine with foreigners on an individual basis, but taken collectively the aliens seemed a mortal threat. When people are afraid for a long period of time, it changes the way they see the world. Eventually, it also changes whatever it is they fear. Sensing the reaction it has provoked, the object of fear responds defensively, generating more fear. That's what happened in L.A. as the Proposition 187 campaign drew to a close.

On November 1, 1994, more than ten thousand Latino high school students took to the streets of Los Angeles in one of the most widespread protest demonstrations in the city's recent history. With no prominent leaders or a strategic plan, they walked out of classrooms all over the metropolitan area to voice their anger over Proposition 187. They marched down major thoroughfares somewhat aimlessly and chanted slogans. Sometimes by design and sometimes by accident, they blocked traffic. Tying up freeways got them attention.

They took to the streets every school day until the election a week later, and with each march, the local television news broadcast images of young people, mostly brown-skinned teenagers in baggy pants and hooded sweatshirts or tight jeans and tank tops, swaggering down the street, shouting, and being angry. But most of all, the newspaper and television coverage emphasized a single image: The barrio kids carried Mexican flags. Ballot initiatives do not usually produce good visuals, and the local media could hardly resist the demonstrations. Morning, noon, and night, the Mexican tricolor was on the tube. Red, white, and green became the colors of opposition to Proposition 187 as the campaign came to a close.

"We carry this flag because it is the flag of our parents. We belong here because our parents came here, and many others have come here," said Leonardo Hernández, sixteen years old, as he marched down Whittier Boulevard in East L.A., a busy street where Spanish has served as the language of commerce for an entire generation. "They always let everyone in when they need us, and then they think they can get rid of us later. But we've always been here, and we'll always keep coming here."

The public opinion polls had shown Proposition 187 losing support as voters began to focus on the real implications of their choices. That had happened before with California ballot initiatives that seized on popular causes but applied drastic solutions, and the proposition's opponents had begun to believe that the public would again respond to a last-minute wake-up call. Then, soon after the first student demonstrations, the polls began to swing back the other way and the proposition gained strength in the final days of the campaign.

Supporters of the initiative could hardly hide their glee as the students marched. Alan Nelson, the former INS commissioner who helped draft the proposition, denounced with relish the display of Mexican flags. "People can draw their own conclusions," he said at a Sacramento news conference. "But I would say that's un-American."

Nelson's epithet, "un-American," has not usually been applied to purely external threats. It typically applies to an enemy within.

Anglos and blacks and not a few native Latinos in Los Angeles hardly needed a reminder of how the Latino immigrant population had grown, but the Mexican flags confirmed fears that a foreign people had taken over the streets of the city. The student marchers stirred up images of an inexorable procession of Mexicans headed north from across the nearby border. Fear of these numbers combined with the fear that the United States was weak and vulnerable and incapable of absorbing so many foreigners. It was the fear of swamping, of being overwhelmed, of seeing all that is familiar and valued somehow swept away by people who are different.

Fear on one side engendered fear on the other. The backers of the proposition meant it to be a declaration of war on illegal immigrants. Large numbers of Latino young people—citizens, legal immigrants, and illegals alike—took it to be a declaration of war on them. They felt under attack because they were the sons and daughters of workers who always got jobs but always stayed poor.

They felt excluded because they were the new people. They were the makers of the great barrio that had taken over so much of the city and that lived connected by deep channels running south to Mexico and Central America.

"How can they say we cannot go to school and learn like everyone else? They are happy to let us go to work and go shopping. That is all right with them, but now they say we cannot go to school," said Rubisella Zabala, eighteen years old, as she marched down Whittier one sunny morning with about two hundred of her classmates.

"If they threw us out, there would be no one to work here. There would be nobody to put food on the table, or to build houses or anything. If they threw all of us, the Mexicans, out, this place would be empty," said Rubisella, who came north three years ago. "They want to punish us. They want to get rid of us. But they can't live without us."

The flags did not assert some kind of simple nationalism. The students were proud of coming from Mexico, but that is also the country they had left behind. And it was not "Remember the Alamo" in reverse, some kind of Mexican revanchism reclaiming conquered land as if Los Angeles could somehow come under Mexico City's sovereignty again. They wanted to be in L.A. They did not want to be back in Mexico. But they were willing to go to the streets to stand up for Latino L.A.

The students were not playing the minority-group game. They were not holding up the U.S. Constitution and demanding rights. Nor was it a statement of ethnic pride. They were not saying that Spanish is beautiful.

The Latino youth of Los Angeles felt threatened not as Mexicans but as migrants. It was not Mexico that was under assault, but Latino L.A. They marched in defense of their homes, the ports of entry, the places beyond borders and beyond nationalities, the places of transition. They marched in defense of mixed families, of homes where legal and illegal immigrants lived under one roof, of lives that mixed Mexico and the United States. They held up their flags and marched in defense of the barrio.

On Election Day, November 8, 1994, Proposition 187 passed 59 percent to 41 percent, with overwhelming white support. Latinos went against it nearly three to one, while African-American and

Asian-American voters split. The vote said that America was ready to start closing the doors. It said that Latinos should stop coming and that some already here should just go home.

The student marchers of 1994 demanded recognition of their rights as children of a new migration. They were not claiming to be Americans, but they *were* claiming to have earned a place here by virtue of the work their parents had done in this country. They were not claiming to be legal, but they asked for fairness under the law. They called themselves Mexicans but wanted to be appreciated for what they had become and what they were becoming in the United States. They demanded recognition of the fact that they had arrived, that they had become part of the place, and that they were not going back.

And that is why the voters rejected them. White Californians are not threatened by Mexico, but they are afraid of Mexicans in the United States.

PART III

BUILDING BARRIOS

Dos patrias tengo yo:
Cuba y la noche.
O son una las dos? . . .

— José Martí, "Dos Patrias"

Two homelands have I:
Cuba and the night.
Or are they one and the same? . . .

C H A P T E R   8

◆·◆·◆·◆·◆·◆·◆·◆·◆·◆·◆·◆·◆·◆·◆·◆·

Los Angeles:
People in Motion

◆·◆·◆·◆·◆·◆·◆·◆·◆· $\mathbf{A}$ s Manchester Avenue leads east out
of South Central Los Angeles, past the old
bungalows, the run-down storefronts, and the burned-out lots, it
assumes a grander name, Firestone Boulevard. Not long ago, it
showed the way to a big tire plant whose jobs gave people a reason
to move west to California.

When it reaches the workers' suburb of South Gate, the Boulevard is lined with hamburger joints, bowling alleys, and auto deal-
erships that announce themselves with neon typefaces from the
prosperous 1950s and 1960s. That's when South Gate belonged to
America's blue-collar heartland. Now the union wages are gone: The
Firestone plant is gone, along with the GM plant that was a little farther out. Also gone are the Goodrich, Goodyear, Uniroyal, Ford, and
Buick plants. The old factories have disappeared, along with their
promises of lifetime employment. Instead, there are now many

smaller plants where the management goal is flexibility and quick
turnaround. Many of the people who worked in the old plants have
left, too, replaced by new immigrant Latinos, who have been hired
for the new jobs because they are so anxious for dollar wages that
they will agree to be temporary and disposable workers.

More than a million whites left Los Angeles County in the 1980s
and more are leaving. Nearly a million and a half Latinos arrived in
the 1980s and more are coming. Economic change and demographic
change have worked in tandem here and across the United States.
The net effect is visible in the emergence of communities—barrios
populated by immigrant Latinos—that are transforming the urban
landscape. The barrios are products of structural change in American society, and they reflect new relationships between workers and
employers in a postindustrial economy, new means of seeking political power by minorities at the waning of the civil rights era, and
new plagues like multibillion-dollar drug trafficking. The barrios
are also home to the most newly arrived Latinos, and so these places
are the products of the ever-changing process by which immigrants
become Americans. No one barrio can serve as a model for all
because, not surprisingly, people of different nationalities arriving
at different places and times have produced a variety of results. It is
important not only to look out across the country at several different barrios but also to look back thirty years or more to understand
how these communities were built and how they will shape this
nation's future.

Firestone Boulevard may not rise much above discount merchandise now, but it does not descend to boarded-up storefronts, and
some gaudy new neon appears amid the old. Far from being abandoned like so many streets in other industrial burgs, Firestone
Boulevard is crowded and alive. The newcomers kept South Gate
alive and reinvented it. On Firestone Boulevard, the impact of
Latino immigration is not so obvious by day, but at night it rattles
your bones.

By about 10:00 p.m. on a Saturday night, Firestone clogs up
around the Lido Dance Hall. Suddenly, it becomes a real boulevard.
Traffic stops while two drivers of the opposite sex, traveling in
opposite directions, exchange *piropos* (propositions disguised as
compliments). Pickup trucks polished to a high gloss reflect the
streetlights. At the Lido, parking lot attendants slip big old Ameri-

can cars into narrow spaces. One after another, the vehicles are parked bumper-to-bumper, two deep, then three deep, then four deep, until the lot is covered with metal. No one comes to the Lido for a drop-by. It costs ten dollars to get in, and it is an event. The attraction is *banda* music.

Banda is an artifact of the Los Angeles barrios, the vast barrio that has its heart in East L.A. and then stretches across two hundred square miles from downtown to the San Gabriel valley and out into Orange County and all the smaller barrios scattered in pockets and swaths all across the rest of the nation's largest metropolitan area. *Banda* is the product of the superbarrio that embraces all of the region's 5 million Latinos. The new communities being built by Hispanic immigrants are not sharply circumscribed by geographical boundaries because movement is one of the defining characteristics of Latino immigration. People move constantly within a metropolitan area to take advantage of housing and work opportunities, and they constantly move back and forth to their home countries. *Banda* is the sound of immigrants who skip across national borders, picking up music—*corridos,* hip-hop, rock and roll—wherever they go. *Banda* is the music of an immigrant community living in a freeway city.

Banda doesn't have a blue note or a 4/4 beat or a lineup of instruments to identify it, but *banda* has a look and there is a dance. For women, dressing for *banda* is simple: skirts, jeans, blouse, and tank tops, regardless of the color, all tight, very tight, as tight as possible, even when tight means compressing buttocks until they look like balloons ready to pop, and tight also means revealing, as revealing as tight will allow.

But it is the men who define the look. They call it *tejano* (Texan): boots and well-pressed jeans; big belt buckles; a cowboy shirt—bold stripes are good, but so is plain white—and a hat, fine bleached straw, stiff, broad-brimmed, white, bright white. The hats are not made of *paja,* the softer, natural-colored straw in the sweat-stained hats that *campesinos* (peasants) back home wear when they work the fields. Instead, these are spotless, never worn for work, dress-up American cowboy hats. The men at the Lido are costumed to look like Garth Brooks. But everyone speaks Spanish as they go through the metal detectors and get their pat-downs in the lobby.

Because this is Los Angeles, the capital of style, two fashion

accessories have been added to the costume, and these add-ons help
set the style and make it something new that belongs to the barrio.
Hanging from each man's belt is a *cuarta* (quirt), a little riding whip
maybe a foot long made of braided *latigo* leather. There's a loop at
one end of the braid and at the other end the leather cords just dan-
gle loose. That's not something you see on American cowboys very
often. And to make the statement complete, men have got a *pañuelo*
(kerchief) hanging out of their right hip pocket. These are special
kerchiefs. The cloth has the name of a Mexican state embroidered or
printed on it in vertical letters so that when it is folded a certain
way, the name of the state—Jalisco, Zacatecas, Sonora—cascades
down the faux cowboy's blue-jeaned butt. Like some kind of "I
♥———" bumper sticker, the *pañuelo* announces where a person
came from before he headed north.

It is a glance back across the border with pride, and the *cuarta*
drives the message home. The style may be L.A. urban cowboy, but
before there were cowboys, there were *vaqueros,* the Mexican cat-
tlemen who rode the West when it was the North. The *cuartas*
belong to them and to the Villistas, the revolutionary bandits who
rode the border with Pancho Villa. But you will not readily find
cuartas and *pañuelos* in Mexico. This is a fashion fad of people
who are building a new community even as they continue to live
between two countries.

On the stage of the Lido, the Spanish-speaking emcee introduces
the first band of the night: "Just arrived in Los Angeles from a triumphant tour of Sinaloa, welcome back, Los Patrulleros de
Durango." Instead of launching into a song, the lead singer pumps
the crowd cheerleader-style by saluting *"nuestros amigos de
Jalisco,"* our friends from the Mexican *estado* of Jalisco. Then he
does Sinaloa, Michoacán, and Chihuahua, and with the name of
each state, he draws cheers from couples seated at tables on three
sides of the huge dance floor. Men at the bar, situated beneath a
giant blue mirror, compete to let out the loudest howls. It is a pep
rally for the places left behind.

They are Mexicans in Los Angeles, and the Lido is their place
tonight, and no one is making any excuses for who they are. The
dance hall is filling. Together in big numbers, they can be whatever
they want to be.

The first set of music is *norteño,* the music of northern Mexico, with the accordion up front. The old time oompah beat is almost gone. The songs are still waltzes and *cumbias* even though the beat is faster. The steps are the ones they learned from their parents, but bouncier. And after each song, the lead singer shouts the names of a few *estados* and cheers grow as a stream of people pours through the security check.

When the music starts up again after a break, Los Patrulleros sound very different. With a few flicks of the synthesizer, they suddenly have a brass section, and some riffs sound like Caribbean-American salsa music. Then the two electric guitars weigh in with enough rock and roll to sound like Bill Haley and the Comets with a little extra twang. Along the way, the singer raps a few verses of a song. The core of the sound is still *norteño,* but it is going a lot faster than anyone figured it could and a lot has been added to it.

Banda is eclectic because it is the product of a migration. The best bands from all over Mexico travel north to tour American barrios, earn dollars at places like the Lido, and get their records on American Spanish-language radio. The lucky ones make it to *Johnny Canales* or *Sábado Gigante* or one of the other big variety shows on the American Spanish television networks. And then they go back again to their home audiences in Mexico. *Banda* music is made both in Mexico and in the United States and most of all it is made in the travel back and forth. The musicians are the product of the great *mestizaje,* the mating of Spaniard and Indian that gave birth to the New World's new race. They are embarked on what may become the next great *mestizaje,* the mating of Spanish-speaking barrios and English-speaking cities, but that has not happened yet. *Banda* reflects the culture of a place in between, a port of entry where people are coming and going, a community that is still evolving. Every barrio lives on the treadmill of constant immigration. No matter how far a community progresses in adapting to America, it is always helping to settle the most newly arrived. Along with those who go back and forth all the time, the newcomers keep the sounds of the south fresh in the barrios and rekindle the Latinos' group identity as a community of foreign origins. It is both rejuvenating and exhausting.

For immigrants at the beginning of the century going from Europe to the United States meant going from one world to another, from the old to the new. Time and distance were real barriers that had to be overcome physically, and yet the Europeans kept close links to their home countries. Despite the voyage, many still managed to go back and forth several times in a life of sojourning. They read the news of their European homelands in dozens of native-language newspapers. In American cities, they gathered at beer gardens, churches, and fraternal organizations to express their opinions, and when there was a revolution or a civil war across the Atlantic, they would fight among themselves as if they were still in Dublin, Naples, or Vienna. So then what kind of home country ties can be expected of people who can simply walk from one world to another?

Time and distance have different values for Latino immigrants than for the European newcomers of long ago because they can visit home for the weekend or phone a loved one whenever they feel the urge to hear a familiar voice. Latinos come from close by and their migration has occurred at a time when technology is bringing all places closer together. Time and distance are not barriers for Latino immigrants; rather, they are part of an easily negotiated continuum.

The Statue of Liberty stands as a symbol of the European migration because it represents a terminus. There is no terminus for Latino immigrants. Latino immigrants pass through borders. Then they create barrios that are borderlands.

Gloria Anzaldúa, a Chicana poet whose book *Borderlands* extols the ambiguities of Latino life in the United States, draws this distinction this way: "A border is a dividing line, a narrow strip along a steep edge. A borderland is a vague and undetermined place created by the emotional residue of unnatural boundary. It is in a constant state of transition."

At a time of quick and ready travel, the borderland can be anywhere. This holds for all immigrants today, but the ambiguities are most intense for Latinos because of the proximity of their homelands. The barrios are borderlands not because foreigners live in them, not because they are filled with exotic smells and voices. Instead, they are borderlands because of a constant traffic of goods and people, a give-and-take, a constant hybridization. The human traffic between the United States and the Latin American countries that send it immigrants, especially Mexico, has achieved a size and speed unimaginable a few years ago. So many people in these countries are so closely linked and move back and forth so much that they create transnational spaces. These are not cactus-strewn deserts somewhere out in the Southwest, but chunks of American cities where national identities and geographic boundaries lose their relevance. These are barrios where Latinos invent new kinds of music and new identities and where a new generation of Americans is trying to define itself while living in a constant state of transition.

As the dance hall, the bar, and the adjoining restaurant at the Lido fill with what seems to be more than a thousand people, a song is drowned out by a rumbling that shakes the whole building. It is the sound of hundreds of boots all stamping on the floor in unison. The patrons are doing a *zapateado,* a sort of tap dance that has gotten very fast and funky, so that it is a cross of Mexican cowboy folk dance, flamenco, and frug. The crowd gets excited and in sync.

During a slightly mellower but still fast-paced tune, there is a collision and crash on the dance floor and the crowd parts as angry words are exchanged. A tightly focused flashlight beam shoots down from a balcony and behind it I can see two men, one of them talking into a radio. On the dance floor, five security men in red shirts dart through the dancers and in a moment they converge on the altercation. These are the perils of *la quebradita,* a dance that takes its name (the little break) from a move in which the girl bends as far backward as she can while the boy, with his hands around her waist, swings her around like a limp doll. It takes practice. The collisions on a crowded dance floor are not just painful but also resented.

By midnight, the dance floor is a sea of hats, some black felt ones amid the straw, that are going up and down. Dancing to *banda* music is all in the knees and vertical, unlike salsa, which goes from side to side with the hips. Around the tables, more English is being spoken. Some men have appeared with earrings; a few others have a buzz cut on the sides of their heads and a ponytail growing off the top and back.

These are Chicanos, native-born Latinos of Mexican descent. Their families could be Angelenos and English-speaking for a generation at least and with no more connection to Mexico than Mario Cuomo has to Italy. Yet here they are dressed *tejano,* down to the *banda* scene on a Saturday night, hanging out where most of the people are immigrants still speaking Spanish.

"All we ever used to listen to was hip-hop, rap, techno, sometimes rock and roll oldies, but we never heard Mexican music except maybe at family parties," said Erika Cobian, a recent high school graduate, eighteen years old, from the Latino-Asian suburb of Montebello. She and her friends find that *banda* is better for dancing and makes for livelier parties. "This stuff peps you up," Erika says. "You want to dance and learn the steps and show off what you know."

But *banda* is more than just backing off the hard edges of rap or the retro appeal of dancing to a melody. "This is like the music we grew up with when we were little and they played it at birthdays and stuff when relatives came over, but now people play *banda* on their radios. They played it at pep rallies at school this year and people even began dancing. People aren't afraid to show the Mexican in them anymore."

When the lead singer of Los Patrulleros does his thing with the states' names, Erika cheers for Jalisco. "I was born here in L.A., and so I really don't have a place in Mexico to cheer for," she says, "so I cheer for Jalisco because that is where my father's family is from."

Erika usually does the *banda* scene as a member of a floating dance club called Si Tu Boquita (If Your Little Mouth), after a song lyric. Parties are held at members' homes, often in the driveways. The two-dollar admission pays for a deejay, nonalcoholic refreshments, and some decorations. Adults—there are a lot of young parents—teenagers, and even small children come. When *banda* was just taking off, hundreds of such clubs sprang up around the barrios.

"One big difference between *banda* clubs and regular parties is that when people do *banda,* they don't bring guns, so everything is peaceful, no one gets shot," Erika said.

Banda's success with Mexican-Americans is the reverse of the usual cultural flow. Even as immigrants move toward their more assimilated countrymen who have been here longer, native Latinos are also adopting immigrant ways. Barrios are not just immigrant communities where newcomers become Americans. They are also places where native Latinos live and have lived, sometimes for generations before the current wave of newcomers began arriving. Now a multifaceted transaction is under way that involves dealings between native and immigrant Latinos as well as the larger interchange between the newcomers and American society. This farrago of influences produces new forms of cultural expression like *banda* as well as expressions of cultural confusion like the bilingual international street gangs proliferating between Los Angeles and San Salvador. It produces new forms of community building as well as new forms of crime because the barrios are in the process of inventing themselves with no template to operate from and no predictable outcome in sight. For now anyway, the Spanish sounds are the predominate influence. The immigrant influences are ascendant simply by virtue of the number of newcomers arriving in these neighborhoods every day. Assimilation goes on all around, and eventually the acquisition of American ways will become the predominate drama, but for now the barrios are still in an age of arrivals that will continue for years, perhaps for decades, because the influx has so much human momentum behind it. The barrios are places of uncertainty, movement, and conflict, and these are the places where America's Latino future is taking shape.

It took forever to get out of the Lido parking lot, and the traffic was crawling on Firestone. Just down the block from the Lido, a police car was pulled up part of the way on the sidewalk so it wouldn't block the street. One cop stood very close to a young boy shirtless in the night air and they were both speaking at once. The other cop was bent over a body, which lay facedown, bleeding. As I made my way down the boulevard, there seemed to be sirens coming from several directions at once.

❖•❖•❖•❖•❖•❖•❖•❖•❖•❖•❖•❖•❖•❖•❖•❖•❖•

CHAPTER 9

Houston: Cantina Patrol

❖•❖•❖•❖•❖•❖•❖•❖• Late at night, in a bar in a dark corner of Magnolia, a young man wearing work boots had just started kissing a woman in a sequined miniskirt when America made its presence felt in the form of six uniformed officers of the Houston Police Department.

The cantina patrol was on its twice-a-month rounds of the sweaty little places where immigrant men drink beer with salt, shoot pool, and pursue other forms of recreation. Standing by the doorways for a moment, the men in uniform scanned the room in case anyone made a move to dispose of drugs or a weapon. The four-piece band stopped a gregarious polka in mid-oompah. Under twinkling Christmas lights and tattered crepe decorations, there was a sudden stillness and silence in the Friday-night crowd.

A look of annoyance passed across the woman's face as she rearranged her shiny clothes. With a forlorn expression, the young man in the dirty boots stretched forward to continue his pursuit, running his hands up the panty hose flecked with gold. Before he could reach his goal, the policemen had spread out, checking behind the bar for license violations and accosting every man who looked as if he might have had too many beers. Puzzled but quietly obedient, the men stood up as commanded and tried to balance themselves on one foot to prove themselves sober, holding their arms out to their sides like children playing Simon Says. And even as they had their limbs akimbo, the police asked rapid-fire questions in Spanish. "What time did you get here? How many beers have you drunk?" The cops' uniforms set them apart as representatives of English-speaking America, but their language and their familiarity with the place marked them as operatives of the barrio itself. Most of the cops are Mexican-Americans. Many grew up in Magnolia. It was an older part of the barrio policing the new arrivals.

As the interrogations continued all over the cantina, flashlights were shining in people's faces and sharp voices barked orders, but the young man in the dirty boots was unrelenting. He had his hand almost to the woman's crotch. Her mouth was buried in his neck. That was evidence enough for Sgt. Art Valdez, so he asked him the question of the hour. *"¿Casa o cárcel?"* ("Home or jail?") It was a simple choice, but the man in work boots seemed confused. He slammed his dirty hands against his temples, then ran his fingers through his hair, as if that would help him focus better.

"I'm just here for a few months working construction and then I'll go home," he said in a sullen monotone.

The sergeant, speaking in a soft voice, told the man he did not have to go home to Mexico but that he did have to go wherever he was staying in Houston. Then the cop asked whether he had a family in Mexico and the man bashfully admitted he had a wife and children back there.

"You came here to make money, right? Then why are you in here spending it on this?" said Valdez, casting a disdainful look at the woman in sequins. "Think of your family at home. Think of what your wife would think if I had to send her word that you had finished up in a place like this with a knife in your belly."

The man grew wide-eyed and with exaggerated nods of his head put a few crumpled dollar bills on the little table next to the woman and walked out.

The officers hit eight cantinas in a few hours around midnight and sent about twenty men to the downtown lockup for the night on charges of public drunkenness.

Valdez started the cantina patrols in Magnolia in 1978 and thereafter led every outing for more than a dozen years. A tall, heavyset man whose gut and muscles bulge beneath his powder blue uniform shirt, he is a by-the-book cop who drives everywhere fast, sees a world full of bad guys, and uses a lot of paramilitary jargon when he talks in English about his work. Valdez was born and raised in the barrio and has never really left it. He spent virtually his whole career as a Houston cop in Magnolia and kept coming back to lead cantina raids after he switched over to the state liquor control board.

When Valdez talked about the cantina patrol, there was none of the remoteness or disdain you often hear in cops' voices when they talk about the streets they work. Perhaps that was because he could recall his own fathers' visits to the cantinas. "He'd set us in the back of the pickup with a bag of potato chips and a soda, parked out front of the cantina while he had a beer with his friends." He remembered men who did much worse, drinking and whoring until all their money was gone or getting into fights and either killing or being killed.

The first time I watched Valdez and his men in action, I thought they were just harassing immigrants who did not know enough to complain. That night, Valdez readily admitted he would never get away with the same kind of roust in a white or African-American neighborhood. "They'd have my fanny in court, and they'd be picketing and protesting about their rights."

By way of explaining why it was different in Magnolia, Valdez said, "You've got people here who understand all about the Mexican thing and who understand you've got to keep a handle on such things, and they are people who care about the community, who build up the community, and they support us one hundred percent." He was talking about the residents of Magnolia who feel rooted enough here to see the new arrivals as foreigners.

Magnolia sits along the banks of the Houston ship channel, and it has always been full of warehouses and docks and saloons for working men. Valdez seemed to take special pride in raiding cantinas where he found familiar faces.

Kicking up gravel and dust, four squad cars screeched to a stop in front of a roadside place so ramshackle that it must have been there back when there was swamp instead of city all around. Valdez was first through the door, holding his big flashlight over his shoulder like a hunting club. Inside, most of the light seemed to come from beer displays and a pair of bare fluorescent tubes hanging over a pool table. A young man with long hair took a shot that he had been lining up when Valdez and his crew burst in. The sergeant pointed his light into the boy's face, making him squint, and yelled "Drop it," as if the pool cue were an automatic weapon in disguise.

Over by the bar, a woman too old for her tight-fitting clothes went to the jukebox, punched up a tune, and began to sing along. It was a frisky Mexican ballad in which the singer boasts of his banditry and mocks the *federales* who put him in jail. The four or five other people in the place were frozen, trying as hard as they could not to attract attention to themselves and averting their faces from the cops' inquiring looks.

Through heavy makeup, the woman never stopped smiling and singing and never took her eyes off Valdez. She pranced over to the pool table and clutched the young man with long hair and started dancing with him. He was no more than a teenager and his blunt face seemed deadened until she began whispering in his ear, all the while working him back to a dark corner. Then with an abrupt nod of his head, the sergeant directed another officer to roust the suddenly enlivened young man right out of the woman's arms. Looking at Valdez, she mouthed a silent message that I couldn't quite make out.

Later, back in his car, racing to the next target just down the street, Valdez said, "You should have seen Alice fifteen years ago when she worked the dance halls instead of low-life places like that." For a moment, he laughed to himself. "I bet that kid she picked up was barely walking when she was in her prime. Well, he'll spend the night courtesy of the taxpayers and the poor dumb bunny will never know Alice was about to give him a gold-plated freebie just to piss me off."

Valdez is so familiar with the people and the bars that he sometimes seems like a mean big brother disciplining younger siblings. But he is really more of a big mean stepbrother. He and the other Mexican-American cops are clearly related to the immigrants they bust, but they are not exactly members of the same family. They grew up in the barrio before the current wave of immigration developed much momentum, and they have become guardians of a household beset by a horde of visiting relatives. Valdez assigns himself a special responsibility to uphold American values in Magnolia precisely because his ancestry is Mexican. His uniform allows him to play that role with impunity.

Magnolia is like some ancient city of the Levant that can be explored down into the soil through clearly marked archaeological strata but that bustles with contemporary noises on the surface. Like many older barrios, it is reinventing itself in this new age of immigration, but the new enclave is being built atop an old one.

Driving around Magnolia, Valdez points out two elementary schools, two parks, two public swimming pools, all within a mile of one another. He's the kind of tour guide who likes to ask rhetorical questions. "You know why we have two of everything?" Then, after the obligatory pause, answering himself, he says, "We used to have two of everything around here because one was for whites and one for Mexicans. Now they're all for Mexicans, because the whites are gone."

Mexicans have lived in Magnolia for eighty years, but they shared it until the 1960s. The whites left here about the same time they left all the old city wards and headed for the suburbs. It became a solidly Mexican-American working-class community, a Latino Queens with Latino Archie Bunkers like Valdez. Many of the younger ones have moved on to their own suburbs. Those who remained behind, third- and fourth-generation Mexican-Americans, now share Magnolia with the newcomers.

Some things change. Some things don't. There have always been two Catholic churches in Magnolia. It used to be that Immaculate Conception Church held services in English and was the larger, more affluent church, which catered to whites. Immaculate Heart of Mary was the mission church with Spanish masses for Mexican immigrants. Now that the whites are gone, Immaculate Conception is where Mexican-Americans pray. They are the landlords and the foremen and the policemen and they worship in English. The mission church serves newly arrived immigrants, Mexicans and, most recently, Central Americans. They are the construction workers and janitors and warehousemen and they pray in Spanish.

The two congregations—the natives and the immigrants—share

the barrio, but they speak different languages, listen to different types of music, and eat different types of tortillas. Newcomers are about the only ones who eat corn tortillas; Mexican-Americans eat flour ones. They are two parts of a single community that is divided by income and immigration status. Some of the people in Magnolia are illegal; many used to be illegal and got papers one way or another. Some came as children. Others were born to American parents. And now, with the arrival of the Central Americans, they are divided by nationality, as well. They don't mix at church or on Friday nights.

Valdez can do a typology of Magnolia's cantinas as precisely as if he were categorizing butterflies by genus and species, except that it is a human caste system he describes. At one end, there are the raucous dance halls, some of them big Quonset huts, where younger men, mostly Mexican and mostly illegals, are drawn by the abundant bar girls, most of them now young Salvadorans, who will dance and perhaps do more, depending on the money. When there are fights, they are usually over women.

Then there are the simple bars frequented by older men who remain tied to home, whatever their immigration status. They mostly drink without women and listen to little *conjuntos,* which are minstrel groups with a few guitars and maybe an accordion that play old songs. And now there are the new places that play salsa and other sounds with tropical rhythms rarely heard when the barrio was populated predominately by mountain and desert people.

At the other end of the spectrum are the fancy places with neon lights outside and bouncers in slick suits where Mexican-Americans go. The music is eclectic, some rock, a lot of country and western, but mostly *tejano,* a kind of country-rock combination that originated in south Texas and is sung in Spanish. The customers are English-speaking young people in their twenties and thirties out on dates. Most have come back to the old neighborhood from new suburban barrios. Valdez does not bother with these places.

The ethnic fragmentation so evident in the barrios somewhat resembles the rifts that often developed in European immigrant communities at the turn of the century. Some well-established Mexican-Americans view recently arrived Latino immigrants with a distance and displeasure that recalls the way some American Jews of German descent who had achieved considerable prominence here viewed the influx of Eastern European and Russian Jews. The divisions were much starker among the Jews because of bitter disputes over religious practice and disagreements on the value of assimilation. The parallels are stronger in the economic arena. Then, as now, the newcomers often find themselves working for fellow ethnics who have been here long enough to create businesses, and the competing interests of the two groups leads to friction. There is another parallel in that the native-born—Jews then, Latinos now—have assimilated here enough that they view the newcomers as aliens, and similarly, the recent immigrants disdain their Americanized brethren for having given up so much of their native culture.

These relationships do not remain static but evolve, of course, in response to events. In the 1880s, some organizations representing American Jews sought reduced levels of immigration by Eastern European "paupers," and they made a proud public show of rejecting their coethnics. But over the course of the next three decades, these differences gave way to strong demonstrations of ethnic solidarity. Affluent and assimilated Jews organized settlement houses and other efforts to improve living conditions for recent immigrants, and a profound bonding took place between Americanized Jews and immigrants in response to pogroms and other manifestations of violent anti-Semitism in Europe.

Latinos are still diverging, and their experience is too fresh to suggest a definite outcome. An extensive study of Latino attitudes, the 1992 Latino National Political Survey, found that most people who might call themselves "Latino" or "Hispanic" reject those panethnic terms in favor of Cuban, Mexican-American, or other such designations based on national origins. The survey concluded, "Over all, these groups do not constitute a political community." Nationality is only one aspect of the fragmentation. Like the rest of America, the Latino population is polarized along economic lines, with those who have gained the credentials to prosper in the post-industrial economy pulling away from those who have not, and the divisions are marked by differences in where people live and work as well as by different forms of assimilation to American life. Other contrasts reflect differing political experiences. Many native-born Latinos and long-term immigrants have a deep faith in the minority-group identity and the civil rights tools that go with it because they have seen explicit discrimination and have seen it rolled back. More recent immigrants may have experienced prejudice, but of a more informal sort, and their only contact with the civil rights ethos is through calcified social service bureaucracies or by way of endlessly litigated arrangements that govern the functioning of public schools. Finally, the divisions among Latinos are being reinforced by changes in immigration and welfare law enacted in 1996. Most of those who arrived illegally in prior decades found ways to achieve legal residence, largely thanks to the 1986 amnesties, and many are now becoming U.S. citizens. Today, it is much harder for illegals to fix their status, and there are no prospects for another amnesty. For the newcomer, being an illegal alien is probably not a temporary condition; the recently arrived illegal and his neighbors know there is probably no escape from that caste. Also, welfare reform has obviously affected poor immigrants most of all by eliminating noncitizens' eligibility for various programs and thus heightening class differences among Latinos.

Clearly, America's barrios should not be viewed as homogeneous communities, and the Latino experience in the United States should not be viewed as a continuum. There is no valid reason to expect that the descendants of today's immigrants will end up acting like third- and fourth-generation Latinos who are now thoroughly Americanized and living in the suburbs. The circumstances greeting immigrants today are so different from those of just a few decades ago that the past does not serve as a model for the future. Latinos like Valdez, whose forefathers came north fifty to a hundred years ago, have no common cause with newly arrived Latinos. The Jews and other Europeans found a basis for group identity when confronted with deadly adversity or when it became apparent how solidarity would bring them clear benefits such as greater political clout. Latinos have yet to encounter such circumstances. Instead, they still face forces that pull them apart. To understand the power of those centrifugal forces, one need only listen to Valdez and his police buddies out on cantina patrol.

After raiding several cantinas, the cops took a break for fried chicken, and most of the talk was about how the police department had settled a lawsuit alleging that it had discriminated against blacks and Hispanics in promotion practices. A young sergeant, the son of Mexican immigrants, complained bitterly that other Latinos who did not score as well as he did on the sergeant's exam were going to be hired.

"The white guys at the station say we don't got what it takes to compete and that's why they made special rules to let us score high enough," the young sergeant said angrily. "Well, I put in the midnights with those damn books. I showed the white guys what I was made of, while those other brothers were screwing around. So now because they got themselves a lawyer, now they are going to get in." The young patrolmen nodded their agreement.

Valdez chewed his corn on the cob and listened quietly. Just when the table seemed to have been swayed by the young sergeant's arguments, he spoke up. "Look, you don't know because you weren't here, but it used to be that they played all kinds of games with us to hold us down. They had height requirements to keep us off the force. They screwed around with promotion lists, with work assessments, with everything. We had to fight to get the first Mexican sergeants and the first detective and the first everything. And all along, if we didn't complain, we didn't get nothing."

The young sergeant wasn't buying it. "I think we put ourselves at a disadvantage. I think we are just making excuses for ourselves and the Anglos know it."

Later in the car, Valdez vented his frustration. "He doesn't know anything about the way things used to be, about how the sons of bitches were on our backs, keeping us down all those years. He's young and he thinks he's smart, and that's all that matters to him, but his problem is that he's too young to know anything."

Toward the end of one patrol, I said to Valdez that it seemed the cantinas were a personal crusade for him. He responded as if the comment had been made before.

Speaking in a deep drawl that hid all but the barest accent left over from his immigrant parents, he said, "It used to be we'd get two or three shootings a weekend in the cantinas. You got a lot of illegal aliens and other folks who think they can behave just like they were still in Mexico, and by making the rounds, we kind of remind them they're here in the United States, where the rules are different."

Numbers make a difference, he insisted. "It's not that more of them are criminals than anybody else. It's just that when you get more people, you get more bad guys. And it is not just crime that goes up. People are fed up. They say there's got to be a limit on how many we take in."

As it got toward 2:00 a.m., the computer on Sergeant Valdez's cruiser lit up with calls about burglaries, shootings, and rapes that had been reported to 911. It would be a while before any squad cars rolled toward those blinking addresses, because he had half the officers in the district out on cantina patrol.

"All that other stuff happens every night," he said, pointing to the computer, "but the cantinas, it's like doing maintenance. We go out every other week, and that way we keep a lid on things. Otherwise, this place would look like Mexico or something."

◇•◇•◇•◇•◇•◇•◇•◇•◇•◇•◇•◇•◇•◇•◇•◇

New York:
From Stickball to Crack

◇•◇•◇•◇•◇•◇•◇•◇ This is a joke Puerto Ricans tell on themselves:

A Cuban, a Dominican, and a Puerto Rican are captured by cannibals. They're told that first they'll be eaten and then their skins will be used to make canoes.

The Cuban is taken to the edge of the boiling cauldron. He adjusts his hair and his clothes and then jumps into the water, shouting, *"¡Abajo Fidel! ¡Viva Cuba libre!"* ("Down with Fidel! Long live a free Cuba!").

A martyr at last.

The Dominican is next. He tells the cannibals that their stew needs some potatoes and onions and offers to get them bargain rates at his brother's bodega. They take him to negotiate with their chief.

Spared—for the moment.

When the Puerto Rican is taken to the cauldron, he tells the cannibals he wants a fork so he can savor their brew before jumping in himself. When they oblige, he stabs himself viciously in the chest, legs, and arms, shouting, "Fuck your canoes!"

Into the cauldron.

Cuba, the Dominican Republic, and Puerto Rico—three island places in the sun, all lined up in a row. All three have sent large numbers of people to the United States, but these people have gone to different places at different times and as such have endured vastly different fates. The Puerto Ricans came first and they have done very badly compared to their Caribbean neighbors. In fact, the Puerto Rican migration to the U.S. mainland has produced so much poverty and misery that Puerto Ricans only half-jokingly ask themselves, Was coming north a self-inflicted wound? Would it have been better to stay home? The Puerto Rican experience presents another set of questions, but of broader and more urgent concern: How much of the Puerto Rican disaster was their fault? How much can be explained by what they encountered here? And are today's Latino immigrants likely to suffer the same fate?

Finding the answers requires looking back to the 1950s and early 1960s, when the Puerto Ricans came to New York in substantial numbers and tried to build a barrio for themselves. They began with hope. In the end, some did quite well for themselves, but too many finished in misery. It is important to know why some prospered and whether those who ended up very poor simply lacked the skills, education, and culture to make it in America. Many Latinos who share similar characteristics are now arriving, and many of them are beginning to ask whether coming north has cost them too much. It is important to know whether poor people who arrive here with few skills are destined to remain poor in the United States, because so much of the thinking about poor people and the policy developed toward them is built on conclusions about group characteristics. If one assumes it was a mistake for so many Puerto Ricans to come, then it is a mistake for so many others like them who are coming now, and the United States should bar the door to all those other Latinos with similar characteristics before they, too, hurt themselves and hurt the nation. But if the disaster resulted from circumstances, such as shifts in the labor market or obstacles to political participation, that denied many Puerto Ricans the opportunity to prosper— even as some among them succeeded—then the nation should take steps to ensure that today's newcomers have a better chance.

The Puerto Rican migration is the granddaddy of today's Latino migrations. Between 1945 and 1965, almost a million people left the island. Most of them were poor and had little education. Many came from the countryside, where they had been unemployed too often. And two-thirds of them headed for New York. The Mexican flow is of course older, so much older that it belongs to a different species. The Puerto Rican migration is part of the contemporary flow. The Puerto Ricans were the first large group of Latinos to migrate substantially by airplane, to find a place in an economy that was transforming from manufacturing to services, the first obliged to deal with American blacks as neighbors, allies, and rivals. They were the first to experience a divided fate, splitting between individuals who melded into the middle-class mainstream and a large number who remained isolated in a minority-group culture of poverty. The one great difference between Puerto Ricans and today's Latino immigrants is that Puerto Ricans are American citizens by birth. This should have made it easier for them to be accepted into the American mainstream, and yet no less than any other Latinos, Puerto Ricans remain outsiders. How much of their fate is destined to be repeated?

Start on a hot New York afternoon in 1951. Papo Machicote remembers that it was hot enough for tar to get soft on a tenement rooftop. He remembers that the dictionary felt heavy when he and his buddies carried it up to the roof in search of a name.

"We started going through this big book," he says. "It was all in English and we didn't know the words, but there was lots of little pictures, and when we saw the right one, you know, we all said it at once, 'Minotaurs, yeah, let's be the Minotaurs.'"

Papo and his pals were just learning to play stickball; to play stickball, you had to have a team, and to have a team, you had to have a name. Everyone else had stickball teams—the Italians, the blacks, the Irish, the Jews—and so Puerto Ricans understood that they, too, should do the same.

"We made Puerto Rican teams because back then we was making El Barrio. We was making it Puerto Rican."

Papo remembers that afternoon and many other afternoons in the 1950s because it was the time when Puerto Ricans became New Yorkers. They learned the game of the streets and much else. They began to think of themselves as a distinct group that could join the combat among the many groups that constantly jockeyed for position in the streets, in the schools, and in the factories. Like all the others who had come to the city before them, the Puerto Ricans organized themselves as a group, and like all the groups that had come to New York from someplace else, they claimed a turf. They transformed a piece of Harlem into El Barrio. These were not Puerto Rican things they were doing. They were newcomers absorbing and adapting to the America they saw all around them. In effect, they were trying to do what the European ethnics had done when they arrived in New York a half century earlier.

Every Latino neighborhood can call itself a barrio, but only one rightfully claims the title of "The Barrio." (Outsiders might know it as Spanish Harlem.) Wedged between Italians to the east and blacks to the west, the Puerto Ricans made a place for themselves in New York City. It was a poor and dangerous place, but it was theirs, and in the 1950s, the Puerto Rican migration to the United States was still young and full of promise. That same sense of possibilities infects the barrios now being built all across the nation.

As Papo tells it, the Minotaurs, like all New York stickball teams, were also something of a street gang. With broom handles and rubber balls made by Spalding thus known as "Spaldeens," they contested their manhood against the Vultures, the Pretzels, the Falcons, the Home Reliefs, the Eagles, and the Royal Kings. Occasionally, they fought the other gangs, too. There were knives and zip guns, but fists were still by far the most common weapons. Every gang, every group of ethnics, was trying to define a place for itself according to the rules of the city.

In his 1967 memoir, *Down These Mean Streets,* Piri Thomas writes of those summer days in El Barrio: "All the streets are alive, like many-legged cats crawling with fleas. People are all over the place. Stoops are occupied like bleachers sections at a game, and beer flows like there's nothing else to drink. The block musicians pound out gone beats on tin cans and conga drums and bongos. And kids are playing all over the place—on fire escapes, under cars, over cars, in alleys, back yards, hallways." That book dramatically relates how those streets were also alive with *bolita,* the numbers game, marijuana, heroin, prostitutes, stickups, and bloody battles with Italian thugs.

Many years later, the mean streets of El Barrio are remembered nostalgically by many Puerto Ricans because they evoke a sense of possibilities now gone. Puerto Ricans set out to build themselves an enclave that could serve as a starting point. Like the Europeans before them, they followed the well-worn trail that led to the factories and the docks of the industrial economy and they got into the game of Democratic party politics, trying to be a voting bloc. In the 1950s, the Puerto Ricans had every reason to assume that even if they started out poor, they would eventually prosper and grow out of the enclave and become one of the groups that claimed its share of city jobs and other spoils of political success.

Thinking back to those days, Puerto Ricans remember movie theaters in El Barrio and neon lights up and down Lexington Avenue, shining from stores and restaurants owned by Puerto Ricans. They get nostalgic about La Marqueta, the bustling market under the elevated train tracks where you could get the best bananas and cassavas and salted cod. Some who knew East Harlem then even allow themselves to get nostalgic about the tenements, recalling the tight sense of community that existed when people were poor but still hopeful.

Papo, his hair now thinning and receding, boasts about how easy it was to find work in the old days. "I started after school hauling ice, and then as soon as I was sixteen, I dropped out of school and went down to the Fulton Street docks to become a stevedore. When there was no work on the docks, you could always go to the Garment District and just look for signs, because there was always a loft that was needing a delivery boy. I had more good-paying jobs by the time I was twenty than most of the kids today have in a whole lifetime, and I never spent a day on relief."

In 1960, the labor participation rate for Puerto Rican men was 85 percent—four points higher than for black men and four lower than for Anglo males. Puerto Rican women worked at about the same rate as Anglo females—40 percent—seven points less than for black women. The city had an aging but still substantial manufacturing sector that employed 60 percent of the Puerto Rican workforce in jobs that did not require much training or education. The work was plentiful, even if it did not pay much, and in places like El Barrio, a real community was developing. Puerto Ricans were beginning to buy bodegas, bakeries, restaurants, and other small commercial establishments. By the late 1950s, Puerto Ricans owned some four thousand businesses in New York, more than the black population, which was nearly twice as large. Growing more confident of their place in the city, they started to win offices in labor unions and made quick political gains.

In 1961, a Puerto Rican replaced an Italian as Democratic political leader in a district of East Harlem. Glazer and Moynihan reported this watershed event in *Beyond the Melting Pot*, first published in 1963, noting that "many saw Puerto Ricans entering the same path that Italians took forty years before." That path had led to ethnic cohesion, growing political and economic power, and, eventually, social acceptance. The authors were a little skeptical: "But it is a different city, and a different group, and one can barely imagine what kind of human community will emerge from the process of adaptation."

No one could have imagined that the Puerto Ricans had just passed another kind of watershed: Barely off the bottom, many— but not all—Puerto Rican New Yorkers had begun a long, painful process of decline. In 1960, Puerto Rican family income was nearly two-thirds of the city median. Overall, they were poorer than their neighbors, but that was expected of the newest group. But instead of gradually improving their standing, as all other newcomers had done before, Puerto Ricans as a group would never rate as high again compared with other New Yorkers. New York had changed greatly since the turn of the century, and the Puerto Ricans took a very different trajectory than the Italians, who also started out very poor but reached economic parity with the rest of the city in the third and fourth generations. In 1990, Puerto Rican median family income was barely more than half the city median, meaning that after thirty years the Puerto Rican population of New York overall had become far poorer compared to other city residents, even though there were many success stories that defied the norm.

On the mean streets of East Harlem today, there are burned-out lots, vacant for so long that they are thick with waist-high weeds. *Casitas* (little houses) have sprung up in some of the jungle lots. Put together out of plywood and planks, these little shacks resemble just the sort of sad dwellings that commonly served as housing in the Puerto Rican countryside in the days when people set off to find opportunity in New York. Men with no work sit and play dominoes and tend little gardens as if they were back on their island and the whole migration had simply taken them back to where they were fifty years ago.

By the 1990s, many Puerto Ricans had moved on to midtown jobs and homes in the suburbs or had abandoned New York altogether for prosperous lives in California or Florida. But those who remained in New York and remained poor were about the poorest group of people anywhere in the country, and they represented a huge part of the Puerto Rican population in the city. Depending on which definition is used, roughly between 40 and 50 percent of the 900,000 Puerto Ricans in New York can be categorized as poor. That is about double the city average. It is a level of poverty nearly half again as high as among native-born blacks, and it is a higher poverty rate than for any of the major immigrant groups in New York. In almost every category—unemployment, welfare usage, HIV infection— Puerto Ricans suffer exceptional misery. Two important pieces of evidence—the condition of the family and the levels of educational achievement—suggest that these Puerto Ricans will remain poor for at least another generation and beyond. One-third of all Puerto Rican households in New York are headed by women, again double the rate in the general population. Nearly half of all Puerto Rican children are being raised by women with no spouse present. The poverty rate among these Puerto Rican single mothers is 57 percent, far higher than any other ethnic group and far above the city average of 35 percent for single mothers. Puerto Ricans lag behind other New Yorkers in schooling at a time when upward mobility from one segment of the labor market to another is more dependent on education than ever before. Less than 50 percent of all Puerto Rican adults hold high school diplomas, compared to 66 percent among African-Americans and 83 percent for native-born white adults in New York City. Their relative disadvantage is growing. Several of the new, rapidly growing immigrant groups such as the Colombians, Jamaicans, and Chinese all come to New York with higher levels of education. (Only the Dominicans—by far the largest new immigrant group in the city—arrive with a less educated adult population.) There are no signs that this status will improve markedly anytime soon. Despite significant gains in graduation rates over the past decade, the dropout rate for Puerto Ricans in their late teens is twice the city average and Puerto Ricans are similarly underrepresented among those going on to college.

In *Beyond the Melting Pot,* Glazer and Moynihan wrote, "Nothing—in education, in work experience, work training, or work discipline, in family attitudes, in physical health—gave the Puerto

Rican migrant an advantage in New York City." Oscar Lewis depicted Puerto Ricans as victims of their own "culture of poverty" in *La Vida,* a powerful anthropological narrative published in 1965. Lewis wrote in the introduction, "The people in this book, like most other Puerto Rican slum dwellers I have studied, show a great zest for life, especially for sex, and a need for excitement, new experiences and adventures." This stereotype of the irrepressible, irresponsible Puerto Rican shaped perceptions among Anglos for decades and continues to feed biases today. Describing the household he presents as typical of the Puerto Rican experience, Lewis said, "In the Rios family, uncontrolled rage, aggression, violence and even bloodshed are not uncommon; their extreme impulsivity affects the whole tenor of their lives."

The culture of poverty, Lewis argues, is "both an adaptation and a reaction" to life at the bottom of "class-stratified" society. "An effort to cope with feelings of helplessness" is what he calls it. Although it is supposed to be a response to "objective conditions," Lewis grants the culture of poverty a kind of genetic permanence. "Once it comes into existence it tends to perpetuate itself from generation to generation because of its effect on the children. By the time slum children are age six or seven they have usually absorbed the basic values and attitudes of their subculture and are not psychologically geared to take full advantage of changing conditions or increased opportunities which may occur in their lifetime."

It might not seem that much of an explanation is necessary for the Puerto Rican condition. By this account, they were simply unqualified for life in New York and responded poorly to what they encountered there. A similar analysis can be heard today from social scientists who ascribe broad characteristics to other groups of poor people who are not white, and they predict inescapable destinies accordingly. If anything, prominent scholars are now willing to put even more emphasis on racial and ethnic identity than they were thirty years ago. For example, in their controversial 1994 best-seller, *The Bell Curve,* Richard J. Herrnstein and Charles Murray took the measure of ethnic groups based on their scores on IQ tests. They concluded, "Latino and black immigrants are, at least in the short run, putting some downward pressure on the distribution of intelligence."

A more widely accepted form of analysis depicts the "human

capital" of an immigrant group by measuring educational attainment, income, family structure, and other characteristics in their home country. Harvard economist George Borjas has influenced the debate over immigration policy in the 1990s with extensive writings and congressional testimony that purports to predict how groups of immigrants will fare in the United States based on that kind of statistical analysis. Just as *The Bell Curve* correlated IQ scores and race, Borjas correlates national origins and work skills. After analyzing Mexico's labor market, he concludes in *Friends or Strangers,* "Mexicans in the United States are likely to be unskilled." At the conclusion of that book, published in 1990, Borjas issued a call to arms that has been answered eagerly by advocates of reduced immigration: "The empirical evidence presented in this book indicates that the skill composition of the immigrant flow entering the United States has deteriorated significantly in the past two or three decades; that this decay in immigrant skills justifies a reassessment of the economic benefits and costs of immigration; and that major reforms in immigration policy may be needed to reestablish American competitiveness in this important marketplace."

Borjas argues that conditions in a home country shape the future not only for immigrants but also for the second and third generations in many cases. Thus he concludes that in the long run this flood of unskilled workers "reduces potential national income simply because they are less productive." Demography becomes destiny for newcomers, their offspring, and for the society that receives them.

Like the Puerto Ricans, many of today's Latino newcomers arrive with little education and not much in the way of technological job skills. The main difference is one of scale. The Puerto Rican migration was small enough that the primary victims of the disaster were the Puerto Ricans themselves. Today's Latino migration is so much larger and so much more widespread that the entire nation will suffer grievously if the Puerto Rican fate is repeated. Puerto Ricans made up 8 percent of New York's population in 1960 and grew to 12 percent by 1990. Five million Hispanics—half of them immigrants—lived in the Los Angeles region in 1990, making up a third of the population; their numbers will grow to 12 million by 2020, when they will make up half the population, according to official estimates. If Borjas is right in predicting that current Hispanic immigrants are destined to Puerto Rican–like poverty, then Southern California should have already begun an inexorable slide into a Third World catastrophe. Obviously, it hasn't.

The Puerto Rican case seems to provide a rock-solid precedent for dire predictions, but broad assumptions about the fate of immigrants based on group characteristics are no more valid now than they were when nineteenth-century nativists argued that Europeans coming from despotic states would prove unfit for life in a democracy. A close look at what happened to Puerto Ricans after they arrived in New York exposes two crippling weaknesses in this line of thought. First, it assumes that the United States is an inert receptacle, when, in fact, circumstances encountered here can dictate what direction immigrants will follow. Second, the aggregate statistics used for this kind of analysis do not account for diverse outcomes among members of an ethnic group. Describing a group identity based on average income, median educational levels, or other gross statistical measures misses the exceptions even when they are numerous, and yet this is the predominate form of analysis in American social science as it is applied to ethnic and racial groups, especially immigrants. For Puerto Ricans, the group statistics mask the many third- and fourth-generation migrants who are success stories. Understanding their lives is of more than academic interest; it is critically important in formulating public policy for the future.

When the Puerto Ricans came to New York after World War II, the European immigrants who had arrived in the early decades of the century were rapidly aging out of the industrial workforce. As a result, Puerto Ricans poured into this sector of the labor market just as it was about to crash. Between 1970 and 1980, New York City lost well over half a million unskilled and semiskilled jobs, which accounted for more than half of the total job loss in the city. Hundreds of factories closed or relocated and warehouses and wharves went idle as the demise of Rust Belt manufacturing hit New York. Puerto Ricans suffered disproportionately because they were so heavily overrepresented in these areas of the labor market. Even after years of decline in manufacturing employment, more than a quarter of the Puerto Rican workforce was still in that sector in 1980, compared to one-sixth of the city workforce as a whole.

When New York's industrial economy sank, the Puerto Ricans sank with it. During the 1970s, family income for Puerto Rican New Yorkers dropped by 18 percent in real terms, while whites, blacks, and other Hispanics experienced gains. Mexican immigrants nationwide experienced a 19 percent *gain* in family income in real terms in the 1970s, riding the oil boom in Texas and the defense spending buildups in California. To make matters worse for Puerto Ricans, the losses in income were five times greater when the head of the household was born on the mainland, compared with those born on the island. The second generation was just entering the workforce, only to find the rug pulled out from under it. Their poverty was born and bred in New York. By comparison, the city's blacks had a bit of a cushion because civil rights initiatives had opened up the public sector and other opportunities. While the overall poverty rate for blacks declined by 15 percent during the 1970s, it went up among Puerto Ricans by the same measure.

While the Puerto Ricans were losing their jobs, they also lost their neighborhoods. Rather than creating a successful enclave, building up real estate holdings and a retail sector that could cushion the community against bad times for wage earners, many relocated repeatedly, sometimes by choice but often not. The villains of the true West Side story are demolition crews rather than street gangs. Whole Puerto Rican communities were eliminated to make way for the construction of Lincoln Center and the regentrification of the Upper West Side. Huge chunks of El Barrio were leveled to build public housing projects. Puerto Ricans got their share of the new apartments, but the price they paid was that whole shopping areas where they had begun to show some entrepreneurial zest simply disappeared. In the 1970s, the Bronx and Brooklyn became home to the largest concentrations of Puerto Ricans, but they arrived just as those areas began to burn in a firestorm of arson widely blamed both on slumlords who sought escape from unprofitable properties and on the work of Puerto Rican vandals. The area of the South Bronx with the highest Puerto Rican population lost 57 percent of its housing units in the 1970s, causing 120,000 people to relocate, most of them for the second time in the space of a few years. And, for the many thousands who remained, the South Bronx was a place of devastating poverty.

Because so many Puerto Ricans were displaced persons within

the city, they never had a chance to develop the kind of enclave economy in which dollars are recycled through retail shops and other small businesses, gradually allowing a community to develop its own base of entrepreneurial capital and credit worthiness. This, in turn, meant that Puerto Ricans were all the more dependent on wage employment and welfare. They never had a chance to build the kind of kinship networks and local organizations so typical of Latin communities, including El Barrio at one time. Without that web of churches, informal associations, and small institutions, economic losses translated into social losses much more quickly. In addition, the displacements diluted the Puerto Ricans' political strength by scattering them through many electoral districts.

When they did play the political game, Puerto Ricans suffered a major handicap. They were designated nonwhites, but they never matched the blacks in moral standing, quality of leadership, or organizing abilities. The blacks never embraced them as natural allies, nor did the European ethnics. As a result, Puerto Ricans have lived in a state of perpetual ambiguity while trying to survive in a rough game of ethnic politics.

The Puerto Ricans' handicaps and their blunders are clearly illustrated in the many battles over the city schools. For the better part of a decade, starting in the late 1960s, one enduring fight involved a dispute over whether control of the schools should rest with local boards or a centralized bureaucracy. One of the most bitter conflicts pitted black community groups against predominately Jewish teachers' unions. The Reverend Joseph P. Fitzpatrick, S.J., a Fordham University sociologist who extensively chronicled the early decades of the Puerto Rican experience in New York, politely concluded, "The relationship of the Puerto Rican community to the decentralization controversy was neither clear nor consistent." In his 1987 book, *Puerto Rican Americans,* he describes how the Puerto Rican leadership frequently split on the issue, angering all sides. When it finally came time in 1973 to vote for members of the now-powerful local school boards, the United Federation of Teachers and European ethnics working through Catholic parishes outorganized the Puerto Ricans. The Puerto Rican leadership failed to turn out its own voters, according to Fitzpatrick's account. "As a result, in many predominately Puerto Rican areas, few if any Puerto Ricans were elected to the community boards." In American politics, the failure to define a clear and consistent position often leads to a loss of power, but for Puerto Ricans, that reflects something inherent about their place in the New York mosaic.

In the schools and in city politics overall, many Puerto Ricans wanted to follow in the Europeans' footsteps, but the reality of minority-group politics dictated otherwise. Glazer and Moynihan noted this distinct character in the message and tactics espoused by Aspira, an important Puerto Rican community organization that primarily worked to help students through school. In 1963, they said of Aspira, "Its identification is with the Jews or Italians of forty years ago, rather than with the Negroes of today." But Fitzpatrick concluded nearly twenty-five years later, "Although Puerto Ricans may be uncertain about their identification with blacks, they find that because of their social, political and geographic proximity, they must work with them." The result, he concluded, is "serious tensions" between the two groups and an ongoing identity crisis among Puerto Ricans.

Despite Aspira's open emulation of the Europeans, it won its single greatest victory after filing a civil rights lawsuit against the city Board of Education and winning a consent decree in 1975 assuring bilingual education to Spanish-speaking students. Taking stock of what had been accomplished as of 1987 with decentralization and the decree, Fitzpatrick concluded, "In brief, the situation of Puerto Ricans in the New York City schools is as bad, if not worse, than it has ever been." The Europeans, and to a lesser extent the blacks, gained advantage because they adapted politically, even ideologically, to the circumstances they encountered in New York, becoming adept at the city's distinctive forms of labor organizing and Democratic machine politics. They also produced successful leaders and political organizations. The Puerto Ricans did none of these things in sufficient measure to ameliorate their situation.

Perhaps the most ironic concurrence of events to befall the Puerto Ricans occurred when many simply gave up on New York and decided to go home. Starting in 1948 with an economic development plan named Operation Bootstrap, Puerto Rico underwent a period of industrialization and modernization that was brusquely successful. From the launch of the program through 1970, more than one thousand factories were opened on the island, directly creating some sixty-eight thousand jobs and contributing to the creation of sixty thousand more in services or trade. Like most rapid economic growth, this spurt displaced a great many people even as it created opportunities. The churning gave Puerto Ricans reason to migrate, but it also gave them reason to return. They traveled both ways in a constant circular flow facilitated by ninety-nine-dollar fares on the *puente aéreo* (the flying bridge) that connected New York and San Juan.

When unemployment and burned-out neighborhoods became a way of life in the late 1960s, many Puerto Rican small-business owners cashed in whatever they had gained, abandoned New York, and went home in search of good economic times and a simpler life. But those new arrivals in Puerto Rico were greeted by economic crises even more severe than the one in New York. Industrialization had not fully cured the island's chronic poverty, and yet its economy had become tied to the mainland. During U.S. recessions unemployment rates regularly went beyond 20 percent in Puerto Rico as business failures on the island skyrocketed. Of the Puerto Ricans who had gone home to avoid the demise of the New York barrios, many prospered and helped build the island's middle class, but many others eventually headed north once again and not just for a visit. By then they had lost all that they had earned.

"The first time I went to New York, I was chasing my dreams. The second time I went, I was trying to survive," said Jimmy Pabón. He first came to East Harlem in 1957 without a dime, and by 1971 he was the proud owner of a restaurant and nightclub in El Barrio. Soon afterward, he grew concerned about how the neighborhood was going downhill, so he sold his property and returned to Puerto Rico, where eventually he went bust. He ended up back in New York, penniless, much older, and in a city that had become a tougher place with a surging crime rate and an industrial economy in demise.

Just as Puerto Rico had been a safety valve when prospects started turning dark in New York, New York became a safety valve for what happened on the island. The availability of ready escape routes meant that many Puerto Ricans never confronted problems in either place, and they paid a price for their inconsistency.

"If all of us had stayed here and fought for El Barrio instead of taking our money out and going to Puerto Rico, I know this would be a different place, because we never got back what we lost," said Pabón.

Although no data specifically measures circular migration, a number of indicators have led experts like Fitzpatrick to estimate that hundreds of thousands of Puerto Ricans have divided their lives between New York and Puerto Rico, with long sojourns in both places. The Census Bureau found that 5 percent of the island's population in 1980—more than 137,000 people—had lived on the mainland prior to 1975. And a 1987–1988 survey by the Puerto Rican government of airline passengers leaving the island found that two-thirds of those stating an intent to live on the mainland for an extended period of time reported that they had done so at least once before. While it is difficult to know how many people lived in one place and then the other, there is no doubt there was an enormous and constant traffic back and forth.

"There is an element of Greek tragedy about what happened to the Puerto Ricans in New York," said Fitzpatrick as he reflected back on the years he spent trying to unravel that drama. "It seems that every move they made was predestined to bring them grief. They are exemplary in showing how things can go wrong despite the best intentions."

Coming to America became a wicked transaction for the Puerto Ricans: The situations Puerto Ricans encountered here—like the collapse of the industrial economy—greatly exacerbated their liabilities. Their lack of qualifications meant they suffered more and made it harder for them to bounce back and find new work. They brought loose family structures with them and encountered the corrosive effects of the welfare state, a permissive society, and frequent displacement. The Puerto Ricans were weak exactly where the dangers were strong. It was the interaction of group characteristics and circumstances that shaped their fate. But even as one tries to balance identity and history, it is important to remember that individuals sometimes evolve through several different identities over the course of a lifetime.

George and Lucy Garcia* were born in New York and grew up in East Harlem households made up of a mother and children fathered by several different men. They both understood the workings of the welfare bureaucracies at an early age. Statistically speaking, for most of their lives they would have been counted as

*George and Lucy's names and those of their relatives have been changed at their request.

among the failed cases of the Puerto Rican migration. They still live in East Harlem, and the most prominent decoration in their dim, dark apartment is a glossy poster-size copy of their wedding portrait. It as if they are making a statement. They are both in their early twenties, and they seem determined to take a new direction.

"Like almost everyone else around here, I went through a time when I was pretty much living the life of the streets," said George, who speaks English with an accent that is all New York and very little Puerto Rican. He leaves no doubt that he was on the wrong side of the law for a while but insists that he never physically hurt an innocent person and never went to jail. His older brother, Pepe, died while still a teenager, but he will not talk about that except to say, "Drugs did it." Eventually, George got work at a hospital, first as a janitor, then as an orderly. There he met Lucy, who was a high school graduate and had taken some business college classes. She worked in the billing department as a clerk. When I got to know them, George was preparing for his high school equivalency exam and had been taking courses that would qualify him for work in rehabilitation therapy. Lucy was within sight of her bachelor's degree and had received several promotions at the hospital.

Asked why they have managed to do so well, compared with so many others in El Barrio, George answers without hesitation: "Lucy started my life over again for me, and then this one really got me going." He is pointing to their one-year-old daughter, Angela, who sits in a playpen that occupies most of the open space in their tiny living room. Clearly, George and Lucy have a powerful bond based in part on their mutual desire to get beyond their troubled beginnings. That partnership and the motivation they now draw from their daughter is one factor in explaining why they seem able to have changed their fates, and it is a nugget of human serendipity invisible to the statisticians. George's mother, Maria, who is forty-four and has had three children by three different men, lives in another apartment in the same building, and on workdays she looks after Angela as well as her own youngest child, who is just two. As convoluted as her life has been, Maria has managed to maintain a sense of family. She has lived in East Harlem since she came from Puerto Rico twenty-five years ago, and she has developed a network of friends and relatives that on occasion has helped her and her older children find work. She hints that some of these neighborhood people saved George from serious trouble at one point during his delinquent days.

Although these factors may not have actually boosted George and Lucy's chances of success, they did help them survive circumstances that have sunk others. Well aware of what they have had to overcome, the two of them brimmed with plans and expectations. "The health industry is where it is at, and we are positioning ourselves to take advantage of all the growth there is going to be," said George as if he was discussing a Wall Street prospectus. Lucy smiled and said modestly, "It is good work."

In assessing their chances for success, George rendered a blunt assessment: "Lucy can pass, but I can't, so she is the one we are counting on." What he meant was that she is light-skinned and can pass as white. George has fine features and straight hair, but his skin is brown enough that he looks clearly Latino. "When Lucy puts on her work clothes, she can sit down at her computer and no one thinks she is anything but a red-blooded American white girl," George said proudly.

Lucy interrupted and upbraided him. "You look down at the corner at the guys you used to hang with who are dealing crack and shooting people and there are some lighter than you are and so you know damn well that's not what makes the difference. There are winners and there are losers and that's all there is. You go one way or the other. You choose."

Fifty years after they began their migration to New York, Puerto Ricans are indeed a fractured people divided into winners and losers. During the last decade and a half, mainland Puerto Ricans underwent an extraordinary ethnic mitosis. Roughly speaking, about half did well socially and economically. Upward economic mobility carried many to the suburbs and to the Sun Belt. The other half remained poor and sometimes got poorer, and the poor half was concentrated in city ghettos, not just New York's but also in places like Allentown, Pennsylvania, and Lawrence, Massachusetts.

Puerto Ricans began as one people, but those born here produced at least two very distinct groups. In the 1980s, one of them became the poorest of all ethnic groups; the other enjoyed the largest increase in median family income of any major ethnic group, nearly a 30 percent jump. Similarly, Puerto Ricans and blacks claim the largest percentage of households headed by single women, about 31 percent, but at the same time the percentage of Puerto Rican women employed in professional and managerial jobs, 23 percent, is not far behind the mark for white women, 28 percent.

This split outcome can be explained to some extent by changes in the New York and U.S. economies in the 1980s. Whites made up a shrinking share of the population in cities everywhere but especially in New York during this period. At the same time, however, a new urban economy was developing around financial, business, and legal services, telecommunications, and computing. Roger Waldinger, a UCLA sociologist, has shown how the declining number of whites opened up opportunities for Puerto Ricans, blacks, recent Asian immigrants, and others. For those who had the right qualifications, white-collar jobs became available to an extent unthinkable a generation earlier. In his 1996 book on New York labor markets *Still the Promised City?* Waldinger argues that America's perpetual race consciousness creates an ethnic hierarchy so strictly segmented that he compares it to a totem pole, with the groups most desirable to employers on top. As economic growth, suburbanization, and other factors pull the topmost groups upward, those below them advance in the pecking order. Although this analysis gives significant weight to elements of American culture like discrimination and events such as economic restructuring, it gives an almost deterministic value to ethnic-group identity. "The continuous recourse to migration as a source of low-level labor, so characteristic of the United States, has made ethnicity the crucial and enduring mechanism that sorts groups of categorically different workers into an identifiably distinct set of jobs." Group identity is so powerful in Waldinger's view that home-country experience and culture can determine where immigrants establish their niche in U.S. labor markets, and once niches develop, the children of immigrants are channeled into them. "Just as with the first generation, the second generation's search for advancement takes on a *collective* form."

Nothing is quite so neat and simple, especially in a place like New York, and Waldinger accounts for the possibility of messy competition and conflict among those at the bottom of the economy. Puerto Ricans who lacked qualifications for the new jobs found it ever more difficult to hold the old jobs as a massive influx of new immigrants created greatly increased competition for low-wage, low-skilled work. The newcomers underbid the Puerto Ricans and used their strong networks to take over whole job categories, such as working in industrial laundries, sewing garments, and driving cabs. Contrary to Waldinger's heavy emphasis on collective fates for ethnic groups, some Puerto Ricans managed to climb up several stages of the totem pile, while others were sliding ever further down.

A split of some sort among Puerto Ricans has been forecast for decades. In the 1950s, some scholars predicted that light-skinned Puerto Ricans would assimilate to life in the mainstream American white community, while the dark-skinned ones would become part of the black community. More recently, conservative writers like Linda Chavez have argued that Puerto Ricans and other Latinos cannot achieve prosperity until they leave their barrios and adapt themselves to America's white, English-speaking mainstream. Remaining in the enclaves and clinging to ethnic forms of social and political expression can only be ruinous in this view, and the dismal state of Puerto Ricans in New York is offered as evidence.

The out-of-the-barrio scenario ignores obstacles to mobility, such as skin color, and it oversimplifies the Puerto Rican experience. The Puerto Rican population did split, but the split is not neatly defined by either race or geography. Success does not simply belong to those who are light-skinned or those who went to live among Anglos. And it is a cruel joke to cast blame on those who chose to live in a barrio, because every time Puerto Rican New Yorkers began to build an enclave, they lost it to arson, urban renewal, circular migration, or some combination of all these factors. They never had a place comparable to Houston's Magnolia or L.A.'s Boyle Heights, where for fifty years or more one generation after another of Mexicans built up barrios that have a dense network of social and economic interconnections and long-standing institutions.

In fact, Puerto Ricans have done well when they have had something like a successful barrio experience. The South Bronx has begun to show important signs of rejuvenation in the last decade, in part because the population there eventually stabilized. Community organizations have carried out sustained efforts to improve the quality of life, and some skillful political leaders, like Bronx borough president Fernando Ferrer, have reached positions of power and have helped promote economic redevelopment. Under these circumstances, significant public and private funds have been invested in once-neglected communities.

Finally, there are no signs that the winners are simply trying to abandon their Puerto Rican identities, any more than that the losers are clinging to a self-destructive ethnic consciousness.

George and Lucy are anxious to leave East Harlem, and they are saving every dollar they can to finance an escape. But when they talk about their dreams, they envision joining some of Lucy's relatives in Florida, where some of the nation's fastest-growing and most prosperous new Puerto Rican communities have developed around Orlando and Miami.

"Florida has got a future that includes us," said George. "It is a place where you can be natural and not have to worry about how some Ivy League Yuppie is sizing you up. The people we know who got down there have cars and houses and the best salsa clubs in the world." Rather than fleeing a barrio to seek their fortunes in the wide-open spaces of the American mainstream, these Puerto Ricans are contributing to the expansion of Florida's unique Caribbean culture.

Like all ancestral portraits, this one offers an inexact but telling image of the present. The Puerto Rican story helps establish a perspective that makes it easier to understand the Latino experience at the end of the century. It shows how dangerous it can be to rely on the kind of social science that paints group identities on the basis of census data and then predicts outcomes. There is no way of knowing how today's Latino immigrants will end up simply on the basis of the human capital they bring with them. They arrive as Spanish-speaking peasants. They become citizens of postindustrial America.

A great deal of the debate over Latino immigrants and their long-term impact on this nation is colored by statistical portraits that pretend to assign group identities on the basis of big aggregate numbers. Predictions that Mexicans are destined to end up poor and dependent in the United States emerge from a kind of reasoning dangerously close to the type of prejudice that employed science to prescribe identity on the basis of race. What is most perilous about the American obsession with group identities at a time of immigration is that it assumes that the receiving society, the host, is a level playing field. It also falsely assumes that circumstances remain static and that the host society is unable to improve the immigrants' chances of success. As the Puerto Rican experience demonstrates so tragically, the United States—its economy, its culture, and its government policies—can exercise a powerful force over the fate of an immigrant group. For example, the extent of education immigrants bring with them may be critical in determining their immediate fate, but the quality of education their children encounter in American schools will have a greater effect over the course of several decades. Demography is not destiny, and both the newcomers and the hosts have it in their power to shape the immigrant future.

That lesson also applies to a very different group of Latinos who came a little bit later and who received a warm and generous welcome here. The Cubans of south Florida are in many ways a world apart from the Puerto Ricans of New York, but it is the similarities they share that are the most telling.

❖•❖•❖•❖•❖•❖•❖•❖•❖•❖•❖•❖•❖•❖•❖•❖•

Miami: A Barrio
Without Borders

❖•❖•❖•❖•❖•❖•❖•❖•   Sometime in the early 1950s, Miami
International Airport became the place
where the United States and Latin America crossed paths. South-
bound travelers had to go there to catch the roaring DC-7s for the
long night flights to Panama and beyond. In Miami, these voyagers
got their first taste of hot, damp air, their first earful of foreign languages, their first sight of men in starchy white shirts and combed
black mustaches. For those headed north, it was the essential gateway to the United States. Once past the formalities of entry, Miami
International was the place where everything started becoming
neat, orderly, and modern.

In the first months of 1959, shortly after Fidel Castro's triumph,
fistfights erupted at the Miami airport as two sets of exiles crossed
paths: The first exiles fleeing Castro's revolution debarked flights
arriving from Havana and crossed paths with Castro's allies, exiled

by the former regime, who were waiting for departing flights to take them home. The angry encounters by the airport gates have become part of the creation myth of Cuban Miami, a fitting legend, because since then, the whole of South Florida has become a massive transit lounge. It is a place of constant arrivals and departures, an entrepôt familiar to people comfortable straddling two cultures without committing themselves to either one.

Nearly half a million Cubans settled in South Florida in the first twenty years after Castro's revolution, and they built the only barrio where a lot of people have become rich, influential, and respected. More than a quarter of those who came in the first two decades had annual incomes of more than fifty thousand dollars by 1990, exceeding the national average, and in the highest brackets, they almost rivaled Anglo affluence. Cuban Miami is the only barrio with country clubs, but, like the others, it remains a place apart from the rest of the country. Well into its fourth decade, Cuban Miami is still a port of entry, a borderland between north and south.

A *Time* cover story about Miami in 1993 proclaimed, "For if the go-go '80s was New York City's and Wall Street's, the globally minded '90s belong to Miami, 'the Hong Kong of Latin America,' perched on the rim of the fastest-growing region in the New World." The article justified its claims by noting that international commerce is a $25.6 billion business in Miami, having grown by 20 percent in 1992 alone. Like Hong Kong, the city is in fact a giant enclave. South Florida has become a destination for the entire Western Hemisphere and for Europeans as well because it is physically attached to the United States but not really a part of it. Miami prospered as a transit lounge for money, people, and ideas, but the city never realized its full economic potential in part because the Cubans remained locked in their glorious barrio.

The Miami Cubans prospered, and they have also remained apart from America. The Cubans' story shows that the separateness of other Latino immigrants is not simply a product of poverty. Their story shows how the migration itself, the ongoing link between north and south, defines the Latino identity in this country today. Like most other barrios, Cuban Miami is not a collection of urban neighborhoods. Cuban Miami is a barrio without borders because it is a frame of mind and a network of relationships that is interwoven throughout South Florida and that stretches across the water down to Cuba itself. Cuban Miami is a place where people reinvent themselves, a marketplace of transactions between an old land and a new land, and in that, it is like all other barrios.

The Miami Cubans are exceptional among Latino immigrants because the initial migrants, the builders of the barrio, came from the upper and middle classes and brought with them high levels of education, business experience, and familiarity with the United States. But that does not entirely explain their success. The so-called golden exiles did indeed arrive with a rich store of human capital—and then, significantly, America showered them with opportunities to make that capital grow.

The anti-Castro Cubans who came after 1959 received a warmer welcome from the United States than any other group of foreigners who have ever come to this country. In addition to economic and political largesse granted them as Cold War heroes, they also benefited from accidents of history and geography. Just as the Puerto Ricans were cursed at almost every turn, the Cubans were blessed in nearly everything they did. In addition to their material success, the Miami Cubans have also enjoyed a demographic triumph of sorts. They are the first Latinos to become the dominant population in an important metropolitan area—the first but not the last. Latinos will become the largest group in metropolitan Los Angeles and many smaller urban areas before long. The Cubans gained the opportunity to govern quickly, within the lifetime of the first arrivals, but they have not bothered to lead Miami. Instead, they have helped fragment the city. Locked inside the mental enclave that is Cuban Miami, they so ignored the opportunities around them that they put their success at risk.

The Cubans were able to build a strong barrio and eventually define an entire city because they landed at the right place at the right time. Such coincidences are crucial in the history of immigration.

The European immigrants arrived in New York when it was growing and prospering as a terminus for transatlantic trade. The Puerto Ricans arrived in time to ride the city down as that role declined. Just as New York became the key point of contact between the United States and Europe because steamship routes and telegraph lines ended there, Miami grew starting in the 1960s because it served as the hub for inter-American air travel and telecommunications. Like the European immigrants who helped fuel and define New York's ascent, the Cubans proved the ideal human ingredient for the Miami boom.

"When the Cubans got here, Miami was in a tailspin and ironically that created opportunities for them," recalls Monsignor Bryan Walsh, who directed the Roman Catholic Archdiocese's refugee relief efforts during most of the Cuban influx.

Entering the 1960s, Miami's only substantial enterprise was as a winter resort, and the advent of easy airplane travel had brought killer competition with newly accessible island destinations in the Caribbean. For vacationers, Miami became a place to change planes. Otherwise, it lived off the retirees who had fled from the Northeast and had made Miami the butt of shuffleboard jokes.

In 1961, Walsh remembers, the Miami United Way didn't fulfill 60 percent of its annual fund-raising goal. The city had hit bottom. Anybody who could was getting out. Meanwhile, the Cubans were getting in.

Instead of having to fight for a turf like most newly arrived groups, the Cubans found an empty space in a neighborhood just beyond the shadow of downtown where there was a lot of pre–World War II housing interspersed with bakeries, bottling plants, and warehouses. As working-class whites fled the declining economy, the Cubans moved into the stucco bungalows and clapboard saltboxes. The neighborhood soon became known as Little Havana to outsiders, while the Cubans referred to it as Calle Ocho, after the main commercial thoroughfare, Southwest Eighth Street.

"You had occupancy rates down to thirty percent in Calle Ocho when they [the Cubans] started coming," said Walsh. "It wasn't the nicest place in the world, but it allowed the Cubans to establish themselves as a community right from the beginning."

One of the people who helped build that community is Luis J. Botifoll. An attorney and newspaper editor in prerevolutionary Havana, he became a banker in Miami, rising from loan officer to chairman of the Republic National Bank. When I asked him about the early days, he pointed out of the window of his office atop the bank building. Calle Ocho seemed small and compact and shady compared to the Sun Belt sprawl all around it. "If we had been scattered around a big city, we would have been lost. The geography here was essential to our success because it allowed us to concentrate our resources on creating our own economy. Our businesses thrived because our own people provided them with loyal clients and employees."

He was describing the classic formula for the emergence of an ethnic-enclave economy. Little Havana gave the Cubans a place where they could adapt to the United States, build their networks, and accumulate capital. Unlike what happened to Puerto Ricans, no one tried to bulldoze them, burn them out, or buy them out. While they got on their feet, no one else moved in to town to compete for housing and jobs. For other Latinos, the barrio has been a place to survive. For the Cubans, the barrio was a means to prosper.

When Cubans progressed enough to seek better housing, they did not have to go far. Miami is sufficiently compact that they were able to move out of Calle Ocho without scattering and losing their sense of community. The Cubans not only created a successful enclave but they managed to avoid one of the great pitfalls that others have suffered. Barrios like Magnolia, Washington Heights, and East Los Angeles have remained stuck at a level of working-class poverty in part because the most successful residents are always moving to distant suburbs and breaking off all ties with those who remain behind. Capital, both human and economic, is removed from the barrio, and local businesses lose talent, investment, and clients.

As they expanded out of Little Havana, the Cubans created many new economic enclaves, from the working-class strip malls of Hialeah to the upscale suburban boutiques in Kendal. But, wherever they went, the Cubans stuck together. They remained loyal to one another not only in the choice of a neighborhood store but also in picking car dealers and insurance agents, subcontractors and suppliers, even if that meant driving back to Calle Ocho to make a purchase. In Miami, the Cubans extended the economic benefits of a tight-knit enclave both geographically and across the spectrum of business activities. Meanwhile, Calle Ocho took on a new role. Retaining a run-down fifties look against all the shiny glass and tropical pastels of contemporary Miami, it has become the historic old town of Cuban Miami with its restaurants and bookstores, its ceiba trees and its memorial to those who fell at the Bay of Pigs. Now Calle Ocho is a place of memory and identity.

Most major Latino communities have been stuck on the treadmill of continuous immigration for decades and have constantly

expended energy on absorbing the latest arrivals. The Miami
Cubans never faced that challenge because two mutually hostile
governments limited the human flow, allowing only a few relatively
brief blasts of immigration. In between, the Miami Cubans enjoyed
stretches of a decade or more when almost nobody arrived. These
pauses served as important breathing spaces that allowed them to
absorb the newcomers and then continue the work of building a
barrio.

In addition, the content of the migration also shifted in advanta-
geous ways over time. As the sociologists Alejandro Portes and Alex
Stepick have noted in several studies, the Cubans who came
between Castro's takeover in 1959 and the Cuban missile crisis of
1962, which shut down the influx for the first time, were better educated and more skilled than those who came in the next wave
aboard the "freedom flights" of the late 1960s and early 1970s. And
they, in turn, surpassed those who came during the four-month
Mariel boat lift of 1980. The early arrivals built the barrio and set
up the enclave's businesses. Then the "declining social gradient,"
as Portes and Stepick described it, neatly filled Cuban Miami's
growing demands for new workers and new consumers without
overburdening it at the onset.

The Cubans had another huge advantage: They received a generous welcome.

"Never in the history of the United States did any immigrant or
refugee population receive the kind of help that was made available
to the Cubans during their early years here; I am confident that is a
very safe statement," said Monsignor Walsh, who helped adminis-
ter that help.

One federal effort alone, the U.S. Cuban Refugee Program, spent
more than $1.5 billion helping settle some 486,000 Cubans who
sought assistance during the first twenty years of the migration.
Another federal program provided special scholarships for Cuban
college students. The University of Miami created a course just to
prepare Cuban physicians for the licensing exams that would allow
them to practice in the United States and organized a loan fund that
helped the doctors while they studied. The Dade County public
schools launched a crash program to recertify Cubans who had
come with teaching experience. Many were then put to work in the
first, and some of the most effective efforts at bilingual education
undertaken since the days of the European migration. The Miami

schools took it as an obligation rather than a burden to help Cuban children make a smooth transition from speaking Spanish to speaking English.

The extra help continued long after the enclave was established. Between 1968 and 1980, for example, 46 percent of the Small Business Administration loans in Dade County went to companies owned by Cubans and other Latinos, compared with only 6 percent for black-owned firms. During the construction of the Metrorail rapid transit system in the late 1970s, half of the contractors were Cuban, while blacks got only about an eighth of the work.

In addition, thousands of Cuban exiles were either fully employed or received extra income from the Central Intelligence Agency. Congressional inquiries conducted in the mid-1970s revealed that the creation of a small army for the failed Bay of Pigs invasion was only the beginning of the agency's expenditures. Building up the Miami station until it became the largest CIA operation outside the agency's Virginia headquarters, the CIA employed its own Cuban legion for many years in an extensive secret war against Cuba, involving sabotage, infiltration, and assassination plots. Even in the late 1960s, the operation was so large and well financed that a single small counterintelligence operation had as many as two hundred Cuban paid informants and a budget of more than $2 million a year, according to congressional testimony.

While the myth of Cuban Miami extols the self-reliant exile who arrived with no more than the shirt on his back and who made a fortune through brains and perseverance, the truth is that the Cubans built their enclave with massive public assistance and then continued to draw government subsidies well after they had established themselves here.

The Cubans also had the law on their side. Until President Clinton changed the policy in 1995, the federal government welcomed all Cubans into the country and automatically granted them permanent legal status after they had been here a year. No matter if they entered the country illegally, they could still live and work in the United States forever. Cubans were allowed in even if they freely admitted that they simply wanted to be with family here or improve their economic condition. And it didn't matter how many showed up, because by "voting with their feet," they testified to communism's failings.

No other nationality received such a ready welcome from the

U.S. immigration system. Thousands of Vietnamese languished in refugee camps for years before they could get to the United States. The number of Soviet Jews granted refugee status was subject to specific annual limits. Hundreds of thousands of Haitians and Central Americans were denied asylum on claims of political persecution that were later found valid by the courts, and millions of family-sponsored immigrants from other nations around the world spent as long as a decade on waiting lists before they could get visas.

Finally, the Cubans had a historical advantage. In Miami they never had to adjust to structural changes in the U.S. economy. Latino newcomers elsewhere started out in old-style manufacturing jobs and then had to struggle when these jobs disappeared. The Cubans participated in the creation of a new economy from the ground up and rose with it. During the first twenty years of the exiles' sojourn in Miami, the job market there grew by 74 percent over the national average. No one else was arriving in Miami during those years, and in fact whites were leaving the increasingly Spanish-speaking city. As the unrivaled suppliers of new workers to a hungry labor market, the Cubans prospered.

The Cubans proved doubly fortunate because this new economy based on business services, finance, and tourism has proved exceptionally resilient. During bad times, rich Latin Americans stash their money in Miami, and during good times, they go there to make deals. Miami has another kind of insulation, as well: Drug money is immune to business cycles. When the debt crisis of the 1980s devastated many U.S. businesses that had bet on Latin America, Miami was booming with narcodollars.

This argument is not meant to diminish the many acts of ingenuity and sacrifice by Cuban exiles. But given these advantages of geography, timing, financing, and history, any Latino group—even one with much less human capital—could have done well in Miami. The Puerto Ricans' fate, for example, would undoubtedly have been much different if they had encountered the same circumstances and had enjoyed the same generous handouts as the Cubans. The Cubans, in turn, would have had a very different experience if they had been wedged into a slice of Harlem and given no help except a welfare check. Though one is a saga of triumph and the other of defeat, both the Cuban and Puerto Rican stories demonstrate that the circumstances encountered by immigrants will influence their ultimate fate every bit as much as the qualities they bring with them.

Aside from the importance of circumstances in the United States, the Cuban experience teaches another lesson, as well: Material success in this country does not guarantee that immigrants will focus their attention on life here. Rich Latinos remain ambivalent toward America just as much as poor ones. In fact, wealth may make it even easier to avoid full engagement with the new land, while poverty sometimes forces attention to one's surroundings. With the Miami Cubans, this is most evident in the political realm. Even though doors were opened to them, they chose not to pass through them.

The Cubans' wealth, the moral authority they carried as Cold War exiles, and eventually their concentrated numbers in an important state added up to tangible political power. That influence could have been exerted on many different types of issues: international trade and telecommunications, overall refugee policy, small-business development, bilingual education, and other matters of immigrant assimilation. The Miami Cubans potentially had interesting things to say on all these matters and were in a position to make their voices heard on a national level. Instead, they have focused their energies almost exclusively on Cuba and an obsessive desire to bedevil Castro. They have created a single organization, the Cuban American National Foundation, that dominates political discourse within the enclave, and its single-minded focus is the liberation of Cuba.

Dissent is not tolerated in Cuban Miami. Even in the 1990s, as the Bay of Pigs veterans head toward old age, anyone who speaks out for accommodation with Castro faces the danger of public denunciation and ostracism. In the past, repeat offenders risked being silenced violently. Blowing people up in their cars was a favorite sanction, although threats usually sufficed.

The bombs, the weekend warriors who go to the Everglades to train for the next invasion of Cuba, and the anti-Castro protest marches are the most dramatic manifestation of an identity crisis that has preoccupied Cuban Miami from the outset. Like all migrants, the Cubans are battling to prove that an unknown future will be better than a familiar past. It is the same struggle for self-justification that preoccupies anyone who leaves home to make his life else-

where. Even when an economic or political disaster forces departure, accomplishments in the new land are measured against an idea
of what might have happened by remaining in the old country. All
migrants are travelers in time as well as in space, going back to their
past to justify the future. In the Cuban case, this part of the voyage
is starkly defined because it is expressed in political terms. Castro's
triumph on January 1, 1959, marks a clear line between the past and
the beginning of the migration.

Unlike most other Latinos, the Cubans were unable to return
home for visits during most of the time they were building their
barrio. That seems to have made them even more preoccupied with
their past, even as they gained wealth, position, and power in this
country. Achieving prosperity was a way of vindicating their decision to leave, according to Arturo Villar, a publisher and business
consultant.

"Once we realized that we were not going to ride right back to
Havana, there was a very conscious feeling that we had to do something important here, that we had to show the bastards that had
kicked us out that we were better than they were, that we could
recoup, that we could build something, and the best part about it is
that we ended up believing our own propaganda. It became a con-
viction that we were chosen for this," says Villar, referring to the
material success achieved by those who came in the early era of the
exile.

Like many other Latino immigrants, the Miami Cubans began
their journey simply thinking of survival, but over time the migration took on other purposes. Building the barrio became a surrogate
for defeating Castro. Like other immigrants, the Cubans measured
their success in the United States by the amount of admiration and
envy it generated back home. Just as Juan Chanax worked overtime
in Houston to build a house in Totonicapán that would dispel all the
slights inflicted on him as a Maya, the Miami Cubans strove for
achievements in the United State to *sobresalir* (surpass) their losses
in Cuba.

More than any other Latinos, the Miami Cubans seem to have
followed the model defined by the European ethnics, achieving
the kind of economic success, social stability, and political influence typical of middle-class white America, but the Cubans did it in
a single generation. And yet in other ways, they clearly fit the

African-American model, maintaining an identity that marks them as separate from the mainstream, pursuing narrowly focused group interests, and making their sense of shared historical adversity the prime source of political energy.

Due west past Woodlawn Park Cemetery, where two Cuban presidents are buried, Southwest Eighth Street is no longer Calle Ocho, but U.S. Highway 41, the Tamiami Trail. Here, the barrio takes the form of suburban strip malls and cul-de-sacs. Out in this part of Cuban Miami, almost in the Everglades, there is a school built of unadorned concrete in that modern bunkerlike style popular some years ago.

The school lobby delivers a bit of a surprise. Covering most of one wall is a monumental mural-sized photograph of an ornate neo-classical building that is all porticoes and pillars. American cars of the 1950s are parked in its driveway beneath huge palm trees. The aerial shot has been blown up so much that it has lost a little focus, and the huge white building with all its ornate decor has taken on a dreamy quality. In pre-revolutionary Havana the building in the picture was known as "The Palace of Education." It once housed the Belen Jesuit School, which was founded in 1854 under a royal charter from Her Majesty Isabel II, queen of Spain. Belen was the elite boys' school. For Cuba, it was Groton, Andover, and Exeter all wrapped into one. Fidel Castro went to Belen, as did Luis Botifoll and many of the other men who tried to overthrow the revolution.

In May 1961, just a month after the Bay of Pigs, Castro's troops seized the white palace and expelled the Jesuits. That September, the school reopened in Miami with many of the same students and faculty, almost as if nothing had happened. After nearly twenty years on Calle Ocho, Belen followed its students to the suburbs and built its new campus. All along, the Jesuits performed the same function of preparing young men to become Cuba's leaders.

"We have had to adapt in some things because we are now preparing boys for life in America, but that doesn't mean we have to become like an American school in every way. You can't lie about who you are," said Father José Izquierdo, who made the trip from Havana as a young teacher and became headmaster of Belen in Miami.

The old priest can remember worrying in the 1980s that the

Cuban identity would fade away. "We were seeing the first generation that was born and entirely grew up here, and we were worried that they would prefer American ways over our Latin culture. But they saw that they can live here in a Latin society, maintaining their Cuban heritage, and not have to give up anything."

Cuban Miami offers the best of both worlds to the second generation. Belen educates boys to be bilingual. Many grow up speaking English as their first language, even speaking it at home to parents who themselves were raised in Miami and may only have childhood memories of Cuba. But all the students are also taught Spanish, and not just as the language of holiday celebrations and visits with grandparents, but as one of the languages of the enclave and an essential tool for success in Miami.

"This generation now doesn't have to prove to anyone that they are Americans, and so they are even more confident about their Cuban identity. They know who they are and they know they belong here," says Izquierdo.

He introduced me to several of his top seniors one morning not long before graduation. These boys spoke flawless English, and yet they were deeply steeped in the lore of pre-revolutionary Cuba and the righteous exile. One of the teenagers could recite the address and phone number of his grandparents' house in Havana, an ancestral property abandoned nearly twenty years before he was born yet which he was expected to reclaim one day. Not surprisingly, the boys said they only dated Cuban girls; Anglos might be cute, but they were not good to bring home to mama and papa, and the boys said there were some things about being a Cuban man that an Anglo girl would never understand or put up with. The next fall, the students would be going to schools like Duke, Tulane, and Vanderbilt, but to a man they insisted that upon graduation they would move back to Miami, marry Cuban girls, and live there forever.

All of them had good summer jobs, mostly with businesses owned by family or friends. When I asked how they got these jobs, a handsome lad blurted out a one-word answer that made the rest laugh: "¡Palanca!" Literally, it means "leverage," but it translates better as "clout" or "pull." One of the others who was going to work as a researcher in a county office explained, "When you are Cuban in Miami and you have friends, you have palanca, and if you have palanca, it can get you a lot."

Another added quickly, "If you are Cuban in Miami and you have *palanca,* why would you want to live anywhere else?"

A third said, "Our parents had to hassle with Anglo society, but we don't. This is our city."

Over the past decade, other Latinos have come to Miami in numbers large enough to establish their own barrios. The Cubans paved the way for them—Nicaraguans, Brazilians, Colombians, and the rest—by creating a place where you could be successful while speaking Spanish. But Cuban Miami has remained apart. Its memory and its identity, its past and its future do not transmit to outsiders because they are not part of its history and they have no place in the relationships that hold it together.

During a long and illustrious career in two nations, Luis Botifoll counts as his gravest disappointment the night he spent waiting for news from the Bay of Pigs. He was among the group of exiles ready to declare themselves the new provisional government of Cuba the moment the invasion force had gained a secure beachhead. Instead, he spent the next day informing wives and mothers in Miami that their men were dead or missing.

As one of his great achievements, Botifoll recalls his tenure in the early 1970s as head of the loan committee for the Republic National Bank. "This was the time when people were settled enough to open their own businesses here, and our community had taken the decision that as long as we were here, we would build something of our own."

Fellow Cubans would come in asking for relatively small commercial loans from fifteen thousand to thirty thousand dollars, and Botifoll would grant them even when the borrower had no collateral and no credit history in this country. "We made loans exclusively on the basis of my knowledge of a person's character. Many were people whom I knew personally in Cuba. I had gone to school with them or members of their family or I had done business with them." With a little *palanca,* the barrio built on itself.

A decade later, when much of Nicaragua's business class fled the Sandinista revolution and ended up in Miami, the Cubans offered a great deal of comfort, charity, and political support. But when it came to *palanca,* the Nicaraguans did not have it and the Cubans would not give it to them. Botifoll by then was the chairman of the largest Hispanic-owned banking institution in the United States, but he did not cut the Nicaraguans any slack. "I cannot do for a Nicaraguan what I did for Cubans, because I don't know them," he said.

The barrio opened doors for its own but not for others, and after a while it did not even open its doors for its own. Like Juan Chanax and the Guatemalan grocery store workers, Cuban Miami functioned best as a network in which everyone had some connection to everyone else. Settling newcomers was easy so long as the population of the enclave was relatively small and cohesive. But by the time of the Mariel boat lift in 1980, that connectedness had started to break down. The Miami Cubans rallied to get the Marielitos out of Cuba because their flight repudiated Castro, but the Marielitos joined the enclave only as the low-wage employees of those who had come before. More of these newcomers were black or of mixed race, compared with the early exiles, and they were not members of the pre-revolutionary elite. A decade after the boat lift, 40 percent of the Marielitos had annual household incomes of less than fifteen thousand dollars, compared with only 30 percent of the Salvadorans who arrived in the United States during the same period and 37 percent of the Mexicans. By contrast, the Cubans who arrived in the early waves had much higher incomes than any other Latino immigrants and rivaled the affluence of Anglos. Among the Cubans who came before Mariel, 11 percent had annual household incomes of more than $75,000, compared with 9 percent for the total U.S. population.

Cuban Miami did not exactly shun the Marielitos, but it didn't embrace them, either. The next time a flood of Cubans escaped the island, however, the enclave virtually turned its back on its countrymen. On the evening of August 19, 1994, a delegation of community leaders from Cuban Miami led by Jorge Mas Canosa, the president of the Cuban-American Foundation, was slipped into the White House. As they waited in the Cabinet Room, a flotilla of Coast Guard and navy ships in the Straits of Florida was implementing a new policy that would send Cuban rafters to internment at the Guantánamo Bay naval base instead of to a new life in Miami. President Clinton, dressed in blue jeans and a plaid shirt, slipped away from his own birthday party to sell the Miami Cubans on the Guantánamo plan. No Latino group—and perhaps no other immigrant group—had ever been treated with such deference. Clinton would have been happy if the Cubans had just agreed not to interfere with the operation at sea and not to launch massive demonstrations in Miami, according to administration officials. Instead, Mas Canosa enthusiastically endorsed the internment policy so long as it was accompanied by a tightening of economic sanctions against Cuba. In the following weeks, the Clinton administration put nearly forty thousand Cuban rafters in the camps at Guantánamo and then eventually cut a deal with Castro so anyone trying to get out in the future would be summarily returned to Havana. This reversed thirty-five years of welcoming policies, and hardly anyone in Cuban Miami protested.

Within the enclave, the prevailing political argument held that Castro used both Mariel and the rafters as an escape valve for malcontents. Many in Miami felt suspicious of anyone who had managed to spend most of their lives under communism. The old-timers asked, Aren't these just opportunists leaving Cuba because the Soviet Union isn't around anymore to subsidize the revolution? Finally, the residents of the enclave refused to open the doors as a matter of self-interest. By the time of the rafters' exodus, the Miami Cubans did not need any more low-wage workers, and they certainly did not need the political hassles of resettling a big group of newcomers just as anti-immigrant sentiment was building all over Florida.

The Miami Cubans, the most nationalistic of any immigrants in the current wave, did not base their identity merely on nationality. Being Cuban was no guarantee of admission to the enclave. As immigrants, they were no longer merely Cubans. They were *Miami* Cubans, and that identity was stronger and more specific than nationality. It was also much narrower than the broad ethnic identity expressed by terms like *Hispanic* and *Latino.* Cuban Miami did not embrace Colombians or Hondurans just because they were Latinos. It did not embrace Nicaraguans in the 1980s just because they were fellow refugees from a left-wing regime. Being a Miami Cuban involved a very specific set of characteristics that combined ethnic identity, nationality, economic class, political beliefs, and the experiences of this one barrio. It started out as a place where desperate exiles found refuge, then became a charmed circle closed to the city around it and to outsiders who didn't belong. That kind of isolation carries a price.

. . .

In the spring of 1993, swaths of Miami looked like a
manic gardener had hacked the great green foliage with dull prun-
ing shears. Piles of debris on the curbs and tangles of electrical
wires overhead heightened the sense of disrepair and gave hints of
decay. Amid these lingering wounds from Hurricane Andrew, the
Miami Cubans completed the work of building their enclave. In
local elections that spring, six Hispanics won seats on the Metro
Dade Commission, the powerful countywide ruling body, along
with four blacks and three whites. That racial breakdown was the
result of a federal court ruling that overturned the old voting setup
as discriminatory against blacks and Hispanics, including the
Cubans, who were treated as an aggrieved minority. The Cubans'
victories in the courtroom and at the ballot box capped a decade-
long effort to extend the enclave's influence into the political
sphere. In previous years, they had elected Cuban mayors of Miami,
Hialeah, and other municipalities. Two Cubans had been elected to
Congress, and Cubans had taken over important administrative
posts such as superintendent of the county schools and president of
Florida International University.

For nearly four decades, Miami had been a backdrop as the exiles
wrote new chapters to their history of Cuba. They had built a barrio
that encompassed an entire metropolitan area. They had schools,
businesses, and shopping areas that belonged to them, even pieces
of local government. During that time, a new generation had been
born and raised within the nourishing confines of the enclave. And
Miami itself had grown up. It was no longer a southern backwater,
but a big, complicated metropolis that needed leadership to ensure
peace among ethnic rivals and some semblance of equal opportunity. In an increasingly diverse and fragmented metropolitan area,
the Miami Cubans had become an imposing force. Only the Anglos
exercised comparable sway, and that was because they had dominated the city's civic and business institutions for so long. Anglo
power lay in the past. The Cubans could draw political strength
from the future.

Hispanics had been the largest population group in Miami since
the early 1980s, and as the largest and most powerful of the Latino
groups by far, the Cubans could be expected to exercise leadership.
But leadership requires neighbors to talk to one another, and Miami

has never been that kind of place. The Cubans assimilated to what they found there. When the Cubans arrived in Miami and during the time they built their barrio, an old white business and social elite ruled the city and kept it segregated by race and class. Like Latinos elsewhere, the Miami Cubans became both victims and accomplices of the American system of discrimination.

Although they received a hero's welcome on a national level, in Miami the Cubans were shunned by the local whites. This was most evident in the realm of politics. Until recently, they enjoyed much greater influence in Washington than in Tallahassee. They had become a factor in the Republican party's presidential nominating process when they were still fighting to get fair representation on the local county commission. Following the Mariel boat lift, a grassroots Anglo backlash against the new immigrant wave produced a local initiative that made English the official language of Dade County even though native speakers of English were rapidly becoming a minority of the population. The hostility that the Cubans encountered from Miami's white establishment had unintended benefits, however. Being shut out of the old downtown simply obliged Cuban entrepreneurs to create vibrant new businesses out in the suburbs where the city was growing. And when Cuban professionals were ghettoized to deal only with Spanish-speaking clients, that merely positioned them for Miami's boomtown role as the business center for Latin America.

The experience of being shunned, however, did not make the Cubans sympathetic to other victims of discrimination. It just made them determined never to let themselves be victims again. The Cubans, who were overwhelmingly white in the early stages of the migration, came from a society that had a tradition of some racial discrimination against blacks. As they gained economic position, the Miami Cubans stepped to the privileged side of the racial barrier in the United States. Along the way, the newcomers did nothing to change the old dividing lines in Miami and merely added new ones instead. The city's blacks took notice.

During the time that the Cubans consolidated their enclave, Miami's black neighborhoods erupted into violent protests and rioting in 1980, 1982, 1984, and 1989. The cumulative toll amounted to eighteen hundred people arrested, twenty-five killed, and nearly five hundred injured. The message seemed clear enough. Some analysts began to speak of "the Miami syndrome," which involved an intense frustration among African-Americans, who saw their economic, political, and cultural fortunes declining as newly arrived immigrants achieved success. Other commentators wrote about the "double subordination" felt by Miami blacks. As blacks saw it, the Cubans arrived just when the civil rights era was about to free African-Americans from institutionalized racism. Instead of freedom, Miami's blacks felt they ended up suffering discrimination by both whites and Cubans. While a few prominent Miami Cubans have shown an interest in building bridges, many others have shown a blatant disregard for black sensitivities.

In June 1990, African National Congress leader Nelson Mandela received a hero's welcome in the United States. Recently released after twenty-seven years in South African prisons for opposing apartheid, Mandela had acquired the status of a modern political saint. Then, during a long TV appearance with Ted Koppel of ABC News a week before he was due in Miami, Mandela freely acknowledged his admiration for several fellow revolutionaries, including Fidel Castro.

The Miami Cubans reacted as if he had admitted the most barbaric crime. Five Cuban mayors of towns and cities in Dade County, including Miami Mayor Xavier Suarez, issued an open letter saying that Mandela's comments were "beyond reasonable comprehension." Although Mandela was coming to town only to address a union convention and had no local invitations, the five mayors "uninvited" the living symbol of the struggle for racial equality. A few hundred Cubans held a noisy protest demonstration outside the Miami Beach Convention Center during Mandela's appearance there. Several thousand blacks rallied in support of Mandela, some of them holding signs that read WELCOME TO MIAMI, HOME OF APARTHEID.

In any other city, any group showing such disregard for black sensitivities would have risked being labeled racist, but by 1990, the Cubans felt they owned Miami and could treat African-Americans as they wished. Miami's black leaders demanded an apology from the Cuban mayors, and when none was forthcoming, they organized a boycott of Miami's tourism and convention industry. The boycott lasted three years and became an ongoing symbol of black alienation. The Cubans never hinted at regret.

In May 1993, Miami's blacks called off the boycott in a deal nego-tiated with the city's white business establishment. The blacks were promised a package of loans, contracts, and training programs to increase their role in the tourism business. In exchange, they dropped their demands for an apology from the Cuban officehold-ers. The deal was guaranteed by an ad hoc group of fifteen commu-nity leaders and businessmen called Miami Partners for Progress. Only two Latinos were on the panel. No Cuban elected officials or major business figures showed up for the news conference announc-ing the pact. On Radio Mambi, the most popular Spanish-language station in town, commentator Armando Perez Roura denounced the deal as "blackmail" and insisted that Cuban political prisoners deserved more admiration than Mandela.

During nearly forty years in Miami, the Cubans had never really had to deal with African-Americans. Building the barrio into an economic enclave enforced their separateness, and in seeking politi-cal power, Cubans viewed all other ethnic or racial groups as rivals. Those were the rules of the game the Cubans encountered here. Given their own obsessions with Castro and the racist predilections of their native culture, it is not surprising that the Cubans fell in step with the continued subordination of African-Americans. What is a little surprising is that the Cubans continued to bully Miami's black community even after the city's reputation for racial tensions had become an obstacle to attracting investment and tourism. Going into their fourth decade of life in Miami, the Cubans remained so locked into their own self-enclosed space that they lacked any broader sense of the common good or any long view of their city's future.

Paralyzed by a municipal corruption scandal that toppled several Cuban politicians, Miami struggled with groaning budget deficits in the late 1990s while many other American cities enjoyed surpluses and tax cuts. In the midst of a national economic expansion Miami's unemployment rate consistently exceeded the average for compara-ble cities, and in 1997 a task force of civic and business groups rec-ommended urgent efforts to attract new businesses and create jobs. A lack of political leadership, strained race relations, and a high crime rate had all tarnished the city's image, according to the report *One Community, One Goal*. It suggested that, because upscale employers were fleeing Miami, the city might lose its position as the

premier business center for Latin America; already the losses in professional services had been particularly damaging for the city's
young people. The multinational corporations and foreign investors
that had once ensured employment for the best and the brightest of
Cuban Miami were abandoning the city. No matter how much
palanca they enjoyed, the third and fourth generations might find
themselves forced to move elsewhere because the Miami their parents created could not sustain them.

The Miami Cubans became strong as a group precisely because
they were inward-looking, defensive, and resentful. Like all immigrants, they gained a sense of purpose by looking homeward, and
yet when they used Havana as a mirror in which to measure themselves, they became blind to what was happening around them in
Miami. Like other ethnic or national identities, the identity of
Cuban Miami was forged in part as a defensive reaction. Solidarity
developed as an important tool to deal with the pain of exile and the
difficulties of forging a new life in a new land. The barrio kids of
Los Angeles marched with Mexican flags when they felt threatened
by Proposition 187. So, too, the Miami Cubans had often paraded
their Cuban flags down Calle Ocho to protest some misdeed by Castro or some perceived softening toward him in American foreign
policy.

The Miami Cubans were socially and politically conservative,
intensely entrepreneurial, eager participants in the American political system, disciplined, and educated. Given these qualifications,
they ought to have been the ideal immigrants. In principle, the
more they succeeded, the more they should have blended in, adding
to the cohesion of American society, rather than detracting from it.
But instead of assimilating to gain position in the United States,
they gained power by resisting assimilation. As the Cuban enclave
grew stronger and more powerful, its walls became thicker. If isolation, an inability to come to terms with other groups who share a
city, and continued preoccupation with the homeland are the
results of nearly forty years of material success, then what should
be expected of the Latinos who start out poor and get poorer in
the United States, who do not receive a hero's welcome but instead
get caught in the maws of economic restructuring and an anti-
immigrant backlash? The story of the Dominican enclave on the
northern tip of Manhattan points to the answer.

◆•◆•◆•◆•◆•◆•◆•◆•◆•◆•◆•◆•◆•◆•◆•◆•◆•◆•

New York: Teetering on the Heights

◆•◆•◆•◆•◆•◆•◆• Up on Manhattan's high ground, nearly 250,000 immigrants from the Dominican Republic are taking a stand. In the 1970s and 1980s, they built an enclave that once seemed as cohesive and as vibrant as any the city had ever produced. Their neighborhood, Washington Heights, at the northern neck of the island, was a world apart. While other parts of New York decayed and were abandoned, this hilltop remained crowded and pulsating with life. When the Dominicans could not find jobs, they invented new ones. When others would not hire them, they opened businesses of their own. Undaunted by the ethnic jockeying of New York City politics, they organized themselves and gained influence.

For a while, it seemed as if Washington Heights might serve the Dominicans as a point of transition into the American mainstream, but instead the barrio became a trap. Too many Dominicans came north thinking they would go back. Convinced they were just in New York for a sojourn, they neglected what the city was doing to their young. By the time they began to suffer regrets, their community had been corrupted and they had been painted as outsiders.

One Sunday afternoon when the sun came out after a long, cold spring rain, the towers of midtown a hundred blocks to the south glowed in the yellow light. In between and below, Harlem was lost in a mist. As soon as the weather broke, the Dominicans were in motion, like bees building a hive in crowded chaos.

A shopkeeper unfurled an awning on Broadway. He hauled out boxes of sweatshirts and blue jeans. Plastic trees holding baseball caps filled the vertical space. Then came balloons and a display of cheap toys packaged in bright primary colors. The storefront became an avalanche of merchandise cascading onto the sidewalk. As a final touch, the shopkeeper fired up a stereo, and a loudspeaker hanging over the doorway blared the sound of trumpets and conga drums.

On side streets lined with fine brownstones, little clusters of young men assumed their posts, eyeballing anyone who turned into their territory. Even as they kept watch, they took time for mock slap fights among themselves and to mutter unsubtle suggestions to a few girls who walked by in tight miniskirts. As a stranger, I attracted a different kind of attention. My steps would be accompanied by odd shouts, like *"Bajando"* ("Coming down") or *"Pajarito"* ("Little bird"). The guys on the corners would start it as soon as I entered one of these short, narrow crosstown blocks, and other young men sitting on stoops relayed the alert until all the lookouts were certain that it had been heard all up and down the block. Cocaine dealers don't like surprises, and they rule their streets like sovereign territory.

On Broadway and the other commercial avenues, people with overloaded shopping carts plied the sidewalks and accosted passersby. Anywhere else in Manhattan, they would have shouted the beggar's chant—"Spare change? Spare change?" In Washington Heights, the street people are peddlers and they cried, *"¡A peso! ¡A peso!"* ("For a dollar! For a dollar!") They were selling, rather than soliciting. Their wares included fruit drinks, sandwiches, baked goods, batteries, pinwheels, and other cheap toys, even underwear. Women sold cookies and sweet cakes from trays. Some men stood on corners with nothing but a big bag full of oranges and still they tried to get the attention of every passing car. Washington Heights is a barrio. People are poor, but they all work.

On a sidewalk in front of a bodega, two men set up a little table and a pair of folding chairs so they could play dominoes. Four boys began a basketball game beneath a milk crate tied onto a lamppost. Before the streets were even dry, there was a crush on the sidewalks of Broadway. Elsewhere in New York, the streets might be quiet on a rainy Sunday afternoon and people might fear being alone, but in Washington Heights, no one is ever alone and the streets are always crowded.

Since it was Sunday, there were meetings, because the Dominicans are organizers above all else. Sports leagues were meeting to plan the baseball season for their youth teams. A social club for immigrants from the city of Santiago gathered to plan a dinner dance that would raise money for the schools there. I chose to attend a gathering of gypsy cab drivers who met in a little community center on Amsterdam Avenue. About twenty of them sat on metal folding chairs and talked about their problems. Soon I began hearing tales of how the fate of the whole neighborhood had always depended on the bold men who drove the streets of Manhattan.

The Dominicans first came to New York in the mid-1960s as whites were leaving, and that created opportunities. In neighborhoods like Washington Heights, apartments became vacant and rents dropped. The city was changing in other ways, as well. Crime became more fearsome than before. The yellow cabs, the only ones permitted to operate then, stopped driving anywhere but in the nice parts of Manhattan. Blacks, Puerto Ricans, and Dominicans started unlicensed car services where the yellows would not venture. It was often dangerous work, but for young immigrants, particularly if they were illegal or did not speak English, it was inviting. Eventually, there were so many unregulated cars that the city enacted new ordinances in the 1980s to bring the gypsy cabs under its control.

Dominicans came to dominate the business in northern Manhattan. With Washington Heights and other barrios growing wildly and with the city regaining some of its lost economic glitter, driving a gypsy cab got to be good business. The cars operated out of dis-

patch services often set up as cooperatives by the drivers. As they
prospered, the cooperatives invested in restaurants, car-repair
shops, and bodegas, sometimes operating enterprises both in New
York and in the Dominican Republic. Men would go back and forth,
driving a few months at a time in Manhattan to raise capital and
then returning home to tend to family farms and businesses.

The drivers had gathered this Sunday afternoon because several
of their colleagues had been shot in a spate of robberies. But the
Dominicans did not just bemoan hard times in the city; they had
plans to join forces so they could bargain with insurance companies
for lower rates and lobby the city for better police protection. It
seemed a fine example of a mature immigrant community organizing itself to deal constructively with American institutions. After a
few minutes, the discussion turned away from the agenda and
developed into an abstract debate on such issues as the differences
between individual and corporate ownership of taxi dispatches and
the proper role for independent drivers in collective arrangements.
Speaking in earnest, bombastic tones, the men took turns addressing such questions in an almost-parliamentary fashion. After an
hour, the meeting concluded, with no signs of progress on any practical matters.

Listening to their arguments, I was mystified and not a little
bored. These men and the entire community had a lot at stake in the
future of the gypsy cabs, and yet they had spent a Sunday afternoon wrangling like a bunch of college freshmen who had just read
Marx for the first time.

When it was over, I went to one of the organizers of the event to
get an explanation. Nelson Díaz, a veteran driver and dispatch manager, said ruefully, "It seems everything is frozen and nothing can
be done until after the elections." In response to even greater puz-
zlement on my part, he explained that he was talking about upcoming elections in the Dominican Republic, not any in the United
States. Díaz explained that each of the major speakers represented a
Dominican political party or labor federation. Their ideological
debate was a way of saying that no consensus ventures were possible until after the upcoming electoral campaign.

Díaz explained that his taxi cooperative was associated with the
Partido Revolucionario Dominicano, the Dominican Revolutionary
party, known, like all Dominican political parties, by its initials,
PRD. He himself was best known around the barrio as "Camacho,"

the nom de guerre he had adopted as a young activist in the rough-and-tumble of Dominican politics. When I asked Camacho what role, if any, American political parties played in Washington Heights, he smiled under a graying thin mustache.

"The Republicans don't exist here," Camacho said, "and as for the Democrats, they are important, but almost every Dominican party is stronger. My party alone is much better organized in this community than any American party." Camacho proudly reported that in Washington Heights the PRD had fourteen precinct organizations, each of which collected dues and held monthly meetings. He personally headed the Frente de Taxistas–PRD, the taxi drivers' front of the PRD, which raised money, covered cars with campaign placards, and held rallies. Getting Dominicans to volunteer their time and open their wallets for a presidential campaign back home was easy, he said. A lifelong activist, he was proud of that. But he was more than a little perturbed that the partisanship was so intense that taxi drivers of different parties would refuse to work together even though their lives were at stake.

Active participation in home-country politics is a common trait in immigrant communities, and the involvement can continue for several generations. Some Americans send contributions to parties in the Northern Ireland conflict even though their ancestors crossed the Atlantic more than a century ago. Such a preoccupation becomes a problem only when communities remain so completely tied to the home country that it impedes engagement with the realities of life in the United States.

"Maybe one of the mental errors we have made is always keeping our minds focused on home," Camacho told me after his failure to organize the taxi drivers in New York. "That's because we are always thinking about going back. The first thing everybody does as soon as they make some money here is to buy a house back home and then a car. Dominicans don't buy houses here because they don't think they live here. In fact, they don't care if they live in a cheap little apartment here as long as they are building a nice big house back home. So when problems start developing here, even problems that affect their children or their own safety, they don't always pay attention, because they think, I'll be gone in another year. But then a year passes and they are still here and they have serious problems."

Among the Miami Cubans, an obsession with Castro undoubtedly isolated them even as it drove them to excel in their new land. Among the Dominicans in Washington Heights, preoccupations with the home country also provided the means and the motives for material success. But, unlike the Cubans, the Dominicans constantly traveled back home, so their links were real, not symbolic. The Dominican Republic was not their past, but very much part of their present, and they thought of their enclave as a transit zone where they could make quick profits and be gone. This proved to be a dangerous distraction when the United States treated them much more harshly than it did the Cubans. By the time the Dominicans realized that their future lay in Washington Heights, they were on the brink of losing all they had built.

Driving down Broadway, St. Nicholas Avenue, or one of the other shopping streets in Washington Heights, it looks like the Dominicans have done everything right. There are restaurants, travel agencies, and bodegas on every block. Glittery little shops with phone booths lined up against the wall offer cut-rate calls to the Dominican Republic. This is a neighborhood with a lot of poverty and a high crime rate, but it still has movie theaters, florists, and toy stores. Here the only storefronts not open for business are the ones undergoing remodeling. People are out on the commercial streets late into the evening. On weekends, the restaurants are crowded. Most significant, the patrons, the personnel, and the owners of these establishments are all Dominicans and they are all neighbors.

By any measure, Washington Heights has avoided the economic losses and communal frustration that develops when the local retail sector is in the hands of outsiders. In New York, many African-American and Puerto Rican communities have felt drained and exploited by absentee merchants, first European ethnics and later Asians. Local residents turn wages and welfare checks over to the businessmen, and the merchants spend and invest the profits elsewhere.

Washington Heights represents a textbook example of how a successful enclave economy is built. The key is that money remains in the neighborhood and changes hands several times among residents. Even small businesses can develop an economic momentum of their own when the merchants live among their customers and form part of a coherent community. Money spent to buy food at one shop then gets spent to buy shoes at the store down the street, and then it goes to the travel agent and then back to the food store. Once this dynamic is under way, it draws new immigrants to the enclave because it creates job opportunities, and in turn the stream of new arrivals ensures that the enclave is an expanding market. That's the way it worked for many of the European ethnics when they established themselves in American cities, and that's the way it worked in Washington Heights until the early 1990s. The barrio built on itself.

Like Koreans and other Asians, the Dominicans effectively pooled resources among friends and family to create seed capital for new businesses. The same kinship networks provided a source of trusted employees. Newly arrived Dominicans would work in a relative's bodega for a while, learn the business, and eventually open one of their own. The bodega economy even took advantage of the community's deep and active links to the Dominican Republic. Having created a market for Dominican specialty goods in New York, the *bodegueros* established strong commercial relationships with suppliers back home.

The same system operated for more sophisticated businesses, such as travel agencies and money exchanges, as well as simpler ones, such as clothing stores, beauty salons, and laundries. Tightly knit networks of fellow immigrants operated in each sector of the retail trade, exchanging information, loaning one another capital, and forming clubs or associations that brought people together for social or political events. People relied on one another and could count on help. They fueled one another's success and magnified their overall accomplishments. The barrio developed institutions and a social structure of its own that gave the community a sense of permanence and texture even as it became more efficient as a port of entry for new arrivals. The Dominicans had seemed to become self-sufficient.

The barrio built on itself, but it also fed on itself. All the bright storefronts on Broadway were a sign of weaknesses as well as strength. All that entrepreneurship made for an efficient enclave, but it did not create a community.

"The business of the bodegas was to buy them cheap, get them going, and sell them in a year or so," said José Delio Martin, a

prominent businessman and head of a merchants' association in
Washington Heights. "One family would manage the place, two or
three others would provide the capital, and with luck you could
divide fifty thousand dollars when you sold it."

A dapper fellow sporting a brown fedora on a winter day, Delio
Martin draws respectful greetings from most of the customers who
enter the restaurant where he sits many mornings drinking thick
black coffee from little cups. Rattling off addresses machine
gun–style, Delio Martin lists all the bodegas he has owned in part or
in whole since he came to New York in 1968, and then he pauses to
remember a few more. He describes a fast-moving, quick-profit,
high-turnover kind of business. By the early 1980s, the Dominicans
had saturated Washington Heights with bodegas and had begun
branching out to other Latino neighborhoods around the city.
According to the most reliable estimates, a decade later the Dominicans owned more than twenty thousand small businesses in New
York, including about 70 percent of the city's bodegas.

As he recounts the fabled growth of the Dominican business
empire, there is a note of nostalgia in Delio Martin's voice. He is
clearly talking about the past. "The problem is that it all comes to a
stop when no one has the money to buy, and that's what's happening now," he said.

The Dominicans' vaunted economic enclave turned out to have
been a highly speculative enterprise. Like stocks traded on Wall
Street, the value of bodegas was based on what someone would pay
to own them more than on the inherent profitability of the business.
The *bodegueros* were brokers managing the capital funds accumulated by family networks. The restaurant tables became trading pits
where shops were bought and sold for prices set by the market. It
all depended on a steady influx of immigrants who would work in a
relative's shop for a while, get to know the business, and then
quickly become anxious to get a shop of their own. These newcomers created the demand that kept the price rising. The turnover was
generated by people looking for short-term capital gains. This had a
number of drawbacks.

Banks had little interest in financing this kind of activity, especially in a highly mobile immigrant community. So when family
funds no longer sufficed, *bodegueros* often relied on loan sharks, and
the hefty interest rates increased the pressure for quick profits.

Some businessmen turned to neighborhood drug dealers, who had large supplies of ready money and needed ways to launder their cash.

In addition, the Dominicans overmilked the cow. Business owners cashed in their profits as soon as possible rather than making long-term investments in Washington Heights. Most sent the money back to the Dominican Republic, while those more committed to life in the United States bought homes in the suburbs and became absentee owners in their own community. By continually drawing money out of the enclave, they ensured that it would never make the quantum leap into real prosperity, even in good times. And because so much of the bodega economy was built on speculation, the bad times hit extra hard.

The 1990s brought a recession, the ongoing effects of economic restructuring, competition from other immigrant groups, and a near saturation of markets that had once offered easy pickings. As a result, the trade in bodegas came to a standstill, and the thousands of Dominicans who owned them struggled to protect their investments in an increasingly difficult environment.

Like the Puerto Ricans before them, many Dominicans lacked the skills to find work anywhere but in the low end of the manufacturing sector. They competed with the Puerto Ricans and took over certain job categories, such as garment pleaters. This proved to be just as much a dead end for the Dominicans, except they reached it faster. In 1980, about half of the New York City Dominican workforce held factory jobs, but after a decade of rapid decline in manufacturing, that was down to only a quarter. The result was unemployment rates higher than for any other major component of the city's population and average earnings that rose more slowly than anyone else's. For the *bodegueros* and all the other business owners in Washington Heights, that meant their main pool of clients had less and less spending power.

As New York again became a great port of entry for immigrants from all over the world, the Dominicans found themselves squeezed from all sides. Skilled newcomers from East Asia, Europe, Africa, India, and the West Indies competed for the better jobs sought by Dominicans. Meanwhile, an influx of low-skilled immigrants from China and Latin America made it harder to get entry-level jobs and kept wages down. Wherever Dominicans looked for new retail opportunities in the New York area, they encountered Koreans, Jamaicans, and other rivals who had set up effective self-help networks of their own.

The Dominicans had persevered on the economic front almost as model immigrants, embracing the American virtues of entrepreneurship, competition, and self-reliance, even as they were building a barrio with a multitude of civic organizations and self-help networks. By the late 1980s, twenty years after they had first landed in Washington Heights, the Dominicans were the largest immigrant group in the city and they should have been taking the first steps toward acceptance by the Anglo mainstream. But instead, the Dominicans got exclusion. The name Washington Heights became synonymous with cocaine. Dominicans became typecast as criminals. The NYPD became the chief representative of American society in the neighborhood, and conflict with the police came to signify the way the whole community related to the outside world.

"I can't compete anymore," said Angel, a tall, dark-skinned forty-year-old man standing beside an almost-empty refrigerated meat case in his bodega on St. Nicholas Avenue. "I used to get a whole tray of chicken parts and another of meat and sell them both every day, and now there is just this." He pointed to a single chicken that looked a bit too yellow and a coil of sausage sitting undesirably alone.

Angel's bodega is only about twelve feet wide and it is packed to the ceiling with dry goods, canned foods, and bins of yucca and plantains. Pots and pans hang from the rafters. Twenty-pound sacks of rice are stacked in the corner. The shelves behind the counter are loaded with fancy bottles of Florida Water, bay rum, and other toiletries favored by Dominicans.

Sales slips with names scrawled on them are taped up all over the back of a display case by the cash register, forming a ticker-tape cascade of IOUs. "My customers are very loyal, mostly from the apartment building next door, but I can't give anyone more than three dollars' credit anymore because I need the money to buy merchandise. I used to order from the wholesalers week by week, but now I have to buy almost day by day."

From his front door, Angel can see three other bodegas, along with a meat market and a small supermarket. "There are a lot of people in this neighborhood, more every day, it seems, but there are too many bodegas, too much competition, and so now more and more *bodegueros* are taking the easy way."

Supplementing grocery store sales by participating in the numbers game has been a way of life in New York since long before the Dominicans showed up, but now there is another easy way that is much more profitable. Police officials and community residents have long contended that some bodegas operate primarily as a means to launder drug money. No one, not even the neighborhood's most ardent defenders, disputes this fact. People simply disagree over how many are in on the game.

"When a *bodeguero* takes the easy way, he can also sell for less. He doesn't worry about his profit because the main thing is to keep money moving through the place. One guy like that, if he is close by, can ruin you."

A young man wearing a silk shirt walked into the bodega, looked around, bought a pack of cigarettes, and made a phone call. Angel stopped talking and ignored me the whole time the young man was in the store. He gave me a kind of "coast is clear" signal as soon as the visitor was gone. Looking toward the door and shaking his head contemptuously, he returned to our conversation.

"The worst thing here is that the authorities do not take control. The police know who is here and who is doing what. Do they think these guys can dress in silk and gold because they work for a living? Everybody sees them every day, and the police just drive by. When they do stop, it is just to bother ordinary people. So what are we supposed to think? That the police are stupid? Or are they *vendido* [sold out] to the drug traffickers?" Angel grew worried about what he had just said and pleaded that he not be identified in any way that could lead the dealers or the police to him. But then he continued.

"What we Dominicans are trying to build here in Washington Heights could be a very beautiful thing, but we could lose it all because, like in any family, there are some bad characters here. The way to save this community is to do what you would do in your own family—come in with *la mano dura* [the hard hand] and sweep all the evil away. They should come in here with soldiers, if the police will not do it, and say to these guys, 'You, you, and you—we know what you are doing with the *coca* and we are taking you away and you will never come back.'

"If the Americans do not do this, it is because they do not want to, because they are perfectly happy to let people sell drugs right here on the streets of Manhattan."

Angel never mentioned the possibility that the Dominicans themselves might have been a little too happy to let the drug dealers thrive, and he certainly never suggested that they could do anything about cleaning up their own neighborhood. Most Latino immigrants, like many European immigrants of an earlier time, have come from countries where governments are powerful but arbitrary and where police agencies in particular are rightfully feared and yet assumed to be corrupt. In the United States, those attitudes can translate into a presumptive suspicion of American authorities. Combined with the nationalistic loyalties common to an immigrant enclave, the result is an inherent tolerance for misbehavior by fellow immigrants. To the newcomers, it might seem innocent at first; they see themselves as poor people surviving by getting around somebody else's rules, but the enclave breeds an acquiescence in the sins of fellow immigrants so dangerous that the newcomers do not realize what they have done to themselves until it is too late. Aside from the direct costs of living with criminality, an entire immigrant community can be stigmatized by the criminal behavior of a few. It happened to the Italians and the Irish. The twin perils of corruption and stigmatization are particularly grave for Latinos today because most illegal narcotics come to the United States from their countries and because the drug trade now spawns exceptional levels of violence, profits, and addiction.

To the casual observer, Jerry Giorgio would appear no more than a graying sixty-something businessman in a department store suit, maybe an accountant or an insurance adjuster, no doubt a harmless kind of guy. That would be a mistake. Giorgio has investigated homicides for the New York Police Department since 1972, mostly in upper Manhattan. He is also well known throughout the force for his skill as an interrogator, and he is legendary for his doggedness. He has repeatedly broken cases long given up as unsolvable by other detectives. He spent thirteen years piecing together clues in one murder before he finally made an arrest.

Giorgio is a proud man who is approaching the end of a long career. He is proud of his reputation, of the young detectives who have learned their craft by working with him, and of the satisfaction he has given victims' families. Nothing has frustrated him more than working among the Dominicans of Washington Heights.

"You get cases where a respectable, hardworking family man gets shot dead on a busy street in broad daylight, and when you go looking for witnesses, no one has seen anything, nada, zero. Here's a dead guy on the sidewalk, who was not involved in narcotics or anything criminal, and a dozen people must have seen what happened to him, but no one talks.

"You ask his family to put out the word. You ask them to tell people that they can make anonymous calls and that all they have to say is that the shooter was tall or short or anything. You wait for the calls, but nobody calls."

Giorgio insists that no other community is quite so hard to work in.

"I'll break ninety-eight percent of Harlem cases. You give me a Harlem case and I promise I'll get some people to give me something. It's not me. Any detective worth his salt can get some cooperation in Harlem. Up here, we get fifty percent of our cases, and I'll tell you, we sweat blood—we sweat blood to get them."

Giorgio has many explanations for this.

"There is a lot of distrust and I think a lot of it is based on their cultural background. There's a lot of corruption down there where they come from. When you tell these people you are a cop, they immediately think you are looking for money. These people feel or believe that cops sell cases, that they go after people who have got money, and it's very hard to talk them out of this because that is what they are used to back home."

Some of the problem, he says, is caused by the drug trade.

"There're a lot of people making money out there from cocaine, even if it is just kids working as lookouts. The money goes to families and lots of it gets shipped back to the Dominican Republic. You see all the money that is going around this community, and—come on—this is not being earned by the mechanic and the bodega owner. It doesn't take a genius to see that you got a lot of people up here with a stake in what's going on."

He concedes there is another side to it, as well.

"The other side is that our credibility stinks. We don't have a positive image out there, and who do I blame? I put the majority of the blame on the media. The media would much rather run with the story that a police officer brutalized a youngster than a positive story about how the police have done a good job for the community."

Giorgio returned to the terrible suspicion that the Dominicans harbor of the police.

"There's this impression that we allow the drug trade to flourish. Well, the public doesn't know the restrictions we operate under. We can't go up to anyone and search him. We can, but it will be a bad search, and it will leave you open to lawsuits. And these people have learned about that already. God forbid you make one false step out there, even half a false step; they will sue the jock off you. The frustration level is unreal up here, unbelievable."

Amid all the indecipherable scrawls, all the goofy, loopy script spray-painted on walls, doorways, and even sidewalks, there is a kind of graffiti in Washington Heights that struggles to convey real human feelings. An eerily rendered outline of a sprawled body is neatly painted on the sidewalk outside the entranceway to a charcoal gray apartment building on Amsterdam. Alongside it in block letters is the inscription RIP—WASTED I LOVE YOU. The side of a building just off Broadway is decorated with a painting of a huge mauve tombstone remembering a man named Pepe. All around it, overblown signatures form a giant sympathy card. These are memorials to victims of a crossfire that bloodied the streets of every major American city when two distinct and unrelated events overlapped in the 1980s: the arrival of Latino immigrants and the arrival of crack.

During the worst years of the crack epidemic—1985 to 1990— the number of murders in New York rose by a horrifying 63 percent, but in the northern Manhattan precinct that encompasses Washington Heights, there was an increase of 115 percent. And, similarly, the number of felonious assaults and total arrests rose more than twice as fast in the Dominican enclave as in the city overall.

Because they came from the south, because they kept up a heavy regular traffic of people, goods, and money to the Caribbean, because they speak Spanish, because they came from a clannish society streaked with corruption, because they are foreigners, a very specific and very lucrative niche in New York's vast drug trade opened up to Dominican criminals. Washington Heights became a

major wholesale distribution point for raw cocaine. Geography
played a major role, according to the police. The George Washington Bridge soars up from the very heart of the neighborhood and
crosses the Hudson River to New Jersey. That means it is just minutes from an apartment house on 157th Street to Interstate 95, the
main north-south highway artery on the East Coast. The riverside
highways that run along the east and the west sides of Manhattan
end up in Washington Heights. And bridges spanning the East
River connect the neighborhood to the Bronx and from there to
other boroughs.

"It is a crossroads community," said Sgt. John McDonnell, who
was assigned to an antidrug task force working upper Manhattan.
"No matter who lived up there, it would be a logical place to set up
this kind of operation. Buyers from all over can just pop across a
bridge, get the stuff, and be gone in minutes."

While Colombian organizations handled the importing, Dominican gangs acted as the wholesale vendors, selling several ounces of
cocaine at a time to retailers who then cooked it into rocks of crack.
A handful of successful prosecutions showed that Dominicans were
no less entrepreneurial about the drug trade than they were with
grocery stores. Rather than create a few large criminal organizations
as Italian immigrants had done a generation earlier, the Dominican
drug dealers in Washington Heights formed many small partnerships that usually operated out of several apartments in a single
building. Each operation had a platoon of lookouts, others who
guarded the cash and the coke, and still other young men who acted
as intermediaries between the buyers and the person who actually
held the coke. An abundance of foot soldiers thoroughly insulated
the dealers from rip-offs and from the police.

With their big payrolls, the dealers could also hope to win some
loyalty on the streets. They certainly made little effort to disguise
their presence. Dom Pérignon champagne became a much requested
item in restaurants where the usual specialties were curried goat
and chicken with rice. Young men streaked around the traffic in
shiny new European sedans or big four-wheel-drive sport utility
vehicles while the rest of the neighborhood plodded along in rusty
clunkers.

Members of one cocaine operation became so brazen that they all
got the same kind of hair treatment and became known as the Jheri-

Curl Gang. The fact that their permanents made them easier for the
police to spot did not seem to worry them. With their black hair
still in tight, shiny ringlets, five young men accused of being the
top members of the gang were sentenced in April 1993 to jail terms
ranging from sixteen years to life. Along with these five, who were
convicted of running the cocaine operation, several dozen other
Dominicans drew jail terms for working as salesmen, lookouts, and
couriers.

Eventually, the Dominican dealers became somewhat more dis-
creet. Once they established their hegemony, the level of violence
associated with the drug trade dropped precipitously, as reflected in
New York's declining murder rates in the mid-1990s. The Dominican
drug dealers and their Colombian suppliers then branched out to a
new product: highly potent, smokable heroin, which appealed not
only to crack addicts and users of injectable heroin but also to white
middle-class kids who found it fit their grungy sense of fashion. In
1996, the Drug Enforcement Administration declared that the same
Dominican-Colombian connection that controlled the New York
crack market also dominated heroin sales in the city and had successfully branched out to New England. The product changed, the
market evolved, and the jails filled, but the steady flow of new
arrivals meant that the same basic dynamic was always at work
within the immigrant enclave.

"There are just a lot of kids who come up here with the idea that
they are going to get jobs and make money, and the easiest work to
find, often the only work they can find, is to sign up with the dealers," said Sergeant McDonnell. "You pick these kids up, and they
don't know what's going on with the law. It's not like with black
and Puerto Rican kids who know the street and who know what
kind of risks they're taking. These Dominican kids are just set up to
do the grunt work, and they are told not to worry about the law."

There is a broad, flat wall near the corner of 162nd Street
and Amsterdam Avenue that lends itself to expansive graffiti
expressions. For several years, it bore a crudely painted triptych.
Hands folded in prayer filled one side and a heart topped with
flames decorated the other side panel. In the center lay an open
book, like a Bible, with the name Kiko emblazoned across it. And
above in large faux-Gothic script was the legend TE RECORDAMOS
(We remember you).

Dominicans and the police alike do indeed remember Jose "Kiko" Garcia, but they have very different recollections of who he was and how he died the night of July 3, 1992. Everyone does agree, however, that the events that followed proved a turning point for Washington Heights and for New York City. The Dominicans of Washington Heights found a new way to assert their identity as immigrants, then discovered how little that would get them.

According to the police version of the events that rainy July night, Officer Michael O'Keefe was on a plainclothes anticrime patrol when he saw a bulge in Kiko's jacket, which suggested to the officer that the twenty-three-year-old man was carrying a gun. O'Keefe approached him. There was a scuffle. Kiko fled into the lobby of an apartment building, where he pulled a gun, later found on his body. The cop shot him twice in self-defense. Accepting this account, a grand jury declined to bring any charges against O'Keefe.

According to the Dominican version, O'Keefe was a marauding cop who, like many other policemen in Washington Heights, spent more time hassling people on the street than he did busting drug cases. Witnesses claimed that O'Keefe beat Kiko and shot him needlessly. Alleging that the gun had been planted on Kiko, they noted that no fingerprints were found on the weapon.

For the police and much of the news media, Kiko was a "low-level drug dealer." He had come to the United States illegally at the age of nineteen and within a year had been caught with a small quantity of cocaine. That encounter with the law led to nothing more than a guilty plea on a charge of personal possession and a five-year suspended sentence. No effort was made to deport him.

For many Dominicans, he was another young man who had come to the United States with few prospects and had done what was necessary to get along. If he had an association with drug dealers, it could not have been too lucrative, they said, because he lived in a run-down one-bedroom apartment with his mother and at least four other relatives.

These conflicting realities provided the spark for five days of violent disturbances in which one man was killed and dozens were injured. Although the crowds that rushed into the street after Kiko's death set several cars and at least one building on fire, the looting, burning, and gunfire were quite limited compared with riots elsewhere. In one sense, it was just another spontaneous urban riot sparked by a police shooting. But it was also a moment of collec-

tive protest that involved many different sorts of people in an organized effort to express their anger and frustration.

Unlike almost any other riot, community leaders were out in the
streets from the beginning, trying to direct the crowds into peaceful
protests against the police. People from the Dominican political parties, prominent figures from the amateur baseball leagues and fraternal organizations, social workers, and ministers all put on yellow
ribbons and went into the street as umpires, often positioning
themselves between angry crowds and police in riot gear. They had
walkie-talkies, command centers, and endless meetings. The goal
was to let people, especially the young people, vent their frustration without losing control of the streets. While the effort did not
entirely prevent violence, the neighborhood never fully exploded
into all-out rioting.

Foreigners together in a strange land seek one another out on the
basis of kinship, business interests, home-country political allegiances, and much else. That is the nature of the immigrant experience. At their best, barrios develop these connections into a rich
civil society that provides structure and leadership. Washington
Heights was highly organized, and so it did not blow up when all
the ingredients for an explosion were present. In this regard, the
disturbances following Kiko's death are a measure of how much the
Dominicans had accomplished during their time in Washington
Heights. However, all these relationships pointed inward, and the
real test of an immigrant community lies in whether these internal
structures allow it to gain a positive relationship with American
institutions and with society as a whole. The Dominicans never got
a chance to find out.

Instinctively defensive when faced with accusations of brutality,
the police drew sharp battle lines. They insisted that anyone who
criticized them was endorsing the criminality of crack dealers.
When Mayor David Dinkins tried to avert further violence by visiting Kiko's grieving family, the Patrolmen's Benevolent Association
took out a full-page newspaper advertisement saying the mayor
had "callously ignored the traumatic plight of the police officer
involved and managed to transform a drug villain into a martyr."
The Dominican leaders who tried to contain the violence were even
easier marks. The PBA said their efforts merely "served to exacer-
bate the rioting, looting and burning, as misguided individuals and
street punks rallied around a convoluted cause."

The Democratic National Convention was about to open at Madison Square Garden that July when the disturbances provided a fresh peg for the obligatory "rotten apple" stories about New York's dark side. Both the local and national media rolled out vivid accounts of the drug trade in Washington Heights, making it seem that everyone in the neighborhood had sold out to the "Dominican drug cartels." The Dominicans, who had attracted little notice in all the years they had been building their enclave, instantly became larger-than-life tabloid fiends.

And yet the Dominicans acted as accomplices in their own demonization. No one could dispute the fact that drug money had penetrated legitimate businesses in the neighborhood, just as it does everywhere there is a drug trade. The Treasury Department announced a crackdown on wire transfers of cash to the Dominican Republic in 1997 after looking at just fifteen money transfer companies in the New York area and discovering that they were sending more than half a billion dollars a year to the Dominican Republic. More than a fifth of the cash came from the proceeds of drug sales, the Treasury said. As blatant as the dealers had become, most of the prominent Dominican spokesmen refused to condemn them explicitly. The whole barrio turned out to march in protest against alleged brutality by the NYPD, but there had never been that kind of public outrage expressed against the drug dealers, whose brutality was indisputable and undisguised. For the people of the barrio, the police were outsiders. The dealers were not.

Proving themselves just as defensive as the police, prominent Dominicans argued that American realities were at fault for fomenting drug usage and permitting large-scale trafficking. It was the same gambit for disavowing responsibility used often by government leaders in Latin America: Get your own people to stop using the stuff before you come bothering us. The Dominicans insisted on collective innocence despite the evidence of guilt all around the neighborhood.

"This is not a Dominican phenomenon. You could put the Irish here and the same thing would happen," said Moises Perez, the head of the largest community service organization in Washington Heights, the Alianza Dominicana.

Defense of the enclave became a patriotic matter, as if defense of the homeland was at stake. For example, Delio Martin, the head of the merchants' association and no rabble-rouser, said, "We did not go to the streets in defense of Kiko, one boy that no one knew. We did it in defense of our homes. We did it not just because of that one act of aggression but to stop all the abuses against our community by all sectors of power."

As in many African-American communities subdued by caravans of squad cars and long lines of mounted officers, the police were seen as an invading power. In Washington Heights, this took on a peculiarly Dominican flavor when the immigrants, like generations of their forefathers at home, protested that they had fallen victim to *yanqui* intervention once more. And the perception of an external threat solidified and energized the Dominicans' identity as a people detached from the American mainstream, just as it did for the L.A. barrio kids marching to protest Proposition 187 under Mexican flags.

Utilizing imported habits of mind and inherited rhetoric, the Dominicans stood up for the barrio they had constructed here. They defended a territorial reality, not an abstract demand for equal justice. Even though a strong element of national pride permeated their rhetoric, they did not pursue grievances on behalf of all Dominicans, just for the Dominicans of Washington Heights.

When some of New York's activist gadflies showed up in the neighborhood and tried to tell the Dominicans that they were "oppressed people" and that they should struggle in solidarity with other "people of color," they were told to go home. The Dominicans never tried to make some broader ethnic claim. They never alleged that they had been victimized because they were Latinos. Indeed, they did not seek and did not receive notable support from the Puerto Ricans or from other Latinos. The people of Washington Heights did not behave like an American minority group. When the Dominicans complained of police abuses, they did not cite events two hundred years old and they did not claim to be victims of some larger evil that infected the whole of the United States. They spoke only about what had happened to them since they had come to New York. They strutted around proud and defensive but not on behalf of an ethnic or political cause. They had built a barrio with considerable enterprise, and they wanted it respected.

But Washington Heights, like many other barrios, was not built as a place where newcomers could start the process of becoming Americans. Instead, the purpose was to allow its inhabitants to become transnationals or simply to remain Dominicans. Both the immigrants and the nation that hosted them seemed happy to let things go that way, and the easy travel home that characterizes Latino immigration prolonged the condition. The Dominicans of Washington Heights, perpetual in-betweens, left themselves vulnerable to the worst of two nations.

Kiko Garcia's death and the Washington Heights disturbances added to tensions that had been developing between the police force and Mayor Dinkins almost since the start of his administration. The cops had berated him for not allowing them to carry semi-automatic pistols. They had complained about his appointment of a commission to investigate police corruption, and they had vehemently rejected his plan to create a civilian review board that would investigate charges of police brutality and other forms of misconduct. Then Dinkins's expressions of sympathy for Kiko's family and his other efforts to calm the Dominicans in Washington Heights were taken as acts of outright hostility by the police rank and file.

Six weeks after Kiko's death and a few days after Officer O'Keefe was exonerated in the slaying, the Patrolmen's Benevolent Association organized a protest rally and march at City Hall. Rudolph Giuliani gladly agreed to appear as a featured speaker. He had never really stopped running against Dinkins following his narrow defeat in 1989 and now as he prepared to challenge Dinkins in 1993, the former prosecutor was taking every opportunity to decry the mayor as weak on crime.

Less than half an hour after the rally began on the morning of September 16, 1992, thousands of cops swarmed across barricades and took over the steps of City Hall. Giuliani made his way to the chaotic rally, found a soapbox, and whipped up the crowd, estimated to number ten thousand police officers and supporters. He sarcastically derided Dinkins's police policies as "bullshit," setting a tone that then reverberated for hours. The crowd repeatedly referred to the mayor as a "nigger." There were chants of "The mayor's on crack" and "Dump the Dink." A senior uniformed police officer was booed down when he appealed for order. Police officers poured into nearby bars and drank openly on the street during the speeches.

According to a *New York Times* account of the event, "The greatest applause was reserved for Officer O'Keefe, who called the aftermath of the Washington Heights disturbance 'a personal attack on you.' Facing his protesting colleagues, he said, 'We are a force. We will be a force for good.'" Eventually, more than a thousand of the police protesters moved to the entrance and exit ramps of the Brooklyn Bridge and blocked all traffic in a raucous act of civil disobedience, which on-duty police officers did little to impede. Acting Police Commissioner Raymond W. Kelly issued an interim report on the incident twelve days later, describing the actions of the police officers as "unruly, mean-spirited and perhaps criminal."

It did not really matter that the official inquiries found the police at fault. At a time when uncompromising toughness with criminals was becoming a hallmark of American politics, the Dominicans had decidedly ended up on the wrong side of that issue. Having winked at the drug traffic when it was taking over their streets, and having brawled with the NYPD, they were extremely vulnerable. Just how much so was evident during a small but bloody episode shortly before the 1993 mayoral elections.

For years, the police had run regular tow-truck raids on Washington Heights to clear narrow streets that often became parking lots, especially around gypsy cab dispatch offices. One such sweep was under way when a man tried to stop a tow truck from hauling a gypsy cab off 175th Street. A crowd gathered. Police swarmed in. A melee erupted, and in the midst of it, Officer John Williamson was struck in the head by a bucket half-filled with hardened spackling compound that had been thrown off a rooftop. As he crumpled, blood pouring from his fatally smashed skull, some people cheered, according to press accounts.

Dinkins suspended the towing operation the next day to let both the police and the Dominicans cool off. Giuliani issued a statement with a very telling use of buzzwords: "This sends a message that the city has given in to urban terrorists and that if you want to get your way, kill a police officer and cheer about it."

A few weeks later, Giuliani narrowly defeated Dinkins and was elected mayor of New York. In a close, hard-fought campaign, he resorted to one of the very oldest gambits in American politics by demonizing recently arrived immigrants as a threat to public safety. The difference is that when Latinos are made scapegoats now in harsh media-driven campaigns like the one in New York in 1993 or in California a year later, the stigma is darker and deeper than when the French were the victims in the 1790s or the Irish in the 1890s. In

American cities at the end of the twentieth century, a community that is marked for exclusion once has a hard time ever winning acceptance again. As mayor, Giuliani extolled the benefits immigration brought to New York, but the taint he had helped apply remained indelible. When Abner Louima, a Haitian immigrant, was allegedly beaten by New York police officers inside a Brooklyn station house in August 1997, he initially claimed to have heard something that stuck in his mind. As a toilet plunger handle was rammed into his rectum, causing critical injuries, Louima recalled, one of his assailants saying, "This is Giuliani time, not Dinkins time." Although it was immediately disputed, the statement acquired a notoriety that revealed widespread fears and biases.

Census data shows that during the 1980s the Dominican population of New York rose 165 percent, to nearly 333,000 people, making Dominicans the fastest-growing major ethnic group in the city; estimates show the growth rate accelerating in the 1990s due to a baby boom among the Dominicans in New York. As a result of this population explosion, every public facility in Washington Heights, from the subway stations to the kindergartens, was overcrowded. Parks, clinics, and police precinct houses operated far beyond their capacities because the Dominicans had crammed more people, especially young people, into the neighborhood than any previous residents. A school district designed for 14,000 students was trying to handle 25,000. George Washington High School had so many students that they had to arrive in three shifts.

Immigration has touched off many different kinds of fears among Americans in this decade, and the backlash has generated many new forms of exclusion. The kind of exclusion the Dominicans experienced was not racial or ethnic, as it was with blacks or the Mexican-Americans of South Texas. Rather, it was derived from a series of specific markers. The Dominicans of Washington Heights were dark-skinned people, poor but entrepreneurial. They were immigrants. They were people who flouted the law and American ways by entering the country illegally. They were corrupt foreigners who fed the American appetite for narcotics. The accumulation of these traits constituted an identity much narrower than broad categories derived from skin color or economic class. At a time of increased immigration, exclusion can be targeted to specific people in a specific place. To have been Irish from South Boston or Polish

from the northwest side of Chicago carried a very particular meaning that did not extend to others of the same national origins even
in the same city. The demonizing that occurred in New York applied
only to the Dominicans of Washington Heights, not to all Dominicans, and certainly not to all Latinos.

Because the ostracism was circumscribed, it could be escaped. A
sizable number of successful business owners and professionals left
the neighborhood for multinational barrios in Queens, where they
could be Dominicans without the cocaine stigma of Washington
Heights. Others left for the suburbs, where they could be anything
they wanted. The smart kids who went away to college never came
back. Once they left Washington Heights, no one called them urban
terrorists.

When exclusion can be escaped so readily by those who are
resourceful, it becomes powerfully self-reinforcing. As the upwardly
mobile depart to negotiate their own private arrangements with the
white mainstream, a barrio is left to serve as a port of entry for new
arrivals and as a warehouse for those who are too poor, too corrupt,
or too old to move on. Many, perhaps most, Dominicans will escape
stigma by moving out of Washington Heights and becoming productive, law-abiding members of the middle class, and their residual ethnic identity will fade with each successive generation. But
up on that hill in Manhattan, there will be other Dominicans who
will remain perpetually poor and who will be perceived as darkly
foreign. Over time, their isolation and their numbers are likely to
grow. The benefits that American society draws from the success
stories may outweigh the costs associated with the poor, but it is the
urban hot spots that will grab all the attention, generate anxiety,
and perpetuate prejudice. That is the case with blacks now and
there is no reason for it to be different with Latinos.

The Dominicans failed to build institutions that could effectively
advance their interests here. They bear a good deal of blame for
what happened to them, and many of them have accepted that. So it
came as very little solace to them when many of their worst suspi-
cions about the United States were proved right.

On July 6, 1994, two years after Kiko Garcia's death, a special
investigative commission issued a final report, concluding that corruption was rampant in the NYPD. The Mollen Commission found
that police officers were deeply implicated in the cocaine trade

throughout the city. They practiced traditional corruption by protecting dealers in exchange for bribes, but also a large number of cops were found extorting drug dealers, stealing from them, and often reselling the drugs themselves. Some officers had become so involved with Washington Heights cocaine dealers that they had made several trips to the Dominican Republic.

A series of dramatic arrests occurred at the station house of the 30th Precinct, which covers the southern part of Washington Heights, including the territory that the Jheri-Curl Gang used to work. Crowds formed to cheer as police officers, five or six at a time, were led away from the station house in handcuffs. Eventually, so many cops were busted for taking part in the upper Manhattan cocaine trade that the precinct earned the nickname "the dirty Thirty."

Some of the Dominicans and some of their American neighbors had connected after all, but it was the dark angels on both sides who found one another. It was the classic process of assimilation, but in a downward cycle. The immigrant culture had combined with something it had found in the new land to create a new identity. The danger is that the same corrupting process, though on a less dramatic scale, could befall many in the second generation. They could learn to be poor and to be outcasts in America.

Despite all the difficulties encountered by the Dominicans of Washington Heights and all the troubles they have brought on themselves, their fate is hardly certain. During their first thirty years in the United States, they learned a great deal and they built a barrio with its own rich web of connections and institutions. If they ever take it upon themselves to combat the drug traffickers, if economic trends work in their favor, if the city halts the deterioration of services and infrastructure, if any or all of these things happen, the Dominicans of Washington Heights might yet find a way to incorporate themselves into the nation around them.

But for the most recently arrived immigrants, as we are about to see, there is less potential for a happy ending because they were struck by the political and economic whirlwinds of the 1990s before they had gotten their feet on the ground, before they had marked off a barrio or made any connections at all.

CHAPTER 13

Los Angeles: From the Churn to the Burn

◆·◆·◆·◆·◆·◆·◆·◆· Knowing eyes make contact. He's marked his prey, a newcomer. *"Llamadas,"* he says, directing his voice like a rifle shot. Phone calls: For cash dollars, he is selling the sound of familiar voices, a mother's long-distance embrace.

The muscular young man with an open-neck shirt and sleeves rolled up above his biceps knows how to do it. Confidence pours forth with every move he makes. He nods in the direction of another young man across the street who is shepherding people around four busy phone booths. A third young man in baggy shorts and a big oversized T-shirt dials in the stolen credit card numbers that are scrawled on scraps of paper that he pulls from his pants pocket.

Next to the phone booths, a fat lady sitting on a plastic crate fans herself as she presides over a wooden tray covered with audiocassettes. Songs in Spanish and English, new and old, are there in the little plastic containers. Badly printed labels advertise the work of pirates. The sound may be scratchy, but the price is right.

Not buying cassettes today? Then maybe cigarettes from the next lady down or cheap watches from the next, or T-shirts or packs of gum. The merchandise is spread out atop cardboard boxes or anything else that can be set up and taken down quickly. More substantial goods are available at a "swap meet"—a permanent flea market—that occupies an old movie theater that has been stripped down to a hulking interior of bare brick. Each vendor has a few tables or racks filled with clothes, toys, shoes. Not much of it has price tags. Everything is negotiable. Everything is done person to person, all cash, no paper, no government.

This barrio deep in the heart of Los Angeles is full of people who have come north since the mid-1980s, following well-worn paths up from Central America and Mexico. They are still fresh from the voyage, rootless, and preoccupied with survival. This is a port of entry twenty miles from the sea. It is also an American city neighborhood ready to burn.

The sidewalks are crowded on a sunny Saturday morning. Waves of people work their way past the vendors. This is an old neighborhood not far from downtown where bits of Art Deco and gingerbread recall the days of the Twentieth Century Limited. The walls of the buildings are busy with signs and lights, billboards and graffiti. Hand-lettered signs in windows advertise SE CUIDAN BEBÉS (babysitting) or SE VENDEN REFRESCOS (cool drinks for sale). Even the alleys are crowded.

MacArthur Park fills up quickly. Families pick a piece of lawn and settle in the fresh air. Radios and boom boxes produce little circles of salsa, *banda,* and rap. Strategically positioned on the top of a slight slope, a boy no more than sixteen years old preaches fire and brimstone over a bullhorn. He speaks so fast that only occasional words come through the screech: *Dios . . . pecado . . . Jesús, Jesús . . . Dios . . . muerte.* He seems desperate, sweating deeply in a black suit, white shirt, and black tie. No one pays much attention except the five adults forming a chorus line behind him. They urge him on with hallelujahs and hold a banner advertising the opening of a new storefront church.

Down the hill, a dice game draws a crowd. A man in a silk shirt, tight pants, and aviator sunglasses acts as a croupier, directing the action with a fistful of cash. Men watch and wait for a chance to get in on the game, and they never stop talking. To the side, sitting on park benches, pushers are selling marijuana and crack. Another man works the crowd, saying, *"Micas"* in a clearly audible whisper. He cocks his eyes down to his hand. Uncurling his fingers, he exposes a plastic photo ID card—a fake green card—in his cupped palm. An illegal alien can use it to get a job. On the sidewalks, in the park, in the flea markets, there are children everywhere. A half a mile away, the streets are quiet, and for dozens of miles Los Angeles stretches out to less hectic rhythms. It is early Saturday morning, after all, and the rest of the city, from Watts to Santa Monica, seems empty by comparison.

In East L.A., the old Mexican barrio, where many new immigrants live among native Latinos, people are tending their yards mustering kids for Little League or opening up their shops. This is a place that has been Spanish-speaking for a long time and there are churches, community groups, self-help associations, political leaders, and long-established networks of people accustomed to solving problems together. By contrast, everything is still improvised in the streets around MacArthur Park. It is not yet a barrio because it is not yet a place that Latinos can call their own. There is still an air of transience about the people here, as if they are just passing through, and many of them are. Indeed, the area is generally known as Pico-Union or Westlake and has no real nickname in Spanish. This place of comings and goings is just one of many rootless new Latino communities that have sprung up all over greater Los Angeles.

The number of Mexican-born people living in the Los Angeles region rose from 900,000 to 1.7 million during the 1980s. The growth of the Salvadoran-born population was even faster, from 50,000 to 250,000. And the same phenomenon, though on a smaller scale, was repeated in several of the nation's largest cities. So many Latinos landed so fast that the existing barrios could not absorb them all no matter how fast the barrios expanded. Like all immigrants before them, these new arrivals settled wherever they found cheap housing and access to jobs, but that did not mean concentrating in the urban core, as it had for the European ethnics, southern blacks, and others who had migrated to cities in the past. Metropolitan regions like Los Angeles, Houston, and Chicago no longer take the form of concentric circles with a downtown business district, an industrial area or port at the center, and residential neighborhoods radiating outward to the countryside. Instead, financial, manufacturing, and transportation facilities are scattered around entire regions in nodes that form around airports, highway interchanges, and residential developments. Latinos landed everywhere, from semiabandoned inner-city ghettos to run-down apartment complexes out on the interstates. In the Los Angeles region, this meant that some moved into old neighborhoods, like MacArthur Park, that were near the downtown office towers and hotels where Latinos worked as janitors and waiters. Others landed where the garment industry and other types of sweatshop manufacturing had sprung up in place of automobile plants and other heavy industry. Still others parachuted out to distant suburbs where new business centers, shopping areas, and light manufacturing created other kinds of opportunities for low-wage workers. As soon as a few landed in one spot, many others followed. During the Latino surge, almost every major metropolitan area has been dotted with Spanish-speaking precincts. Whether they are in the MacArthur Park district, or in Queens, or Montgomery County, Maryland, or Du Page County, Illinois, whether they are urban or suburban, these communities have taken in new arrivals continuously for fifteen years or more with little opportunity to develop much in the way of a social or political infrastructure. Compared to the fixed rhythms and recognizable institutions of Washington Heights or East L.A., the new barrios do not have much to anchor residents to their surroundings or to help define their place in the United States.

When people come to the United States from countries nearby, a new barrio is a place of arrival and transition, of barter and transshipment. Nothing has cleared customs here. Many people arriving from the south will never go through the formalities. Many have never dealt with a government they respected. Many have never worked for a big company that has offices, personnel clerks, and paychecks. They have had little connection to schools or universities or any big organizations except perhaps the Roman Catholic church. It takes time for them to build new institutions. Dominicans have been building a barrio in Washington Heights for thirty years. Mexicans have been in East L.A. even longer. The new Latino settle-

ments will still be new and tender and disconnected for decades to
come.

More Latinos went to Los Angeles than anywhere else during this
latest surge, and it was in Los Angeles that the new forms of settlement first manifested themselves; it was also where immigrants first
burned a port of entry in anger.

Jesús Navarro came north from El Salvador in 1988. He
was seventeen years old, prime fighting age, and he was as afraid of
being forced into service by the government soldiers as by the guerrilla fighters who periodically swept through his town looking for
recruits. Rather than join either side, he fled and eventually arrived
in California, where he became part of another kind of turmoil.

When he first arrived, Jesús hooked up with an uncle in Long
Beach and worked day-labor construction with him for a while. The
work did not suit him very well. Jesús grew his hair to his shoulders
and developed a taste for hard rock. As soon as he got a few dollars
in his pocket, he began to chafe at his uncle's efforts to play parent,
and after a year he moved to MacArthur Park to live with three
other young men. They found an apartment in a building where the
pipes dripped incessantly and holes in the stucco were patched
with plain cement. Two of the men had worked in a furniture plant
and the other in an industrial laundry. The one thing they did not
worry about was finding work.

For nearly thirty years, since the boom in defense spending during the Vietnam War, Southern California has undergone an economic and demographic churn that is an exaggerated version of
what has become the prevalent pattern nationwide for natives and
immigrants alike. Both jobs and people are constantly coming and
going. In the Los Angeles area, traditional heavy industries—auto,
tires, and steel—virtually disappeared, and as the factories shut
down, working-class whites sought opportunities in distant suburbs or outside the region altogether in high-growth cities like Seattle or Las Vegas. As the white population grew smaller, it also grew
more affluent. The Reagan defense buildup and the growth of the
aerospace industry stoked up demand for engineers and other
highly skilled professionals. Southern California also developed a
cluster of corporate headquarters, banks, and insurance companies
that was second only to New York in size and importance.

Low-wage sectors not only expanded but were increasingly filled with foreign-born Latinos. For example, the number of cooks employed in the L.A. metropolitan area doubled in the 1980s, according to census data; Central American immigrants held less than a third of those jobs at the beginning of the decade but had more than half by the end. In addition, the new California economy created plenty of factory work for newcomers—not the unionized blue-collar jobs of before, but sweatshop work. When the state of California surveyed the more than 1 million illegal aliens who applied for amnesties under the 1986 immigration reform law, less than 2 percent reported suffering unemployment while some 400,000 were working in manufacturing.

Jesús and his roommates each paid one hundred dollars for sewing lessons from a woman who had a couple of machines in her garage and taught a few basic operations such as attaching sleeves and sewing seams. Neither Jesús nor any of his three pals had reached twenty yet, none spoke more than a few words of English, none was in the country legally, and none of them had the equivalent of a high school education.

"Sewing is the one kind of work that is pretty well guaranteed. Anyone who wants it can get it as long as you know how to run the machines," Jesús said. Dozens of lofts operated in old industrial buildings clustered around a stretch of Broadway just on the other side of downtown from MacArthur Park. Getting a job usually involved doing little more than asking for one and demonstrating an ability to run a sewing machine. Nobody asked questions about immigration status or Social Security numbers, and there were no forms to fill out. Almost all the people in charge of the lofts were Koreans and Chinese and the workers were almost all recent Latino immigrants.

"The important thing is to get a machine, and then once you've got a machine you have to be ready to be patient with the *chinos*." A shy, quiet young man with pale skin, Jesús explained his work routine wearily but without a hint of petulance. The patience was necessary because Jesús might spend the better part of a day just sitting by the machine waiting for one of the foremen to come by with a bundle of clothes that needed work. "You wait because if you get up and go away, even if there has been no work for hours, when you come back, someone else will have the machine."

More often than not, however, the foreman would come by with blouses or skirts needing a hem or a pocket or a seam, usually a hundred at a time. The workers would keep sewing as long as the garments kept coming; often that meant working past midnight. If there was work to do on a Saturday or Sunday, the foreman would simply tell them to come in. "Sometimes I've wanted my Sundays so badly, just to be lazy or go to the park or go around with a girl, but if they said there was work, you had to go, because if you didn't, they could always find someone else."

By the mid-1990s, the garment industry in Southern California employed more than a quarter of a million workers by some estimates. It grew during good times and bad, and it grew so much during the 1991–1992 recession while all other industries contracted that garment workers became the largest manufacturing workforce in the region. This represented a sharp turnabout, because since the 1960s the American garment industry had been leaving for the cheaper and less regulated labor markets of the Third World. When it returned, it brought Third World wages and working conditions back with it.

Off-the-rack ladies' casual wear had always been a volatile product, changing with every season and in response to fashion trends. But in the 1970s, that part of the garment market grew rapidly and became ever more volatile in response to the changing status of American women. As women entered the workforce in ever larger numbers, they needed and could afford larger wardrobes. As the market expanded, it fragmented. More manufacturers entered the business and produced a greater variety of goods. Retailers kept inventories smaller and more flexible so they could change their racks in response to fads and fashions. The marketplace changed and so did the manufacturing. Producing garments in Southeast Asia or in Central America took too long when the goal was to spot a trend and have those fashions in the store windows within weeks. Designers needed to be able to see the product to make sure the look and quality was right. Weaving the cloth, even cutting it, could be done effectively overseas, but sewing and finishing needed to be done close by. The sweatshops returned to the United States, though to a place apart. Inside the lofts, English was a foreign language, and American law was a formality that barely deserved recognition, let alone obedience. The market changed, the manufacturing changed, and immigration helped make it possible.

"Very often we work until eight or nine at night the six days and then work a half day Sunday. That means you make a hundred and fifty dollars, more or less, for the week, and at first that feels like a lot of money in your pocket, but it really isn't." After a while, Jesús found it impossible to send more than twenty or thirty dollars a week back to his mother in El Salvador; he spent the rest on rent and just getting by. Within a year, he started to experience chronic pains in his back and joints, which is a common complaint among garment workers who spend twelve hours a day hunched over a sewing machine.

"I have started feeling old. I never imagined feeling old when I am still so young," Jesús said, brushing his long hair back off his face, revealing sharp cheekbones beneath sallow skin.

Like all the other Latinos who spent their days in the Broadway garment district and their nights in the old apartment buildings around MacArthur Park, Jesús floated from one employer to another. On any given day, even in the middle of the day, a foreman might simply announce that he didn't need so many workers and then pick a half dozen who should leave and not return. Another change in the garment industry and other forms of manufacturing involved the more widespread use of subcontractors. Hardly anything is put together by one company anymore, not even a skirt; instead, each part or each operation is handled at a different venue. Operating on narrow margins, small manufacturers need to keep costs down and volume up, whether they are making garments or brake pads. Instead of long-term, full-time jobs, the growth has been in piecework, temporary or part-time labor. This is called the "contingent" workforce by the experts, and by the mid-1990s it had grown to nearly 20 percent of all workers. The garment industry may be the worst case, but it is not the exception.

"I could go home to El Salvador, but I don't think it would be any better in terms of work and there I would have to live with my family. It is more difficult here, but I have more freedom in how I live." Jesús allowed himself a little boy's smirk and lit a cigarette. "I do not know what the future is for me, but it is not important for me to know."

Jesús can barely remember the names of his employers and it hardly matters. Ownership of the lofts changes hands frequently, and sometimes the workers are left in the cold when they are owed wages; they often arrive and find a place closed down and locked up. When he loses work, Jesús just walks the garment district with dozens of other young men and women. Jesús remained unattached to a job, but he had steady work; unattached to a home but the full-time resident of an American city. He had learned to live in a part of the United States that is a transit zone and that allows, even encourages, newcomers to live on the margins.

Someday, when people look back on this era, Century City will symbolize Southern California's era of ascendancy. It was designed with that cold, confident Reagan style of nouveau affluence, that glow of unfettered horizons. Its main street was laid out as a broad boulevard studded with fountains, copious flower beds, and swatches of lawn so carefully maintained that they could be putting greens. The thoroughfare was named Avenue of the Stars. To either side, office towers rose from concrete esplanades, each shaft an independent, disconnected space, each a monument to the wealth generated within.

Sitting at the foot of that bejeweled escarpment known as Beverly Hills, Century City teemed with the authors and brokers of the new California economy. From their brilliant high-rises, they invented ideas for killer satellites, leveraged buyouts, and music videos and then translated those ideas into business deals. Concepts and capital skipped around the globe electronically. Markets and factories could be anywhere. Finance it in London, build it in Thailand, and sell it in Michigan.

These cunning, creative people, baby boomers who had come to California from someplace else, constituted one part of a labor force that generated a great deal of money in Century City. Others worked at night cleaning up after them. They worked as printers and couriers. They parked cars, tended gardens, and worked in factories. They were the servants, and, just as much as the authors and brokers, the servants were also part of the great global expansion in finance and business services that has generated so much prosperity for the United States. Studying the same kind of economic development in New York City, Saskia Sassen, a professor of Urban Planning at Columbia University, found it utterly dependent on the kind of labor force created by Latino immigration: "The expansion of the high-income work force in conjunction with the emergence of new cultural forms has led to a high-income gentrification that rests, in the last analysis, on the availability of a vast supply of low-wage workers."

The arrival of fresh Latino immigrants was only one part of all this churning, but because they were so new, so noticeable, and so numerous, they became the face of the change. One of the ways people saw the results was when whole job categories changed hands and newly arrived Latinos suddenly began doing work that had been performed by native-born workers before, usually African-Americans. It happened at car washes and on construction crews, in hotel banquet rooms and supermarkets. At first glance, it seemed easy to conclude that the new Latinos had "taken" the jobs once held by blacks. That certainly seemed to be the case with an important job category that changed drastically in Los Angeles: the work of cleaning offices.

In 1980, many, if not most, of the janitors in big L.A. office buildings were African-Americans, especially in the traditional downtown business district. They could count on wages and benefits worth more than twelve dollars an hour as part of secure, long-standing union contracts. Ten years later, most of the janitors in big buildings, especially in the newly developing areas such as Century City, were Latinos, usually recently arrived, often illegals. They worked for something close to the minimum wage with no contract, no vacation, no health insurance, no benefits, no overtime. The social contract that had provided thousands of black workers a decent wage was broken, and it was replaced with the sweatshop labor of immigrants.

The Latinos who have come north in the recent surge are experiencing the poverty of full employment, but it is poverty nonetheless. Salvadoran and Guatemalan immigrants experienced poverty two and a half times greater than did the rest of the population in the Los Angeles region in 1990, and their wages were a third of what Mexican-Americans earned. By 1990, more than 110,000 residents of Los Angeles County worked cleaning offices, more than double the number of machinists and auto mechanics combined. The jobs had increased, but they had also spread out. Economic change and demographic change were part of the same great churning.

Already a city of several major nodes, Los Angeles, like many other major metropolitan areas, sprouted ganglia of office towers all

over its freeway network during the 1980s. The rapid expansion
and geographic dispersal of the market for cleaning services produced a period of cutthroat competition, mergers, acquisitions,
and eventual consolidation of the companies that provide office-
building maintenance services. Among the by-products of this
growth and restructuring was the disruption of a long-standing
labor-market relationship that had linked janitorial jobs in the old
downtown to African-American workers in South Central, Watts,
and other nearby communities. Meanwhile, new relationships
developed, linking fast-growing and widely scattered business centers all over the region with the equally fast-developing port-of-
entry neighborhoods filled with recently arrived Latinos.

Since the early 1960s, a few big building-maintenance companies
had dominated the janitorial business downtown and in some of the
larger buildings farther out. These were the companies that paid
union wages and benefits to a heavily black workforce. At first, the
big unionized firms did not contest the new suburban market, leaving this rich, expanding territory to nonunionized small and mid-
sized cleaning firms. Out on the freeways, businesses were smaller,
moved more frequently, and paid less rent. Cleaning companies had
to charge less and provide a mobile, often part-time workforce.
They met the demand by paying low wages to Latino immigrants.

Eventually, the big unionized firms had to turn to the growing
suburban market to maintain market share. By then, the rules of the
suburban battleground had been defined, and the big unionized
firms had no choice but to fight back by driving down wages, eliminating benefits, and increasing workloads.

The undercutting of wages began in the suburbs, but then it
quickly spread to downtown and throughout the market. Soon
there was all-out competition throughout the whole metropolitan
area. As the stakes grew, the competitors consolidated into fewer
and bigger companies. Eventually, the stakes got high enough to
attract foreign capital in the form of giant international firms such
as the Danish International Service Systems, which took over many
of the big buildings at Century City, and the German-based Pedus
Group, which made inroads downtown. As the competition moved
from the suburbs to the skyscrapers, so did the use of cheap immigrant labor.

This was the same basic process of corporate restructuring in the
face of globalized competition that took place all across the United

States in the 1980s and that continued into the 1990s. Except during the 1991–1992 recession. Amid overall growth in jobs there was tremendous pressure to increase productivity while reducing personnel costs. At the low end of the labor market, that meant declining or stagnating wages and an increasing reliance on part-time and temporary workers. Eventually, everyone, including top executives, would feel the same crunch.

Displacing the black janitors and breaking the union were incidental results of fundamental change in the structure of an industry. Well-paid workers were not being replaced with immigrant, minimum-wage scabs. Instead, the number of jobs was growing, and the new jobs emerged as low-wage, nonunion slots. Meanwhile, compensation for the old jobs decreased. The defining dynamic was not immigration, but a new form of corporate competition that reduced pay for a whole category of workers. That same dynamic invaded many other areas of low-wage work, including the garment industry and other forms of highly subcontracted light manufacturing, restaurant and hotel services, unskilled health-care jobs, and home-construction laborers. As a result, real wages for many of these jobs have declined steadily for the past decade. This is not to say the abundant supply of immigrant workers was merely incidental. Economic change went hand in hand with demographic change, and one could not have happened without the other. But as Eliseo Medina, executive director of the service workers' local in San Diego, said, "What you have to ask yourself is, Who was in control? Who made the decisions? Who made the profit? It was never the workers, not the blacks who worked before and not the Latinos who came later. The industry set the wage and the wage determined who worked."

Immigrants filled most of the new jobs because they were by far the largest source of new entrants to the labor force. Their sheer numbers allowed employers to expand and lower costs simultaneously. No matter how fast the California boom created low-skill jobs, the immigrants came even faster.

By 1990, a job cleaning offices wasn't worth much. It became a second or third job in many immigrant households because janitors' pay alone would not support a family. In this regard, janitors were no different from many other immigrant workers earning poverty wages. The difference was that the janitors revolted.

· · ·

On May 29, 1990, janitors working in Century City went on strike against ISS, the big Danish corporation that held the maintenance contracts there. The workers demanded a union contract and better pay, but the fact that they were part of a huge immigrant wave meant that they had no economic leverage on their employers.

"The problem with Los Angeles is that everyone in Latin America wants to come here and the bosses know that," said Salvador Hernandez, a shop steward of the Service Employees International Union in Los Angeles. "It doesn't scare them for us to say we are going on strike because if they have twenty-five people working in a building, they know they have a thousand waiting outside who want work."

The European ethnics used strikes often and to great effect. Those immigrants and their children built up the trade union movement, ensured that industrial work was safe and well rewarded, and eventually gained acceptance as valued economic players. But by 1990, the unions had lost much of their membership and their leverage. Changes in federal law and policy made it hard to organize and strike successfully. And the unions, like the Roman Catholic church and the Democratic party, did not align themselves with the economic and ethnic interests of the new Latino immigrants with the same vigor as they had with most of the Europeans. Finally, unskilled Latino immigrants had arrived in such abundance that even large numbers of strikers could be replaced in an instant.

That was the challenge facing the L.A. janitors. They responded with novel tactics. They showed up in glittering banks with big bags of pennies day after day and tied up tellers, who had to count out the coins. Even if they were shuffled to one side, they carried their message to elegant precincts just by being there. It was all on their bright red T-shirts emblazoned with the slogan JUSTICE FOR JANITORS. They disturbed the quiet elegance of the best boutiques simply by standing sullenly on the sidewalks and staring at shoppers inside.

The protesters called themselves Los Justicieros, and they had the outsider's view of what is possible: They were willing to take risks when there was no objective reason to assume the likelihood of success. Such protests by Latino immigrants had rarely been seen before, but these were a different type of Latino. The janitors belonged to the big, complex group of immigrants that came north starting in the 1980s. Instead of the peasant farmers who had dominated the flow from Mexico before, large numbers of more sophisticated, more politically aggressive city dwellers came to the United States during the years of Mexico's economic crisis. Political turmoil and civil wars in Central America and the Caribbean pushed out professionals, teachers, union members, and political activists. In L.A., they proved more imaginative and more aggressive in pressing their demands than immigrant Latinos had been before. The new arrivals fueled the janitors strike and several other labor actions. It was their children who took to the streets to protest Proposition 187, and in L.A.'s darkest days, they presented the most perplexing challenge.

Despite their audacity, however, unsettling the sleek ambience of Century City wasn't nearly enough to overcome the arithmetic of an overabundant workforce. The janitors needed the intercession of the Los Angeles Police Department, with its special talent for heightening social contradictions.

On Friday morning, June 15, 1990, a little more than two weeks into the strike, the Latino janitors, now with help from union organizers, planned a lunchtime rally at a public plaza in the heart of Century City. About one hundred strikers and three hundred supporters assembled in a Beverly Hills park. Many wore red bandannas across their faces, just like labor agitators in Central America who do not want to end up on death-squad lists. In this case, they wanted to avoid identification by immigration authorities.

Banging on empty watercooler bottles as if they were conga drums, they marched toward the fabled office district. As they reached the edge of Century City, the marchers were an alien army invading in broad daylight. The police were waiting to repel them before they could penetrate the sanctum. About fifty cops lined up, blocking the street. They dressed for the occasion in riot gear. With no prior warnings or admonitions, a police supervisor summarily declared the march an illegal assembly. He gave the marchers thirty seconds to disperse or otherwise face arrest. In a moment, the police were prodding demonstrators with their batons. The marchers fell back, linked arms, and re-formed their own line. They chanted the slogan César Chávez made famous when he led grape pickers on strike: *"¡Sí se puede!"* ("It can be done!")

After a few moments, the cops broke ranks. In twos and threes, they went after individual red shirts with no other apparent purpose than to inflict injury. People were knocked to the ground and then hit with batons when they tried to get up. The *Los Angeles Times* reported that forty people were arrested and sixteen injured. Union officials claimed a greater number of injuries, including broken bones, concussions, and a miscarriage.

"The Century City police riot just lit up the issue," said Peter Olney, a union organizer who helped lead the Justice for Janitors campaign. "It put a bright light on the Third World–type contradictions of poverty wages amid such wealth and put it on the screen for everyone to see."

Several TV news crews got long clips of immigrant workers cowering beneath baton blows as some of the most luxurious office towers in the nation glimmered in the background. For days, it was the best action video available at six and eleven. As the images became familiar, the LAPD became a social catalyst. At Century City, the LAPD created a victim, and they did it with the same stumbling swagger they later demonstrated in the Rodney King case.

Armed with videotape, lawyers for the Service Employees International Union, which was by then backing the strike, charged into court demanding a restraining order against further police interference with the Justice for Janitors campaign. The hearings turned into an instant trial of LAPD misconduct. The best defense the police could mount was to claim that they had received some unspecified "intelligence" warning that the immigrants had conspired to block traffic. Unimpressed, the judge imposed severe limits on the cops' ability to interfere with the strikers, and thus, in effect, opened the gates of Century City to the protesting janitors.

The restraining order came down on a Friday. That day, the service employees union and ISS, the Danish cleaning company, began serious negotiations for the first time since the strike began. They held an eight-hour session on Sunday, and on Monday the union declared victory on all fronts. The strike ended with a contract that phased in health insurance, vacations, and sick leave and that immediately increased average pay from $4.50 to $5.20 an hour. The Latino janitors got themselves a union contract, but their new wages still would not keep a family out of poverty. The janitors had braved the LAPD's batons for a raise worth less than six dollars a day.

Five months after the strike, the L.A. Police Commission castigated the cops for being overzealous. Police Chief Daryl Gates accepted the finding with an uncharacteristic admission of guilt. "We broke down our line and that was a break in our discipline," he said.

Three years later, the Los Angeles City Council agreed to pay $2.35 million to settle a lawsuit filled by the janitors against the police. The suit alleged that sixty marchers had required medical treatment and that another eight-five had been hit or falsely arrested when the police interfered with the protesters' constitutional rights. It was among the largest settlements in the city's history.

Every year, the janitors celebrate June 15, the anniversary of the Century City march, as El Día de Acción Política (The Day of Political Action).

"We call it that because this whole campaign has been a triumph of politics over economics," said Olney, the union organizer.

If economics ruled, workers would win such victories when the demand for their labor clearly exceeded the supply. But that was not the case with the L.A. janitors—they were the most easily replaced workers in California. So what kind of politics could triumph over that economic condition?

The immigrants of the 1980s and 1990s arrived in Southern California so quickly and in such great numbers that they did not have a chance to build substantial enclaves, and so they did not represent the kind of turf-conscious political force demonstrated by the Dominicans in Washington Heights or the Mexican-Americans in East L.A. They were not recognized as political refugees, and so they did not get the special treatment afforded the Cubans. They filled new spaces at the low end of the economy, and even though the janitors got help from the service employees union, they could not count on the backing of a broad labor movement.

The janitors' victory did not bring them any closer to the American mainstream. Rather, they won in the role of outsiders. It was not a victory of assimilation but of separation. And it was an accidental victory that could not be replicated elsewhere. But the janitors' strike did illuminate a new kind of politics that will become increasingly prevalent in every city that is settling large numbers of newly arrived Latino immigrants.

The L.A. janitors were poor people seeking fair pay. They were

Hispanics—members of a minority group. Many were Salvadorans and could claim to be refugees from a right-wing, U.S.-supported government. Many were dark skinned. Thanks to the heavy hand of the LAPD, they became well known as victims and won recognition as plaintiffs. The janitors presented a fragmented identity. They were not distinguished by any one characteristic, and they could not demand justice on the basis of any single claim. The janitors projected a somewhat confused convergence of racial, economic, linguistic, and political attributes. They were a diffuse and mobile presence in the city, just as much at the mercy of events in winning improved wages as they were when they gained employment.

Americans rely heavily on biological absolutes—race, ethnicity, or gender—to define social status. And numerical measures—how many women in a job category, how many blacks in a voting district—to determine whether or not justice has been served. No matter how appealing this clarity might seem, it no longer explains social conflicts or helps provide mechanisms for resolving them. At a time of demographic change and economic restructuring, the absolutes and simple measures are merely deceiving.

In Latin America, there is no such clarity. Skin color alone—except perhaps in Cuba—has never defined the fault lines, because most people are products of the great *mestizaje,* which mixed the blood of white Europeans together with that of American Indians and African slaves. As in the United States, the richest and most politically powerful people are usually light-skinned, but people of mixed race constitute the majority and they define the national culture. Latino immigrants arrive here accustomed to the idea that people are marked not just by race but also by class, region, and ethnicity. They understand that people bear multiple markers and that this accumulation of traits defines someone's place in society precisely and inescapably.

Most of those who come north are poor and nonwhite. Once in the United States, they are additionally marked by language and ancestry and sometimes also by immigration status. When Latino immigrants feel cornered or abused, they will defend themselves with the weapons they find on American terrain, but their grievances may not translate neatly into the language of American politics. The Dominicans' protest against Kiko's shooting in Washington Heights differed from other disturbances that have followed acts of police violence. The janitors' strike was not a simple labor action or a poor people's protest or a civil rights march; it became some combination of all three.

Questions of race and poverty are not as straightforward as they were before the Latinos arrived. In 1968, the National Advisory Commission on Civil Disorders, headed by Governor Otto Kerner of Illinois, studied the race riots that had seared American cities the previous summer and reached a finding of powerful simplicity. "This is our basic conclusion: Our nation is moving toward two societies, one black, one white—separate and unequal."

When Los Angeles burned during the Rodney King riots of 1992, the fires gave proof that the nation was moving toward a much more complex fragmentation. The United States was still broken into societies separate and unequal, but there were more than two of them. Latinos and Asians had complicated the interplay exponentially because the dividing lines could no longer be drawn according to something as obvious as skin color. Language, ancestry, immigration status, and economic achievement divided the population into many multifaceted fractions—separate and unequal. After Rodney King, nothing could be so simple as black and white.

Los Angeles, the fountainhead of American visual fables, produced two videotape clips in the early 1990s that became part of the American collective memory. One showed the beating of Rodney King: white policemen swinging batons and kicking a black man all in the course of their normal duties, according to the county jury that found them innocent. The second image was the television news footage of the beating of Reginald Denny: A white truck driver who inadvertently drives into a black ghetto that has just been ignited by news of the policemen's acquittal is dragged into the street and mercilessly beaten by young black men who revel in torture.

Those images are as deceitful as if they had been produced on a Hollywood back lot, because they are archetypes in black and white. The fiery days and nights that followed the policemen's trial shattered all the familiar patterns of racial or economic conflict in America. They rendered the term *race riot* an anachronism. This was not Watts or Detroit a quarter century earlier, where blacks took to the streets over accumulated grievances and unfulfilled expectations. Instead, the flames exploded out of a new urban landscape shaped equally by immigration, the unresolved problem of race, and rapid change in the shape of the economy.

The attack on Reginald Denny became a symbol of black anger against whites, but at the same infamous intersection of Florence and Normandie in L.A.'s South Central district, a Latino truck driver also got a beating that April afternoon. He ended up in a hospital, needing more than 250 stitches in his face. While Denny became a household name for most Americans, Fidel Lopez became known as the "forgotten victim" among Los Angeles Latinos who organized a fund-raising campaign to pay his medical bills and to move him and his family out of South Central and into East L.A.

When Reginald Denny's tormentors were put on trial, the prosecution began its case by calling Alicia Maldonado. She testified that as she approached Florence and Normandie that afternoon, she "had to slow down because traffic was being directed according to the color of your skin. . . . The persons that were allowed to pass were all black, dark." She said her car windows were smashed and her purse stolen after a black man in the street ordered her to halt, shouting, "Get her. She's not a sister."

Blacks and Latinos are often lumped together as "people of color" or as "minorities," but in the streets of South Central, sharp distinctions were drawn between them. Fidel Lopez and Alicia Maldonado were not colored enough. Black violence against Latinos seems to have occurred mostly on that first day of the riot. In 1992, South Central became a synonym for black rage, just as Watts had been a generation earlier. But it was a different kind of black rage, because places like South Central had not existed in the 1960s. Like many other African-American communities, it had absorbed large numbers of recently arrived Latino immigrants in the years after Watts. Latinos not only filled the streets of South Central with unfamiliar faces but they also got jobs where blacks seemed always to be turned away. That became a flash point of political conflict between blacks and Latinos after the riot.

Change and threatening visions of the future generated violence in 1992 as much as resentment over long-held grievances. That was evident in the violence that both Latinos and blacks carried out against Koreans, who as a group were targeted with a singular viciousness: 95 of their dry cleaners suffered damage in the riot, 220 liquor stores, 314 markets, 106 restaurants, more than 2,000 of their businesses in all. That accounts for about 20 percent of all the retail establishments created by one of the most entrepreneurially successful immigrant communities ever to set up shop in the United States.

The Koreans also started out as people of color. They belonged to a race that had traditionally suffered rejection in California. They were foreigners and spoke little English, and yet from behind their store counters, they exercised power in poor communities and seemed to prosper with remarkable speed. The Koreans started out on the wrong side of the racial divide and yet they succeeded. Blacks and Latinos could blame the success of whites on racism or nativism, but not when the Koreans demonstrated an ability to overcome barriers of race and alienage. Their success provoked a more violent anger than the success of whites because it was anger steeped in envy and insecurity.

Once the riot lasted for more than a few hours and the sense of order started to break down around the city, many Latinos became full-fledged participants, but they played no clear role because they played many roles. Latinos were both perpetrators and victims in almost equal measure. Latinos both looted and owned stores that were looted. They were beaten up and delivered beatings. They were killed and arrested. In South Central, they tagged along in a black riot. In East L.A., they stood back and defended the barrio against the violence. But Latinos played the most perplexing role in the great port of entry around MacArthur Park.

Throughout those crowded quarters, people took to the streets on the second day of the riot. They looted; then they burned. At the end of the riot, the intersection of Pico and Union was the only spot in the city where all four corners were left in charred rubble. From one block to another, some very obvious symbols of the Latino migration to the United States burned to cinders. No specific event touched off the Latino violence. Nothing provoked the Latinos directly, such as Kiko Garcia's death had the Dominicans in Washington Heights; the Rodney King verdict certainly didn't have such great meaning to recently arrived Latinos. From these uncertain origins, the violence around MacArthur Park became a self-destructive rage. The Latinos set about attacking the symbols of their own life in the United States, even the symbols of their own limited success.

Swap meets, overwhelmingly owned, operated, and patronized

by Latinos, were hit hard. Several were thoroughly looted and then burned by their regular customers, ostensibly friends and neighbors of the owners. These were places where a person could open a business with just a little money and run it with not much overhead. They also provided a poor, working-class community access to essentials like clothing, tools, or utensils at the lowest-possible prices. The swap meets represented years of hard work by newcomers trying to get a foothold in Los Angeles. In targeting them, rioters aborted their community's efforts to create an enclave economy.

One of the largest businesses destroyed in Pico Union was La Curaçao, a furniture store that specialized in a unique form of the immigrant trade. Customers in L.A. could pick out the sofas or bedroom suites they desired, make layaway payments, and when the purchase was complete, the goods could be picked up at La Curaçao's warehouse in El Salvador. It was the retail embodiment of the transnational existence, remittances by way of furniture. For La Curaçao's customers, all the sweat and sacrifice happened in L.A. on behalf of dreams realized back home. La Curaçao was a big black pile of ruins after its clients got finished trashing and torching it.

A few blocks away, La Atlacatl had been a somewhat upscale eatery for the Salvadorans of Pico Union. It was a restaurant for Sunday afternoons, birthdays, and baptisms. The menu and the jukebox were designed to bring back memories of home and stoke a little national pride. It was burned and looted, but nobody touched the large painting of Atlacatl, the mythic Indian warrior who was the restaurant's namesake and a symbol of Salvadoran manhood.

This part of the L.A. riot was not an event with roots sunk deep in time. Instead, it reflected some very immediate frustrations. The Latinos rioted to protest wounds still fresh and raw. The burning in black neighborhoods resulted from the long, gradual buildup of inflammable materials that were set off by a spark, the Rodney King verdicts. The Latino burn was spontaneous combustion. L.A.'s blacks had taken a journey of centuries—from Africa, through slavery, out of the rural South, and into urban poverty—to reach that kind of rage. The Latinos who took to the streets had accumulated enough bitterness to reach critical mass in less than a decade. They had acquired markers that set them apart by virtue of their poverty, ethnicity, language abilities, and immigration status combined. And they understood that they were marked as a people apart. Not only did Anglos look down on them but so did blacks and Asians and even native-born Latinos.

Worst of all, they had begun to understand that in moving from El Salvador to L.A. they had just exchanged one kind of marked status for another. Migration was supposed to liberate them, but their opportunities for real mobility were limited. Despite their travels, they were running in place. They were still people relegated to a diminished and unhappy sector of society, with little chance of becoming something else. The Latino burn in L.A. reflected the anger of unfulfilled expectations, which can be a very bitter and powerful form of rage. Once those emotions exploded, there was nothing much to hold them back. In places like the MacArthur Park neighborhoods or South Central, too many people were too recently arrived to have developed the kind of community leaders and institutions that can put brakes on a civil disturbance.

"People looked at buildings on fire and at looters running out of stores and they did not think, This is my community that is being destroyed," said Aristides Larin, who was an attorney in El Salvador, fled the civil war, and became a travel agent and notary public in a storefront just off MacArthur Park. "To most people here, this is still a foreign place that belongs to someone else."

All immigrants spend some time floating. Getting settled in a new land naturally involves a period of adjustment and even some alienation. But poor Latinos who came to the United States in the last twenty years didn't have much time to adjust. Right from the start, they had to deal with a changing economy, a shifting population, and a society increasingly uncertain about how to manage its diverse ethnic and racial groups.

While South Central and Pico Union burned, everything was quiet on the other side of the L.A. River in the greatest barrio of them all. Down in the Flats, up through Boyle Heights and into Maravilla, and all through the rest of East L.A., places where Latino young men have been forming gangs for fifty years, hardly a flame flickered in the spring of 1992. All across the Latino heartland of Los Angeles, no more than a handful of businesses were looted.

"There're a lot of people who own their homes around here—maybe not a majority, but a lot—and a lot who have businesses right around here, too, and these folks wanted to protect the neigh-

borhood," said Juana Gutiérrez, president of Las Madres de East
L.A., the community organization. "What little they've got, and it
might not be much, but what little they've got is right here and they
wanted to protect it."

Gutiérrez lives in Boyle Heights, just up the hill from the Flats
and the river, and from there, on the high ground at the western
edge of the great Mexican-American enclave, she and the other
madres mobilized to keep the disturbances from spreading into the
big barrio.

"We could smell the fires up here, and sometimes even ashes
would blow on the wind. Well, our boys here have all the same reasons to be angry and frustrated over how things are going, and with
all that burning going on so close, you had to worry that if someone
lit the first match on this side of the river, East L.A. would burn and
burn and we could lose everything." Gutiérrez had reason to
worry.

East L.A. didn't stay quiet because the people there were more
law-abiding than in South Central, Pico Union, or other neighborhoods that burned. In fact, afterward there were many persuasive
accounts of gang bangers and others who traveled from East L.A. to
the riot zones in order to take part in the looting. The big barrio
remained quiet in part because East L.A. was struck by a healthy
sense of vulnerability and apartness. For once, the geographic separation of the barrio, detached from the center of L.A. by the river,
proved a blessing. In addition, the predominantly Mexican and
Mexican-American population of East L.A., like most of white
America, saw the riot as a black event. This not only distanced them
from the disturbances but also caused them to consider themselves
potential victims.

Several times, rumors swept through East L.A. that black gangs
were on their way to loot and burn the barrio. Whether or not the
rumors had any basis in truth, they put many people in Boyle
Heights in a defensive frame of mind.

"Our *vatos* were out there promising the shop owners that they
would fight to protect the neighborhood against attacks from the
black gangs from Watts and South Central, because that's what
everyone said was going to happen," Gutiérrez recalled. "When it
comes down to it, these are our boys, and no matter what problems
they may cause at other times, during Rodney King they acted real

responsibly because if they were swearing to protect the barrio against outsiders, they couldn't very well be messing it up themselves."

In the end, people in East L.A. had a sufficient sense of ownership not to want to burn their own neighborhood, and they perceived the riot as enough of an external threat to want to protect their turf. Moreover, East L.A. had an extensive and mature network of organizations with which to express that ownership. Leaders from many different groups worked hard to preserve the calm. There were informal associations like Gutierrez's Las Madres de East L.A., well-financed community service organizations, and community development corporations, as well as grassroots political machines linked to elected officials.

All of this civil society has not been able to cure East L.A.'s problems with gangs, drug trafficking, and enduring poverty, but on a day-to-day basis, it helps mitigate those problems, and during Rodney King, this undergirding of institutions and human connections helped save the biggest barrio of them all. The result probably would have been different if the riot had started closer by or if it had been sparked by an incident involving a Latino victim. But the fact remains that the largest barrio in the United States did not burn during the largest urban disturbance in American history.

East L.A.'s peace meant nothing for the newer and poorer Latino neighborhoods, such as South Central, that were engulfed in violence.

"There is not at this time a Latino social service infrastructure within that community" in South Central, said David Lizarraga, president of the East Los Angeles Community Union (TELACU), a powerful twenty-year-old economic development organization that had some $300 million in assets located almost entirely within the boundaries of the old barrio at the time of the riot.

Recognizing that the Latino establishment had neglected the new but already-large Latino communities outside of East L.A., Lizarraga said, "That's our fault. . . . Where can we point the finger but to ourselves?"

As with the Cubans in Miami, an enclave can be a huge asset for the people who belong to it yet provide little help to people outside its boundaries, even when they share a common language and culture. Decades of work and investment went into building civil soci-

ety and public institutions in East L.A., and much of it was justified
in the name of an ethnic cause. Whether they were marching with
César Chávez as *la raza* or fighting legal battles or writing grant proposals or making budget demands, the activists of East L.A. usually
said they were acting as representatives of the Latino population.
But in the case of the Rodney King riot, it turned out that all that
effort had gone to the benefit of an enclave, East L.A., not to an ethnic cause that embraced all Latinos. This was most obvious in the
behavior of the city's top Latino elected officials, the masters of
East L.A.

During the riots, several local black political leaders, such as Congresswoman Maxine Waters, made highly visible efforts to restore
calm on the toughest streets, but there was no similar effort in the
riot zones from the most prominent local Latino officials whose constituencies are centered in the Mexican-American East Side. At the
very moment that the largest Latino community in the nation
needed assertive leadership, it got disclaimers instead.

Richard Alatorre, a city councilman whose district is centered in
Boyle Heights, was quoted in the *Los Angeles Times* as saying, "I
try my best to be an advocate for [immigrants'] concerns, but I
didn't get elected to represent them." And Gloria Molina, the only
Hispanic on the powerful Los Angeles County Board of Supervisors, made an equally stunning admission to the *New York Times*.
Although she owes her political career to a voting-rights lawsuit
brought on behalf of all the Latinos in Los Angeles County, she
acknowledged that she really didn't know much about the Latinos
in the riot areas because they were outside her district, which is
centered in East L.A. "At a time when we really needed to reach out
there, we found that we were not as informed as we could have been
about who the Latino leaders were in that area," Molina said.

For almost forty years, the idea that Latinos constituted a minority group had gained credibility and power. They had confronted
and largely dismantled a system of economic and ethnic subjugation imposed by whites across Texas, the Southwest, and California.
They had battled more subtle forms of discrimination, such as the
redistricting schemes that had prevented Latinos from winning representation on the L.A. County Board of Supervisors and dozens of
similar bodies across the region. All this was accomplished according to rules developed to help blacks win their civil rights, and

those rules required Latinos to present themselves as a single demographic entity with uniform grievances against the majority. That special status remains an important legal tool because the nation offers no other means of dealing with discrimination. But after some Latinos in L.A. burned their neighbors' businesses while others elsewhere guarded their barrios, the idea that Latinos constitute a minority group lost much of its value as a means of describing real life.

When Watts burned in 1965, it was easily labeled a race riot. Even if all the blacks in Los Angeles did not join in, it was assumed that by virtue of their race they all shared some of the anger and frustrations that exploded in the streets. Black leaders were virtually unanimous in depicting the riot as a response to the prejudice and poverty experienced by most blacks, and so the hand-wringing and the remedies that followed could be directed at blacks as a group, not just at those in Watts. As troubling as racial divisions may have been to many Americans in the sixties, the concept of race did allow for an easy diagnosis of the nation's social ills and obviated much of the blame by putting it on the injustices perpetrated by past generations.

Thirty years later, most civil disorders involved immigrants either as protesters or provocateurs, and usually Latino immigrants were somehow involved. The term *race riot* lost its meaning when barrios like Mount Pleasant in Washington, D.C., or Washington Heights, or Pico Union became the scenes of street fighting. Even black protests took on a different significance when they were aimed at Miami's Cubans, L.A.'s Koreans, or New York's Orthodox Jews.

In trying to explain the new dynamics of urban America, some people focused on class divisions as the new fault lines in society, but poor people have never constituted a coherent interest group in the United States and they still don't. The Rodney King explosion was no more a bread riot than it was a race riot. Another popular notion held that social conflict in the 1990s could be explained in terms of "people of color" expressing their common alienation with the mainstream Anglo culture and their shared economic marginalization. But that does not help explain why some Latinos rioted in L.A. in 1992 while other Latinos avoided any entanglement. Nor

does it help explain why some people of color, Koreans, were brutally victimized.

This is not just a matter of terminology. A new portrait of urban
America emerged from the great surge of immigration in the 1980s
and 1990s, but the nation lacked a ready vocabulary to describe that
portrait. If something cannot be described, it cannot be understood.
If a conflict cannot be diagnosed, it cannot be remedied.

The arrival of the immigrants did not erase the old dividing lines.
Black rage was still a potent force, and black/white conflicts
remained the hot, unresolved core of group relations in the United
States. The arrival of the immigrants meant that while old wounds
still festered and still produced challenges to America's social cohesion, other challenges emerged as newcomers tried to find a place
for themselves here.

When Los Angeles burned in the Rodney King riots of 1992, the
fires warned of new inequalities created when the Sun Belt boom
sucked immigrants into California and then left them stranded in
the poverty workforce. The blazes warned of immigrants who have
arrived at a time of extraordinary ambivalence and fragmentation in
America's civic culture. They warned of the second generation, the
native-born children of immigrants, who cannot find any open
doors into their own land.

Like the fires of the sixties, these flames warned of dangers
ahead—not of a fate that has been sealed. They signaled that an era
of opportunity was closing but not yet over. In 1968, the Kerner
Commission also insisted that "This deepening racial division is
not inevitable. That movement apart can be reversed. Choice is still
possible."

With Latinos in the 1990s, as with blacks in the 1960s, the caste
status is not yet irreversible; inherited poverty is not inevitable. A
generation of young people is still in school, waiting to be taught.
In the barrios, there are many expectations not yet defeated by cyn-
icism.

We know now that the warnings of Watts and the other fires of
the sixties were not heeded and that many blacks suffered needlessly for that. If thirty years from now people look back and decide
we squandered the last good opportunities to remedy the current
divisions in American society, the regrets and the pains will be
much greater. The difference will be in the numbers. Already the

Hispanic population is growing more than twice as fast as the black population did between the Watts riots of 1965 and the South Central fires of 1992. The nation can barely endure separation and inequality when the minority is small and not growing. The consequences are far greater when the outcasts are becoming an ever-larger proportion of the population. If the warnings of the 1990s are not heeded, the nation will pay a very large price in the next century. The choice is still possible, but the opportunity is rapidly disappearing.

◆·◆·◆·◆·◆·◆·◆·◆·◆·◆·◆·◆·◆·◆·◆·◆·

PART IV

ACCEPT
THE FEAR

Since the beginning of the nation, white
Americans have suffered from a deep inner
uncertainty as to who they really are. One
of the ways that has been used to simplify
the answer was to seize upon the presence
of black Americans and use them as a
marker, a symbol of limits, a metaphor for
the "outsider." Many whites could look at
the social position of blacks and feel that
color formed an easy and reliable gauge of
determining to what extent one was or was
not an American. Perhaps that is why one
of the first epithets that many European
immigrants learned when they got off the
boat was the term "nigger"—it made them
feel instantly American. But this is tricky
magic.

> —RALPH ELLISON,
> *"What America Would Be Like Without*
> *Blacks,"* Time, *April 6, 1970*

❖·❖·❖·❖·❖·❖·❖·❖·❖·❖·❖·❖·❖·❖·❖·❖·❖·❖·

The City That Worked

❖·❖·❖·❖·❖·❖·❖·❖·❖· In the final years of Richard J. Daley's two-decade reign as mayor of Chicago, his Democratic machine controlled all but two of the fifty seats on the city council. The exceptions were a dissident liberal Democrat and a lone Republican. In advance of a roll-call vote Daley had only to signal the alderman from the First Ward whether to go yea or nay and all the others would follow. The First Ward was Italian. There were Polish wards, black wards, Lithuanian wards, German wards, and, of course, Irish wards. They each supposedly represented individual constituencies, but their aldermen all voted the same way once Daley gave the signal.

One day in 1975, the lone Republican, a portly German named John Hoellen, proposed a totally innocuous measure. Daley gaveled it to the Rules Committee, which meant it would disappear without a trace. Uncharacteristically, the Republican protested and pleaded that just one of his ideas ought to get a fair hearing. Lightly tapping his gavel again, Daley cracked a tiny dismissive smile and mumbled, "Rules."

Like little boys lining up behind a bully, several aldermen mocked Hoellen by shouting the word "Rules" at him in sarcastic tones. Growing red-faced, the Republican persisted; finally, with an exasperated look up at Daley, high in his presiding officer's chair, he said something on the order of "You are like the czar"; then, gesturing to the other aldermen, he added, "And these are your Cossacks. You just order them to ride right over anyone who doesn't get down on his knees to obey you."

Daley's smile tightened but did not disappear. He hit the gavel again. "The czar was Russian," he said in his purposeful monotone; "I'm Irish."

As the mayor sat above them silent and serene, the machine aldermen of every ancestry cheered. Every one of them heard their identity affirmed in his quip, and their identity was a meal ticket.

"I'm Irish." It had taken a long time and a great deal of suffering for that statement to become a declaration of power and inclusion. About the time Daley was born in 1902, the son of immigrants from County Waterford, infant mortality was higher among the Irish in the United States than among the Irish in Ireland. Irish families on this side of the Atlantic still went hungry some sixty years after the potato famine had produced the first massive wave of Irish immigration. Alcoholism, work accidents, and poverty took such a huge toll on Irish immigrants that, statistically at least, it might have seemed that coming to America had been a bad bargain for them.

When Daley was born, many Americans still viewed the Irish as subverters of public morals, a class of people fit only for servitude, and dangerously beholden to the Pope. This marked a time when America was deeply in the grip of racial thinking. In the late nineteenth century, social Darwinism served as a creed for many political and business leaders. It held that some individuals and nations were naturally stronger than the rest. "Survival of the fittest" was considered not only a matter of scientific fact but also a desirable form of social organization. Adopted as an American ideal, social Darwinism extolled unbridled individualism as the key to a better world, and yet it imposed strict limitations on groups of people according to gender, race, and ethnicity.

Asians were excluded first. In the United States of the late nineteenth century, few disputed the idea that they were racially undesirable. As the fear of immigrants mounted, laws attempted to bar entry to the lame, the illiterate, and the political radicals. The next step was to create immigration policies based on a system of racial and ethnic preferences. In 1911, a congressional commission headed by Senator William P. Dillingham of Delaware produced a forty-two-volume report that explored the suitability of immigrants according to their "national origins." Applying pseudoscientific methods derived from the eugenics movement and social Darwinism, it concluded that immigrants from Eastern Europe and the Mediterranean were racially inferior to the Anglo-Saxons and Germans who had originally settled the United States. Mexicans, though deemed undesirable as citizens, were not blocked from entry by the commission after it concluded that they performed valuable work while in the United States and then invariably returned home. Having devised a system for categorizing humanity, the next step was to put the system into law.

"The day of unalloyed welcome to all peoples, the day of indiscriminate acceptance of all races has definitely ended." So said Senator Albert Johnson of Washington when Congress adopted the National Origins Act of 1924. The law constituted a triumph of racism, and it remained the law until 1965, when it was overturned by the reforming spirit of the civil rights era. In the meantime, however, the concept of national origins not only brought a halt to the great wave of European immigration, cutting the influx in half almost immediately, but also shaped the way the immigrants of that era formed their communities.

In Chicago and in other cities, European immigrants did not automatically give up their native cultures or languages. Faced with overt hostility, they actually highlighted and emphasized their differences as a defense mechanism. They came together in common cause and found strength in numbers. Poles stuck together. Italians stuck together. Joining with others who shared a foreign heritage of language and culture was a survival mechanism that became a means to gain power and to become American. So it was for Daley. After playing kingmaker in Democratic presidential politics, after brokering deals for the construction of skyscrapers and expressways, after becoming one of the most successful and powerful men in the United States, Richard J. Daley still knew exactly who he needed to be. "I'm Irish."

Hearing commentators today complain about how immigrants are "Balkanizing" America, it's useful to think back to those days in Chicago when being ethnic was not just good; it was essential. A working-class white was expected to apply ethnic allegiances in deciding where to live, shop, and worship, and, of course, in deciding how to vote. Self-satisfied and defiant, Daley proclaimed, "Chicago is the city that works," never mind that he ruled dictatorially over a city that was highly segregated, intensely corrupt, and always violent. Chicago "worked" because it was efficiently Balkanized.

Driving around Chicago, one didn't need to be a local to see how it broke up into enclaves. All you had to do was read the signs in the store windows. Even when a variety of German speakers or a few nationalities of Slavs shared a neighborhood, each group of European immigrants set up its own churches, temples, newspapers, taverns, and sports clubs that served as centers of social life and of associative activities. The English language and American ways worked fine out in the city beyond the neighborhood, but inside the enclave, immigrants used their native languages and old customs to good purpose. The neighborhoods served as incubators for the Europeans. They developed political power within these enclaves. By living together, they controlled precincts and wards because political power in a representative democracy flows from geography and concentrations of people. Each national group had its own grocers, storefront insurance agents, and Realtors, and this allowed the enclave to develop its own small nest egg of capital. Immigrants remained in the enclave and were offered few opportunities beyond it, but some of their children, and many of their grandchildren, worked their way to downtown and eventually gained access to banks and boardrooms.

It is easy now to call up nostalgic images of this America. The peasant-faced immigrants appear in sepia tones, and ragtime music carries the beat of quaint streets. But the old arrangements were far from benign, and there is no reason to miss them or want them back.

Daley's city worked because it was a complete ecosystem, in which every group had its niche. Chicago insisted on order but allowed for conflict among ethnic and racial groups so long as it was managed conflict. There were predators and prey. People were not merely divided into groups; different groups were assigned a worth. The most basic of these divisions were racial. African-Americans had enclaves, too, but they were slums rather than incubators. Blacks were denied essentials like adequate schools, and their political leaders received just enough city hall patronage to keep them loyal to the machine, but never enough to gain independent power. The system of hierarchy worked in more subtle ways with whites, but people received or were denied benefits according to their ethnic identity nonetheless. A Pole could aspire to a supervisory job in the sanitation or public works department but was unlikely to beat out an Irishman when it came to picking the chief of a fire company or the captain of a police district. If the German workers started getting too demanding in the factories, they might find several Czechs promoted to foreman. Whoever handed out the rewards—whether it was a patronage kingpin or an industrialist—found that the city worked better if all the ethnic groups constantly had to compete against one another instead of looking out for their common interests. The mechanisms that allowed for the incorporation of the European immigrants operated by control and exclusion.

No matter how well it worked, however, this city of enclaves and machine politics could not have served as a melting pot without powerful forces at work on the national level that encouraged the European ethnics to see themselves as Americans. The European immigrants could retain, even nurture, their group identities and still work their way into the mainstream, because eventually a powerful sense of American nationhood arched above the group loyalties and brought them all together. Even while ethnic differences continued to guide social and political thinking at the local level, a broader and more unifying vision developed at the national level.

In the middle years of this century, the United States came to accept itself as a nation of immigrants. However, this cosmopolitan view did not develop because the mainstream suddenly felt less threatened by the newcomers or because the purveyors of racist philosophies suddenly had doubts about dividing people up according to their national origins. Instead, the country's fear of immigrants was overtaken by other fears.

First came the Great Depression and the fear that society might simply disintegrate. Next came World War II, and the nation responded to a life-threatening foreign challenge with a crystal-clear sense of mission. Fear of foreigners gave way to the mythological World War II infantry platoon with its blond midwestern farm boy in the trenches along with the swarthy son of Brooklyn. The GIs came back to a bountiful economy that served all whites as a rising tide, and an entire generation of Americans remained bound together in common purpose during the early years of the Cold War. An Irish Catholic from Boston used tales of his World War II heroics to prove his patriotism, assuage fears of his religious loyalties, and become President. Promising to lead the nation to victory in the long twilight struggle against communism, John F. Kennedy symbolically completed the integration of the European ethnics. After Kennedy's inauguration, anything was possible for the offspring of immigrants. A man could say, "I'm Irish" and it was as good as saying, "I'm an American."

This expansive nationalism was forged in decades of crises, and it was more than just a sense of shared identity. An expansive sense of opportunity held all the component parts together. The new nationalism born in the middle of the twentieth century allowed for a society of many different groups only because each group that made up the white majority felt certain of getting a fair share, and it also required everyone to know their place and stay there. The bonds began to fray when borders broke down and enclaves deteriorated. In Chicago in the 1960s, expressway building and urban renewal broke up neighborhoods. Blacks pressed demands for open housing as their population outgrew the old ghettos. The federal government stepped in on behalf of the blacks. The white immigrants' children ran for the suburbs or the Sun Belt. The old industrial economy began to crumble. By the time Richard J. Daley died just before Christmas of 1976, the magic was fading.

The next summer, a cop shot a Puerto Rican youth in a crowded park on a hot Saturday afternoon. That night, a newly settled barrio burned on Chicago's West Side. Amid the flames, the stores still carried names that rang of the Danube rather than the Caribbean. When the smoke cleared and the curfews were lifted, the old men down at city hall wanted to know when all these Spanish-speaking types had taken over a neighborhood once known for its steam baths and beer gardens.

The cruel arrangements and the exhausted perspectives that served the European immigrants will not work today. The fires that burned through Los Angeles in 1992 should have eradicated any remaining doubts that Latino immigration can be managed by relying on racial thinking and by forcing competition among the least advantaged members of society. Latinos cannot hope to duplicate the experience of the European ethnics, and they should not want to. The old ways allowed for winners but required losers. Many Europeans suffered, certainly, yet blacks were the designated losers who always ended up at the bottom. They gave the system of managed competition among ethnics an essential elasticity. If a European group suffered a setback, it could always take solace in knowing that blacks were worse off. But blacks refused to keep playing the designated losers decades ago, and no other group, Latinos included, will take their place.

The old arrangements will not work with Latino immigrants because they defy easy categorization. Group identities lose their pragmatic value when they can no longer be used to assign group roles. The logic of a group label like "Hispanic" that is based on linguistic heritage breaks down when it has to accommodate people who speak only English, or only Spanish, and who demonstrate a wide range of bilingual abilities. Today some Latinos are moving up the economic totem pole, reaching for higher job niches as they become available, but at the same time others are sliding down it. Some Latinos are becoming Americanized and yet others remain thoroughly ethnic. Some identify themselves with the white majority, other as members of a minority group. Latino immigration does not render ethnic identity less significant, but it does make ethnic and racial differences far less manageable.

It is impossible now to look out across an American city as Mayor Daley once did, divide up the population into competing groups like so many animal species, pronounce that the fittest will survive, and then expect everyone to be bound together by a common national identity. Despite its successes, it was a crude and cruel system for managing ethnic relations. One has to be amazed that it could ever have functioned, and it is all the more remarkable that so many vestiges of it survive. The old belief that the single fittest, most desirable social identity can be defined and achieved lives on among those who would have Latinos simply surrender their identities to some mythic American norm, and it lives on equally among those who militantly resist assimilation and who believe these newcomers can triumph by standing up and proclaiming, "I'm Latino."

The old formulas that worked so well for Daley and his Irishmen were a product of history. The integration of the European ethnics into the American mainstream resulted from a unique combination of social, political, and economic circumstances. The melting pot was a historical event, not a model that can be adapted to a new time and place. The patterns of European immigration at the beginning of the century cannot be replicated by Latino immigration at the end of the century. The immigrants are different and the nation is different.

However, many of the problems are the same. Ethnic rivalries still need to be managed so they do not produce violence. Newcomers still need to define their place within the bounds of American society. And now, more than ever, the nation must confront the challenge of poverty that carries over from one generation to another. The outcome will determine whether the nation's cities work or whether they burn. The following chapters examine some of the events of the 1990s that have begun to shape the new arrangements that will govern urban America in the next century.

❖•❖•❖•❖•❖•❖•❖•❖•❖•❖•❖•❖•❖•❖•❖•

From the Burn to the Backlash

❖•❖•❖•❖•❖•❖•❖•❖•❖ **O**n a sultry summer morning not long after the Rodney King fires, the Church of the Nativity in the South Central district of Los Angeles offered a cool sanctuary. Three elderly black women occupied the front pew, each of them wearing a fine hat and a print dress. They made themselves seem unapproachable even though there was hardly anyone around. As time for the 11:30 Mass approached, several middle-aged couples and a few solitary women, all of them African-American, slipped into scattered pews, but even after the Mass got under way, the church remained cool, quiet, and almost empty.

Following the Mass, one of the women, Ida Coleman, recalled when Nativity was a stronghold for black Roman Catholics. African-Americans packed the pews twice every Sunday morning and a big choir of black voices belted out hosannas. Coleman bitterly regretted the passing of those days. Los Angeles had changed and South Central had started becoming Latino.

"I think the blacks in the church are responding like blacks all over the city," said Coleman, an elegantly dressed woman who spoke of the most sensitive subjects in a calm, steady voice. "They feel threatened by the emerging Hispanic majority. They feel swept aside and squeezed."

Because she was involved in the parish council, Coleman was among the first African-Americans to see that change, and because she is committed to the church, she is more committed than most to reaching a constructive accommodation between the two groups. Other blacks are alarmed and angry.

In South Central and in urban neighborhoods around the country, blacks and Latinos compete for jobs, housing, and government programs. The contest began gradually, almost invisibly, in the 1980s. Most white Americans were far removed from this competition and remained oblivious to it even after it manifested the potential to redefine the way the United States manages its ethnic differences. During the recession of the early 1990s and in the aftermath of the Rodney King fires of 1992, both blacks and Latinos realized they were involved in a battle to avoid being left in sole possession of last place in American society. It is a battle at the bottom that is certain to be bloody even though neither contestant can hope for more than a Pyrrhic victory. Blacks have history on their side. Latinos have the power of numbers.

"What bothers me is how they kind of show up and move in like they belonged here all along," said Coleman, who stood on the sidewalk in front of Nativity Church that Sunday morning in South Central. As she spoke, the human tide that so concerned her began to pass by.

The first to arrive were the musicians setting up for the next Mass, which would be celebrated in Spanish. They carried guitars, trumpets, and drums. Then came the families. Young couples poured by with two, three, or four children apiece. By the time the 1:00 p.m. Mass was about to begin, Latinos jammed the sidewalks as they waited to squeeze through the front doors. Street vendors arrived to sell ice cream, soft drinks, T-shirts, and toys. Part of the crowd never got inside and had to listen from the front steps.

Throughout the service, during the quiet parts and during the singing, there was a peculiar background noise in the church. It was an incessant high-pitched clamor made up of babies wailing, mamas hushing, and children running up and down the aisles. Even before the Gospel was read, the church began to feel warm and the air inside had filled with the damp smell of a big crowd in a tight space.

"One day there were just a few of them and that was not long ago, and now there are so many," said Coleman, who found the influx of Latino parishioners nothing less than bewildering. In South Central, as in the whole of L.A., blacks and Latinos live side by side but inhabit two different worlds. They are neighbors and yet strangers, and the differences go beyond language and culture. At Nativity Church, they are all Roman Catholics and yet the African-American and the Latino parishioners pass by one another every Sunday morning without speaking. They even have separate services on Christmas and Easter, and two separate parish councils.

"We have talked about getting together," said Coleman, a long-time leader of black parish organizations. "After all, we live in the same neighborhood, worship in the same church, face the same problems. But it just hasn't happened."

Coleman expressed a little irritation about how the newcomers had insisted on putting up a picture of the Virgin of Guadalupe on a side altar, but she didn't seem to be much interested in ascribing blame to one side or the other. Instead, it was the situation she talked about, an unnatural situation in which two populations, one native and one newcomer, are living side by side and competing with each other to escape poverty. In the ideal and healthy order of things, the group that is on the bottom works its way up to the mainstream of society and then is replaced by the new arrivals. That's the way it happened for many of the older European ethnics, and it worked that way for a good many African-Americans. But a large part of the black population got stuck at the bottom. Then the Latinos arrived and started jumping ahead of them.

South Central, with its clapboard bungalows, palm trees, and choice location, has served as a haven for laborers of modest means ever since World War II. First, it was a white neighborhood, and then black families moved in when the whites left during the great Caucasian exodus that followed the Watts riots of 1965. Coleman remembers how the parish flourished with the support of blacks who had opened small businesses, won access to civil service jobs, or had risen to become foremen in the big industrial plants. South Central became a magnet for blacks migrating from Texas,

Louisiana, and other parts of the South, and Nativity became a bastion for the Catholics among them.

Coleman remembers this as a time of big midnight Masses and a prosperous parish school. Then the good jobs started moving to the suburbs, and many of the most successful blacks began moving, too. As housing opened up in South Central, Latinos began moving in. In recent years, the neighborhood has been evenly divided among blacks and Latinos. Neighbors who followed the path to opportunity out beyond the city's core are recalled with a restrained envy by those who remained. Many good people left, Coleman says, not the slackers and troublemakers, but the blacks with good jobs and nice kids, and as each of them said good-bye, a Latino arrived.

South Central, like many inner-city neighborhoods, is now home mostly to blacks too old or too poor to move. Those who have remained, already resentful about being left behind by their own people, see themselves invaded by eager newcomers from abroad. It is roughly the same process that occurred in a number of occupations that had once been filled with African-Americans, like janitorial jobs in downtown office buildings. Both the neighborhoods and the jobs declined, and that deterioration opened up possibilities for Latino newcomers. Once this dynamic is established, it becomes increasingly difficult for the remaining blacks to find either desirable employment or housing in places that blacks had once dominated. They become resentful about having to compete against Latino newcomers, and the resentment only makes the competition more difficult for them, because it poisons their attitude with envy and defeatism.

Latinos and blacks relate to the economy in different ways, and as a result they have fundamentally different outlooks about themselves and about the nation. Many blacks experience the poverty of welfare and disintegrating families. Most Latinos experience the poverty of low-wage work and crowded households. Inner-city blacks represent the final victims in the demise of the old manufacturing economy, the hapless by-products. Latinos represent the cheap human capital that jump-started a new economy built on discounted and disposable workers. Poor blacks look at Los Angeles and see the end of opportunity. Poor Latinos see a beginning. When Latinos take over homes, schools, churches, and jobs, many blacks sense a confirmation of white racism. They think the newcomers are being advanced in order to keep African-Americans down. Many Latinos encourage this because they harbor racist perspectives of their own and sometimes view their new black neighbors as lazy, defeated, and corrupt. These two groups are now the chief competitors for jobs, neighborhoods, and political clout in American cities.

That competition became far more obstreperous after the 1992 Rodney King riots. Traditionally, race riots are followed by a period of repositioning as everyone jockeys to avoid blame and gain advantage in the rebuilding. The bigger the riot, the bigger the repositioning. In Los Angeles, blacks tried to claim their traditional place as the number-one minority, and for the first time Latinos directly challenged them. The bout that followed offered a preview of the main event still to come when these two groups go toe-to-toe all over the country.

During the good years of the 1980s, blacks and Latino immigrants gained ground in different segments of the economy, so they were in very different positions when they both had to scramble for survival in a declining economy. Many blacks enjoyed a kind of success during California's boom and that set them up for a hard fall in the bust. Most Latinos, especially immigrants, had found work in areas that provided modest but steadier employment.

Black workers had made gains in old-style industrial manufacturing, such as the auto industry, in the late sixties, after the first wave of white flight, and twenty years later they had a share of good blue-collar jobs about proportional to their numbers in the workforce. At the high end of the income scale, the number of blacks working as professionals, managers, and executives rose quickly in the 1980s, faster than among native-born Latinos and certainly faster than among Latino immigrants who generally didn't qualify. During that decade, median annual earnings for black men increased by nearly 14 percent, which was greater than the 10 percent increase for white men.

The most notable employment success for Los Angeles blacks, however, came in areas where politics and policy directly affected hiring. They made major inroads with government jobs, especially at the local level. In weapons and aerospace manufacturing, they benefited from federal equal-opportunity and affirmative-action programs. While blacks made up less than 10 percent of the Los Angeles workforce in 1990, they held nearly 20 percent of the jobs in the public sector, in the aircraft industry, and in the production of missiles and space vehicles. All of these areas—white-collar work, classic blue-collar, government employment, defense, and aerospace—were among the hardest hit during the downturn of the early 1990s, and they never fully recovered.

During the good times of the 1980s, Latino immigrants poured into sectors of the job market where the number of jobs was rapidly expanding, the low-wage service and retail employment, as well as low-skilled manufacturing and construction trades. In many cases, the newcomers took jobs in fields, such as the garment industry, that had long been dominated by Latinos and that then expanded enormously. In other cases, Latino immigrants settled into suburban areas where new jobs had been created but where there was no black workforce.

Even when Latinos took over a niche once occupied by blacks, such as cleaning offices downtown, it was the result of structural change in the job market rather than direct competition between the two groups. Blacks and Latino immigrants could operate on substantially different job tracks without bumping into one another as long as the California dream was alive. But when unemployment rates hit 10 percent and the state lost nearly 600,000 jobs during the 1990–1993 recession, blacks and Latinos began to notice one another in new ways and their perceptions of one another became more critical. It didn't matter that larger forces were at work. In an era of narrowing horizons and growing insecurity, blame attaches to whoever is nearby.

One morning not long after the 1992 riots, Danny Bakewell, a black real estate developer and community activist, passed by one of the many burned-out buildings in South Central, his home turf. A demolition crew was hard at work, which should have made him happy. Instead, it enraged him and set him to planning protest actions because none of the workers were black. They were all Latinos.

"When I saw that," Bakewell recalls, "I realized that people had not really gotten the main lessons of the uprising—that blacks had been excluded."

In what became a much publicized confrontation, Bakewell

pulled one Latino worker off a tractor. According to news accounts of the event, Bakewell addressed the Latino workers mockingly in pidgin Spanish. *"Vámanos a la casa, No trabajo. Ándale."* ("Let's go home. No work. Get going.")

As president of the Brotherhood Crusade Black United Front, Bakewell had spent years promoting the growth of black-owned small businesses in South Central, with the goal of generating entry-level employment for black youths. He hoped to create a self-sustaining, job-generating business network—just the kind of enclave economy found in many immigrant neighborhoods. "Blacks have been brainwashed into thinking that they are not supposed to work, that they are never supposed to own their own business, and when people start thinking that, and start thinking there is nothing they can do to change things, then a community starts going down-hill fast," he said.

When South Central burned, Bakewell felt sadly vindicated. When he concluded that black workers had been left out of the cleanup and rebuilding, he became angry. A large, dramatic man originally from New Orleans, Bakewell rounded up some of his followers and organized demonstrations at a half-dozen cleanup sites, forcing white contractors to hire African-Americans or risk a tussle deep in a ghetto that still smelled of smoke. "If blacks don't work, nobody works" was the demonstrators' slogan.

Bakewell's protests drew support from many of the most prominent black leaders in California. When he led black contractors on a noisy walkout of a meeting with top insurance industry executives, Congresswoman Maxine Waters, the Democrat whose district covers the core of black L.A., defended Bakewell's campaign to shut down cleanup sites. Pointing at the executives who had hoped to win peace in South Central, Waters echoed Bakewell's slogan, saying emotionally, "If we can't work, you can't work."

Months later, Bakewell sat in his large office full of oversized modern furniture, all glass and metal. The walls were laden with testimonial plaques and photographs. Outside on the streets of South Central, the burned-out lots had been cleared, but nothing new was under construction. Bakewell acknowledged that picking on the Latinos was "a little unfortunate," but he insisted that the protests had realistically portrayed the kind of tensions developing between blacks and Latinos in South Central.

"All the people on the street know that Pedro, Paco, and Maria are working and they are not. That's where the tension is—jobs. Say we've been living together harmoniously, but all of a sudden you are working and I am not, and I ask you, 'Where do you work?' And you can't tell me because you don't speak English. Well, I'm left there thinking, Wait a minute. He can't even speak to me and he's got a job downtown."

Friction between blacks and whites has developed most often over schools and neighborhoods. These battles have been fought face-to-face, and it has always been clear that blacks were attempting to enter previously white domains, usually with the law on their side. Now the workplace has become a major battleground for poor blacks and Latino immigrants. Rather than a conflict between minority plaintiffs and the controlling majority, it is a competition between two groups struggling for economic position and there is nothing clear or direct about the competition. Even when they do not compete for the same jobs, blacks and Latinos see one another as rivals. In what is fast becoming an extremely dangerous form of ethnic competition, blacks and Latinos are not so much fighting one another as vying for the favor of whites who lord above the fray.

The Brotherhood Crusade, for example, had a training and placement program that aimed at getting young blacks hired in hotel catering operations, a job category that had come to be dominated by Latino immigrants over the past decade. Bakewell eventually concluded that blacks, especially young blacks, lost that competition not because they lacked the necessary skills, which are minimal, but because of their attitudes toward that form of work.

"You can make a decent living at these jobs, but no one down here wants to do them because they say they are tired of serving white folks," says Bakewell. "That's an issue we have to deal with all the time. What we can do is try to convince our people that these are service jobs, not servant jobs, but there is an attitude to overcome."

For newly arrived Latino immigrants, working long hours for low wages is rewarding, because even the minimum wage in the United States is many times what they can earn back home. For African-Americans, such labor is an old and painfully familiar experience. They have fresh memories of their fathers and grandfathers, who faced discrimination at every turn and were forced to take jobs far below their qualifications.

Bakewell readily acknowledges cultural differences between blacks and Latinos. "These are very aggressive people," he said of Latino immigrants. "They are motivated to work because they come from places of great poverty. They come and they want to blend into the workplace." But having said that, Bakewell blamed white employers for the Latinos' success, especially in service occupations.

"It is the system that is rejecting one and accepting the other. The one accepted is much more passive and there is this assumption with the employer that there will be less trouble, that more work will get done [with Latino employees]." He concluded, "The fact of the matter is that white people feel more comfortable around Hispanics than they do around blacks."

When unemployed blacks see jobs going to Latinos who are newly arrived, who speak little English, and who may not even be in the country legally, they naturally feel resentful. That resentment grows into something much uglier and more powerful when blacks suspect that Latinos are being used as instruments of white racism and that the newcomers are getting jobs not because they are better workers but because they are not blacks.

In Los Angeles, the blacks' complaints were aimed at immigrant Latinos, but the response came from Mexican-Americans, including the same politicians who had distanced themselves from the immigrants during the riots. After Bakewell launched his demonstrations through the streets of South Central demanding jobs for blacks, virtually the whole of the city's elected Latino leadership sent a letter to Mayor Tom Bradley, himself an African-American, protesting what they called "an effort to exclude the Latino community." While stating that their letter was "not intended to diminish the travesties which have been perpetrated against the African-American community," the Latino officeholders insisted that "the changing demographics of the inner city must be recognized." The city's Mexican-American political leaders would grant the blacks of Los Angeles the moral standing that comes with historical grievances, but they countered with census data showing a Hispanic population growing fast due to immigrants. The Latinos were not claiming to be more victimized than blacks, just more numerous, and they were determined to get their fair share. In addition, some Latino leaders began articulating a new approach to their place in the labor market. They tried to reposition themselves on the racial spectrum so that they ended up closer to the side of privilege and whiteness than to the side of color and minority-group status. It was something you could begin to hear clearly in Los Angeles. You could hear it in the way Latinos talked about jobs.

Ricardo González likes doing hotel banquet work because it doesn't require speaking much English. After a dozen years in Los Angeles, he's been able to acquire legal status through the 1986 amnesty, but he has never had time to learn much of the language because he has been too busy working.

A tall, thin man with a short, neatly cropped beard, González said, "To get the waiter jobs, you must leave the house clean; that means take a bath and arrive fifteen minutes before they tell you to. Then you must work quickly and you have to adopt the spirit of the event. When you see people all dressed very elegantly for a wedding or a graduation or to hear speeches, you should think to yourself, How would I like the waiters to behave if it was my wedding day? For years, I could get this kind of work every night of the week. Just about everyone serving was a Latino, because Latinos know how to be serious about work."

As for blacks, he said, "I only ever saw a few older blacks on the job—never the young ones, who always act like they are important even though they have never done a day's work. They could not do these jobs if their mothers' lives depended on it. For those jerks who stand on the street corners all day, it would be easier to fly to the moon than to serve a table properly."

Even as he worked food service at night, González pursued a separate, parallel career by day. He began as a janitor at a small metal-stamping factory that made brake parts. Eventually, he got a job on the production line, and after six years he became a shift foreman. Even after he was promoted, he kept working the banquet circuit.

González worked at the factory for nearly a decade, and during that time he never saw a single African-American employed there. "I don't think they could have worked in that factory because we spoke only Spanish there. Besides, everyone knows that the first thing a person of color asks about is the money, and they would not have been happy to find out that almost everyone there earned just the minimum wage."

Most whites would be wary of expressing such opinions in public for fear of being labeled racists. Many Latinos have no such inhibitions. They have never been part of America's ugly racial saga. They have never been in a position to oppress anyone because of their skin color, and besides, they are officially considered a minority, the same as blacks. Instead of trying to paper over conflicts, Latino leaders and spokesmen often bring a harsher and more combative argument to discussions of social justice. Post-riot Los Angeles offered an opening for that kind of discussion, and many others are likely to develop in the future.

"Take a close look at South Central and you'll see that the blacks there have a three-to-one advantage over Latinos in high school degrees, but Latinos have an almost two-to-one advantage in labor-force participation rates," said Fernando Oaxaca, a prominent Mexican-American businessman. "What does that tell you? Is it that there is so much more discrimination against blacks than against immigrant Latinos? Does it mean that blacks can't get jobs even when they have a much better education? I don't think so. The difference is that we have a work ethic."

Oaxaca is a political conservative and marketing executive who has worked for Republican candidates, but his ideas about the differences between blacks and Latinos are not a function of ideology.

Starting from a very different political perspective, David Lizarraga, of TELACU, the big East L.A. community development organization, arrived at a similar conclusion. His ideological roots lay in the Chicano movement, which allied itself with, and in some ways patterned itself on, the black civil rights movement. Nonetheless, he, too, drew sharp distinctions between Latinos and blacks.

"The issue for Latinos is not employment, but underemployment. Too many of our people have minimum-wage jobs, so they work but still live in poverty," Lizarraga said. "That is a very different problem from the one in the black community, where a lot of people are poor because they are not part of the labor force anymore."

Following the 1992 riot, Oaxaca helped organize a group called the Latino Coalition for a New Los Angeles, which tried to ensure that Latinos got their fair share of rebuilding money. In part, the group was meant as a counterforce to Danny Bakewell's highly publicized campaign. But instead of demanding help out of a sense of entitlement, Oaxaca argued that Latinos were a better investment than blacks.

"There is a self-confidence coupled with a pride that is at a high level in our society and it is constantly being replenished by people who show great determination in leaving home and getting here. These are people who still believe in themselves and still believe in the American dream. They deserve help in building a new L.A. because they will take the ball and run with it. They have not thrown up their arms and said, 'Feed me,' the way so many blacks have."

To back up such assertions, Oaxaca's group produced books and slide shows full of graphs and charts that illustrated such things as the rapid growth of Latino-owned businesses in Los Angeles, the Latinos' high rates of labor-force participation, and the many households in the barrio with two, three, or even four wage earners. And in almost every case, blacks did not fare as well. These numbers were not portrayed as a great economic success story but, rather, as a demonstration of potential.

In effect, Lizarraga, Oaxaca, and many others like them were arguing that Latinos, especially immigrant Latinos, bring a superior character to their economic endeavors. That character, which values work and self-reliance, makes up for a lack of assets, such as language and education. According to this argument, Latinos deserve help because they will make good use of it.

When Latino leaders proclaim that their people are worthy by virtue of character, culture, and motivation, they imply that blacks lack those qualities. Sometimes implicitly, sometimes explicitly, Latinos endorse one of the most basic tenets of American racism by suggesting that blacks remain at the low end of society as a result of their own failings and inferiority, rather than as a result of circumstances. In the framework of the contemporary social-policy debate, the Latinos hit the hottest button of them all by suggesting that they have values, red-blooded American values, such as an appreciation of family and hard work, again implying a superiority to African-Americans.

In effect, the Latinos propose a bargain not unlike the one that brought the European ethnics into the American mainstream. The Latinos offer hard work in exchange for acceptance. In the context of postriot Los Angeles, it was work in exchange for economic-development money and political clout. But it was not quite a clean bargain.

Almost all of the posturing was done by native Latinos, Mexican-

Americans, who relied on civil rights laws to obtain everything from school funds to favorable legislative districts. They eagerly played minority-group politics when it behooved them, and then they shifted to arguments of economic worthiness when that sounded better. It was native Latinos who were talking the talk of hard work and demographic growth, but it was immigrant Latinos, so conveniently ignored in other contexts, who were sweating through twelve-hour workdays and raising huge families. And it was the native Latinos, especially the political leadership, who played old-fashioned ethnic one-upmanship when it came to dealing with blacks.

A sense of demographic triumphalism spread among California Latinos in the 1990s. It was an arrogant assumption that population growth alone could assure their ascendancy. The extent to which this attitude could be self-defeating is illustrated in a minor but revealing episode involving a man whom some Hispanics like to call "our Danny Bakewell." That man is Xavier Hermosillo, a prominent businessman from the southern Los Angeles suburb of San Pedro who had made unsuccessful attempts at elected office and who had an instinct for controversy. Like Bakewell, he did not bother trying to be conciliatory in the aftermath of the riots, when most public figures were treating Los Angeles like a tinderbox.

When Bakewell shut down work sites because Latinos had jobs and blacks did not, Hermosillo said, in an article published on the opinion page of the *Los Angeles Times,* "These actions and attitudes are racist, pure and simple, regardless of the color of the skin of the perpetrator," and he accused Bakewell of employing "the same barbaric tactics employed by members of the Ku Klux Klan." In addition, Hermosillo was reported to have referred to African-Americans as "*mayates.*" That Spanish word for a small black insect can serve as a racial epithet as ugly as the word *nigger.* He never disavowed the statement. Hermosillo not only took on the blacks but he also preached the message of Latino ascendancy.

Hermosillo was head of a small Latino organization that called itself NEWS for America. In a television interview a year after the disturbances, he delivered the news that California would soon belong to Latinos again, just as it did when it was part of Mexico. "We're taking it back, house by house, block by block . . . ," he said. "We have a little saying here: 'If you're in California, speak Spanish.' . . . People ought to wake up and smell the refried beans: Not only are we the majority of the population, but we are not going anywhere."

Hermosillo did not have strong links to any of the major Latino political factions in Los Angeles, which tended to be liberal and Democratic. He had backed Richard Riordan, a Republican businessman, in his successful 1993 campaign for mayor, while most of the big-name Latino leaders had put their bets on other candidates.

When Riordan nominated Hermosillo to the Board of Fire Commissioners, a civilian panel that oversees the fire department, blacks raised a political tempest that lasted through most of the summer of 1993. The top Latinos at city hall made it clear they would rather see the Hermosillo nomination disappear. They had other priorities. They were taking on the blacks over big issues of money and representation and did not need to waste ammunition over someone they didn't much like in the first place. Some Latinos worried that Riordan was playing a classic game of divide-and-conquer ethnic politics in the best traditions of the Daley political machine. Nonetheless, once the blacks publicly opposed Hermosillo, the Latinos refused to back down, even after it was certain that the nomination would not be successful.

Assemblyman Richard Polanco, among the most powerful Latino politicians in California, came to the hearing to make the case for Hermosillo. He started his speech on an unusual note. "Let me begin my presentation, members," he said to the council, "by prefacing my comments by saying I do not always agree with Xavier Hermosillo. In fact, I often disagree with him because of ideology, because of political differences, philosophically . . . but this issue is much larger than Xavier Hermosillo."

None of the major Latino leaders who spoke up for Hermosillo actually said anything very nice about him. But a fellow Latino, even a dislikable one, had to be protected against what was perceived as black encroachment. The Latinos were going up against the city's African-American community to back a candidate who made no pretense to racial sensitivity. Moreover, the Latino leaders were allying themselves with a white mayor who had been opposed by most black leaders and who had capitalized on that opposition to curry favor among white voters. More than ever before, it was clear that Latinos could assert themselves as a group without relying on a broader civil rights ideology that aligned them with blacks.

But at the same time, the Latinos were not rushing to identify themselves with the white mainstream. Instead, they insisted on defining themselves as an excluded party in their own right, with their own complaints and their own agenda. Forced into competition with blacks for a share of the ever-diminishing public sector, Latinos discovered the value of coming together to fight as an ethnic group.

"In many ways Mr. Hermosillo's frustrations are a reflection of the concerns of many Latinos in Los Angeles that our voices are excluded from decision making, concerns that decisions are made without consultations, concerns that we are often scapegoats for the ills of our city," Polanco said to the Los Angeles City Council.

During the debate that followed, harsh words came quickly from both sides, as if they had gone unspoken for a long time. Now they were irretrievably on the record, videotaped, transcribed.

One African-American speaker after another accused Hermosillo of racism and suggested that the black ghettos could blow up again if he was confirmed. Black community activist Patricia Moore asked, "We wonder how Los Angeles can be taken house by house?" and then, angrily providing her own answer, she said, "It can only be taken if African-Americans are made to feel worthless."

Instead of cowering when they were accused of racism, the Latino politicians gave it back to the blacks, refusing to accept the previously undebatable notion that blacks held some privileged moral ground.

The Latinos knew from the start of the debate that they were going to lose and lose badly because the white Democrats would join the blacks on the council in opposing Hermosillo. But it did not matter to the Latinos. This time, perhaps for the first time so explicitly, they were not going to pay deference to the blacks. Hermosillo's nomination was defeated on a nine-to-five vote. The three Latino council members voted for him. The three blacks voted against him.

Latino politicians were not the least bit apologetic about the way things turned out. Instead, they warned everyone else, especially the blacks, that more of the same lay ahead. Councilman Mike Hernández said, "There is this struggle going on in the city which I

am sorry to say we have to go through, but I think the quicker we
identify it and go through it, the less painful it will be. It is the
struggle between ethnic groups and their ability to have access to
resources to deal with the problems of their communities."

When Riordan came up for reelection in April 1997, Latinos
backed him heavily while blacks went overwhelmingly for his
opponent, Tom Hayden. That marked the first time that the two
groups had split decisively in a mayoral race, and the outcome signaled the final demise of the old coalition of Latinos, blacks, and
white liberals that had run Los Angeles for decades and that had
sustained the careers of former mayor Tom Bradley and many other
black politicians. Riordan's reelection was portentous for another
reason as well. Latinos had voted in higher numbers than blacks for
the first time in a Los Angeles election, and every demographic pro-
jection showed that the size of the Latino electorate was surging. A
Latino political leader toasted Riordan's victory by saying, "He is
the last non-Latino mayor of Los Angeles."

The Latino migration to the United States reached a turning point when Mexican-Americans in Los Angeles challenged
blacks to a political duel so openly and confidently. The riot aftermath signaled a fundamental change in the urban landscape, a
change that began in Los Angeles but that will eventually sweep
every major city. Even as newcomers continue to arrive at historic
levels, barrio residents have begun to make demands. But neither
Los Angeles nor any other city has mechanisms in place to deal with
the Latinos' new assertiveness and the kinds of claims they now
press. More challenging still, no city has mechanisms in place to
deal with the competition between blacks and Latinos that is now
beginning to take shape.

Blacks and Latinos share minority-group status and extensive
poverty. Both groups live in cities being abandoned by whites and
Asians. They suffer together from the same bankrupt social and
education policies, and many of both groups find themselves on
the losing end of economic restructuring. Given all that common
ground, Latinos and African-Americans might become allies in the
future, but what they share most now is scarcity, and so they will
become rivals first. Soon to be two big groups of roughly the same
size, blacks and Latinos are competing on a practical level for jobs,

neighborhoods, and political power in the nation's cities. Neither side can win a conclusive victory, yet their struggle will have consequences for all Americans because, on a broader level, blacks' and Latinos are now vying to define how the nation views poverty and racial differences as it moves out of the civil rights era.

What poor urban blacks fear and what has already produced violence is the possibility that immigrants might simply step over them and acquire the social acceptance that comes with middle-class economic status and membership in the white majority. Such anxieties fueled the black anger directed at Latinos and at Korean shopkeepers during the Rodney King riots, and the same feelings have fueled many of the disturbances in Miami over the past twenty years. As a practical matter, blacks fear that the advancement of immigrants means more blacks will be left behind permanently. When newcomers achieve an upward mobility that eludes, or has been denied, African-Americans, the result is a potent sense of social and psychological subjugation. This is already happening with many groups of immigrants such as those from China, Japan, Korea, the Philippines, India, Pakistan, the former Soviet Union, Eastern Europe, the English-speaking Caribbean, and Africa, who have quickly achieved notable economic success here.

The contrasts are much more complex when it comes to Latinos because they are more numerous and because they compete with blacks on several different fronts. Some Latinos threaten to step ahead of blacks. Others mix it up with them at the bottom of the economic ladder. And all of them together challenge the blacks' preeminence as a minority group.

In California and Texas, a growing number of Mexican-Americans, including some third- and fourth-generation immigrants, are moving into white-collar jobs, middle-class suburbs, and a significant number of political offices. They compete with the black professional and political class even more directly than Asian immigrants because they do so as a native minority group that has a substantial interest in the public sector. It is already clear that even a small middle class of native-born Latinos will fight for protection against current discrimination and the effects of historical prejudice, just as middle-class blacks pressed the civil rights struggle decades ago. In principle, the rights of Latinos and those of blacks do not conflict. It is conceivable that blacks and Latinos might have become political partners during an era of expanding recognition of minority rights and increasing public spending, but that is much less likely when affirmative action is under siege and government payrolls are dwindling. In the coming years, blacks and Latinos will be obliged to fight one another—and in California, both will compete with Asians, as well—for whatever remains of these traditional vehicles for minority-group advancement.

Even if the circumstances were more conducive to collaboration, blacks and Latinos are not natural allies. They do not share the same language, culture, or historical experience. Latino immigrants often bring their own forms of racism to the United States and this stains their attitudes toward blacks. Meanwhile, blacks sometimes succumb to the temptations of xenophobia. The influx of poor Latino immigrants greatly exacerbates these differences. Poor Latinos challenge black communities for control of urban spaces, and they take the jobs that are the natural first stepping-stones up and out of ghetto poverty. They colonize whole factories and vast job niches in ways that effectively lock blacks out of these workplaces. The Latinos are pursuing their own self-interest, but they are also often assisting in the exclusion of blacks in ways that at times makes them accomplices to white racism. Not surprisingly, some African-American leaders consider poor immigrant Latinos a formidable barrier to black aspirations.

Frank L. Morris, former dean of graduate studies at Baltimore's Morgan State University, is the most prominent African-American spokesman for that view. He argues that blacks risk the same subjugation they suffered at the beginning of the century when white industrialists chose European immigrants to man their new factories rather than native-born blacks, who were relegated to a residual labor force. "The result has been similar—a more difficult and depressed labor market for African-Americans in the last part of the twentieth century," he says. Issuing "a wake-up call" to black leaders and intellectuals who have been sympathetic to increased immigration, Morris concludes, "Anything, including immigration, which increases the supply of labor in America works against the interests of African-Americans." Such arguments have proved persuasive. A majority of black voters backed Proposition 187, for example. The NAACP and many blacks in Congress offered vital backing to pro-immigration advocates during the policy battles of the 1980s, but they are now mostly neutral on the issue, if not quietly supportive of restrictive measures. Barbara Jordan took up the cause shortly before she died in 1996, proposing through her Commission on Immigration Reform that the number of low-skilled legal immigrants needed to be reduced drastically in order to remedy the economic plight of poor Americans.

Although it is true that large-scale Latino immigration heightens competition for jobs at the bottom of the wage scale, it is not necessarily true that reducing or eliminating the Latino influx will make it easier for poor blacks to find work. The global economy has created vast exceptions to the law of supply and demand in labor markets. If Mexican immigrants are not available to do industrial assembly work at the minimum wage in Chicago, that does not mean the jobs will automatically go to blacks, particularly if they ask for something like decent pay. The jobs might well go to Mexico. And if blacks now on welfare took over all the jobs in the Los Angeles garment industry, they might end up poorer for it.

Looking to the European influx for an understanding of how immigration affects blacks today is nearly useless. When the Europeans arrived, the great majority of African-Americans still lived in the South. Industrialization did not bypass blacks; it skipped over the entire region they inhabited. Today, blacks and Latino immigrants share the same economic sphere. Looking to the beginning of the century also glosses over the fact that a large black population did eventually migrate north to enter the industrial labor force, and the legacy of that migration shapes the economic condition of African-Americans today. The black underclass developed among the descendants of those migrants decades before the surge in Latino immigration. Since then, black poverty has developed a disastrous permanence in high-immigration cities like Los Angeles and in cities that have not experienced a huge Latino influx, such as Detroit, Memphis, and Philadelphia. Finally, black urban poverty has persisted even during a period of rapid expansion in the low-wage sector of the economy.

The competition today between poor blacks and poor Latino immigrants is not a contest between sets of new entrants to the labor market, each fresh at the starting line, ready for a fair race. Instead, it is a struggle between those already left behind by society and newcomers who arrive with many disadvantages. White preju-

dices, structural changes in the American economy, and black attitudes have already deeply conditioned the position of poor blacks
in the urban workforce. Latino immigration adds a powerful new
demographic factor to the equation, but it does not diminish the
significance of existing forces. Thus there is little to be gained by
wondering whether Latino immigration is a cause of persistent
black poverty. But it is very important to ask whether Latino immigration will help or hurt efforts to remedy the condition of poor
urban blacks.

During the contentious welfare-reform debates of the 104th Congress (1995–1996), President Clinton and Republican legislators
agreed on two points from start to finish: Welfare recipients should
make the transition to work and the money to pay for "workfare"
would come from reducing benefits to legal immigrants. Both these
features found their way into the auspiciously named Personal
Responsibility and Work Opportunity Reconciliation Act of 1996,
which set in motion a new and unpredictable form of competition
between poor blacks and Latinos. President Clinton promised to
move 2 million people from welfare to work during his second term
in the White House. To facilitate the transition, he proposed training programs for the new workers and tax incentives for their
prospective employers. But many of those former benefits recipients
will be moving into the same crowded segment of the labor market
where poor Latino immigrants are already concentrated. That
means the public sector welfare bureaucracy, as well as the array of
community organizations and social service agencies that have blossomed around it, will be locked in deadly competition with immigrant networks for access to the worst jobs in the United States. No
one can win that kind of battle, except perhaps the employers, who
will enjoy a glut of prospective workers and government payoffs,
too.

In the immediate future, welfare reform will fuel demands for
greater restrictions on Latino immigration, especially the illegal
flow. The welfare-to-work plan proposes a marriage between two
parties—employers and welfare recipients. In the past, they did not
end up together for reasons that certainly include deeply ingrained
attitudes on both sides. Now leaders from the entire political spectrum are committed to making this marriage work and the circumstances at the onset are propitious. The plan is going into effect in

the ripe years of an economic expansion. That means demand for workers is still high, even though most of the best prospects have already been hired, unemployment is low, and welfare rolls are declining. All that bodes well for the start of welfare reform. But when the economy slows or goes into a downturn, finding work for welfare recipients will become much more difficult. Calls for tighter restrictions on immigration inevitably gather force during economic hard times because newcomers are viewed as extraneous competitors for a shrinking supply of employment. Welfare reform ensures that the anti-immigrant animus will be particularly bitter in the next recession, because poor Americans will be portrayed as the most prominent victims and because a very important experiment in social policy will be in play. No one should be surprised if under such circumstances poor Latinos and poor blacks see one another not merely as rivals but as foes.

Although the game will evolve, this competition seems certain to become an enduring aspect of American urban life. Not very many poor immigrant Latinos will easily step across the barriers of race and class that divide American society. They will remain a large, clearly identifiable nonwhite group sharing the margins with poor urban African-Americans. Instead of a single multiethnic underclass, the United States will have at least two large populations of poor people, each with distinct characteristics, and each will make its own distinct claims on the society as a whole. When Latinos grow angry at the way they are treated, they usually present contemporary grievances and they make demands based on their numbers or the work they do. Poor urban blacks make a powerful case for special consideration on the basis of long-term neglect and victimization, as well as the immediate experience of prejudice. It seems improbable that blacks will welcome immigrant Latinos into a grand coalition based on a common experience of discrimination. And it is equally unlikely that immigrant Latinos will seek out blacks as allies in a fight for their rights as workers.

The multiform interaction between blacks and Latinos offers a hint of the transformative power and the potential for discord that Latinos bring to American society as they seek to define their place here. After thirty years of steady immigration, this is a moment of flux and contradiction. In Texas, black and Latino civil-rights lawyers are fighting together in the courts to salvage affirmative-action admissions policies at the University of Texas Law School even as black and Latino activists are fighting each other for control of the school boards in Dallas and other major cities. That sort of paradox derives from the complex segmentation of American life in this era of immigration, and it should be welcomed as an opportunity for coalition-building—and for conflict—among members of different ethnic and racial groups based on specific interests rather than broader notions of group identity. But before that opportunity can be realized, and before Latinos can fully assert new roles for themselves in American society, the question of illegal immigration must be resolved. Whether they are dealing with blacks or whites or with the public and private institutions that make up this nation's civic society, Latinos will always be handicapped so long as a large proportion of the Latino population is made up of people who have no legal standing in the United States. To understand how this issue can be addressed and how a successful effort to stem illegal immigration can change the way Latinos see themselves, you have to start in El Paso—which is the oldest port of entry.

◆•◆•◆•◆•◆•◆•◆•◆•◆•◆•◆•◆•◆•◆•◆•◆•◆•

Closing the Doors

◆•◆•◆•◆•◆•◆•◆•◆• **O**ut where the Chihuahuan Desert meets the Rocky Mountains, a spring flows year-round at the end of a little box canyon. A cave on the canyon wall is decorated with a six-thousand-year-old pictograph painted in white on the dark gray rock. It depicts a squiggly arrow rising up through an eight-pointed sunburst. The arrow marks a well-traveled highway up into North America. The pictograph is an ancient signpost in an oasis that has been a way station for a long time. Corn seed and knowledge of how to plant it traveled this route. Aztec traders, Anasazi cliff dwellers, Comanche raiders, and a variety of bandits and smugglers followed the path of the arrow. In this century, millions of Mexicans have come north to the United States along this path, and now interstate highways follow the same route that was painted on the canyon wall so long ago.

The Spaniards called it El Camino Real (the Royal Road), and they

marked its beginning at a place they named El Paso del Río del Norte
(the Pass of the River of the North). That is where the Rio Grande
makes a big turn as it goes around the base of a mountain now
known as Comanche Peak. Downriver, the water runs east for eight
hundred miles to the sea, now marking the boundary between the
United States and Mexico. On the other side of the mountain, the Rio
Grande cuts north up through New Mexico, past Santa Fe and Taos,
all the way to the river's sources in the Rocky Mountain snowcaps.
The upper valley is the north-south highway immortalized on the
wall of the oasis cave. It offers passable terrain and water that a traveler will not find elsewhere for hundreds of miles in any direction.
Looking up from the south, the people who named El Paso saw the
upper valley of the Rio Grande as the gateway to the mountains,
high plateaus, and prairies that lie at the heart of the continent.
Eventually, it became the gateway to the Pacific Coast as well,
because the riverbed at the base of Comanche Peak is the easiest all-
weather route across the Continental Divide in the United States and
today it is crowded with train tracks and the asphalt of Interstate 10.

Human beings began traveling freely through El Paso almost as
soon as they arrived on this part of the continent. The border was a
very late and very small addition to the topography and did little to
inhibit those who wished to cross the river. From the early years of
this century, the railroads, the garment factories, and the growers
came to El Paso when they needed to recruit able hands. Deep into
Mexico, this became known as the place to launch a sojourn in the
United States. Along the river itself, El Paso and its sister city, Ciu-
dad Juárez, grew up like two halves of a whole, with people going
back and forth all the time. Whether they crossed the river legally
or illegally, nobody much seemed to care.

Thousands of years of history changed on September 19, 1993,
the day that the United States first tried to close its doors to Latino
immigration. Acting on secret orders code-named Operation Blockade, some four hundred Border Patrol agents set out from their sector headquarters on the edge of Fort Bliss a little before midnight.
Moving quietly in the dark, they set up new observation posts
along a twenty-mile stretch of the Rio Grande. In their dark olive
drab uniforms and Smokey the Bear hats, they stood within eye-
sight of one another, forming a human chain atop the concrete levees on the U.S. side of the river.

At first light, the crowds started gathering on the opposite bank. The *lancheros* (boatmen) who normally smuggled people across the dank water stood by their rafts in shock. The commuters who usually snuck across the railroad bridges every workday to jobs in Texas wondered what they would tell their bosses. That Monday morning, children going to school, mothers going shopping, and the rest of the ten thousand people who normally crossed the river illegally every day could look to the other side and see that there was no way to get north without getting caught.

Within a few weeks, something unexpected became apparent along the river: The illegal traffic practically stopped. The blockade appeared to be working. The U.S. government had never made a serious effort to control the southern border, and many policy makers, scholars, and advocates had long contended that large-scale illegal human traffic was the unavoidable, almost natural result of a border between a rich country and a poor one. So the blockade acquired the true value of a miracle because it suggested that something seemingly impossible in the physical world could be made to happen given sufficient will and faith.

Within a few months, something else equally startling became apparent. No serious protests developed against the operation on either side of the river. In Mexico, priests decried the injustice of denying poor people the right to a livelihood. Some protesters burned Uncle Sam in effigy, a traditional ritual, and some minor political figures engaged in the obligatory anti-American posturing. But otherwise, the blockade hardly produced a response. On the U.S. side, a few activists, mostly Anglo liberals, made predictable but little-noticed protests. Somewhat louder complaints came from businessmen and government officials who had a stake in the approval of NAFTA, the free trade agreement with Mexico under debate in Congress then. To mollify them, the Border Patrol agreed to change the name from Operation Blockade to the less bellicose Operation Hold the Line. But most significantly, no substantial opposition to the blockade developed among the Latinos who make up 70 percent of El Paso's population. This, too, like the apparent success of the blockade, was so unexpected that it seemed unnatural.

"The scariest part of the whole thing, what really scares you in terms of the results we've been getting, is that moment when you realize that we can actually take hold of the border and control it," said the man who launched the blockade, Silvestre Reyes, the chief of the El Paso Border Patrol. "All these years we've been told and sometimes we've said to ourselves, 'The border is the border. People are going to cross illegally and there's only so much you can do about it.' But now you look out there and you have to say, 'Wait a minute. We've got real options, we can do serious stuff.' Then you ask, 'So what do we really want to do?' and someone way past my pay grade is going to have to figure that out before too long."

Illegal immigration has always produced more rhetoric than strategy, and it was no different after the El Paso blockade. Reyes had acted alone, with no backing from Washington, but Republicans and Democrats alike rushed to proclaim his operation a triumph and then revel in it. The Rio Grande levees quickly became a place of pilgrimage for many kinds of believers. California's governor, Pete Wilson, brought his reelection campaign to El Paso to have his picture taken with Reyes, and Barbara Jordan arrived with her Commission on Immigration Reform to hold hearings. President Clinton summoned Reyes to the White House to deliver a briefing on the operation's success.

Reyes was the first to point out that the blockade could not be readily duplicated, but no one paid much attention to him. He repeatedly reminded his admirers that he had handled a unique stretch of border. At El Paso, the Rio Grande is contained within big concrete levees that run pretty straight, that are readily accessible by car, and that are easily illuminated at night. A single Border Patrol agent can stand on top of the levee on the U.S. side and keep watch over hundreds of yards of river. Anyone dropping down the Mexican side is easily spotted before he even sets a toe in the water. Elsewhere, it can take hours just to find the border. For hundreds of miles at a stretch, the border runs across desert canyon and mesas that are largely uninhabited and totally inhospitable. Reyes warned that maintaining a continuous watch over these areas would require a massive military-style operation and still might never prove totally effective. But the appeal of a quick fix proved irresistible in Washington. At the height of the 1994 election campaign—well after it had become apparent that illegal immigration was the hot issue in California—the Clinton administration gave California its own version of the El Paso blockade: Operation Gatekeeper on the border south of San Diego. Then the same tactics were applied in

Arizona with Operation Safeguard, centered at Nogales. At the height of the 1994 campaign, Attorney General Janet Reno traveled to Los Angeles and promised Californians "a secure border that is fully defensible against illegal immigrants," and on the eve of the vote her Justice Department promised that within eighteen months the entire border from El Paso to San Diego would be closed to the interlopers. Not to be outdone, Congress voted a series of budget increases for the Border Patrol between 1994 and 1996 that would double its size by the end of the decade. All of these efforts and the promises that accompanied them departed from a false reading of what can be accomplished with border controls. Instead of a quick fix, the El Paso blockade pointed to a long, drawn-out struggle to gain control of the border, albeit, perhaps, a struggle that can be won.

A few months after the Border Patrol agents mounted the levees, it became clear that the El Paso blockade was halting only certain types of illegal crossings. The casual travelers who came over for the day to work, shop, or stand on a downtown corner begging for spare change were substantially cut off. Their absence was strikingly visible on the city streets. However, records for hospital admission, school attendance, and employment indicated that most illegals who were living in El Paso remained there. They were just not going back and forth to Mexico as much as before. Reyes soon concluded that when illegals really needed to make a trip north, they circumvented the blockade by crossing through the desert west of town, which was a longer, more perilous route, usually requiring the services of alien smugglers—*coyotes,* as they are known in Spanish—who can provide vehicles, shelters, and knowledge of the terrain.

These findings were confirmed in the 1997 report by the Binational Study on Migration, the massive research project by a team of twenty U.S. and Mexican experts that was commissioned by the governments of the two nations. "The United States border enforcement strategies begun in 1994 are affecting migration patterns, but not preventing unauthorized entry," the report concluded. As one of the most important new patterns, the report cited the greater and more successful use of smugglers by illegal travelers. "The increased use of coyotes generally, and particularly at the border, helps to explain why most migrants attempting unauthorized entry succeed despite significantly more U.S. Border Patrol agents and technology on the border," said the report.

The other important new pattern reported by the study involved the frequency of travel. A series of surveys conducted in Mexico by the Binational Study after the border crackdown found a sharp decrease in the number of Mexicans who went north illegally for temporary sojourns. It is possible, the study reported, that "the increasing difficulty of crossing the border has led temporary migrants to reduce the number of times they move back and forth between the two countries." Less frequent travel will change the fundamental character of illegal immigration in the United States. For decades, Border Patrol apprehension counts dropped in November and December because most of the illegal traffic was heading south as people went home for the holidays. The numbers shot up again in January and February as illegals came back north. The border was insignificant, and it was easy for Mexican illegal aliens to spend relatively short periods of time in the United States earning dollars while maintaining their primary residence in Mexico. The casual attitude toward the border is less viable now that the trip across the border has become something more worrisome and expensive, only to be undertaken when absolutely necessary. This does not mean, however, that fewer people are coming to the United States illegally, but rather, as the Binational Study concluded, that "many people are deciding to establish residence in the United States or to prolong their stay there."

If effective border controls can be sustained for a decade or more, these changes in the patterns of illegal immigration could become permanent and begin to have important consequences. For example, the quick trip home would no longer serve as a safety valve during times of unemployment in the United States, and illegal aliens would need to be more certain about their prospects here before departing. In addition, one can speculate that some of the psychic reward of coming north would diminish if illegals could not readily check on how their remittances were being spent or bask in the gratitude of those who receive money earned in the United States. If the only illegal route into the United States from Mexico involved a long, dangerous and expensive trip through the desert, then wives and children would make the trip once or not at all. All of these developments would reduce the transience of barrio life, and eventually the size of the illegal population would shrink somewhat. Those finite goals are worth the effort, and the alternatives to determined enforcement effort—a return to the chaos that marked the border in the late 1980s—is unthinkable.

Taking control of the border will require more than the massive manpower increases that Congress has authorized so eagerly in recent years. The Border Patrol is perennially overwhelmed and dispirited, and while it undoubtedly needs resources, a hiring binge is not the answer. An important and well-documented difficulty is a pay scale so low that it produces constant defections to the U.S. Marshals Service, U.S. Customs, and even state police agencies. This is the legacy of the many decades that the Border Patrol spent as the poor cousin of federal law-enforcement agencies performing under-valued duties far from view. Rather than simply growing, the Border Patrol needs a long-term program of institutional development that emphasizes improved leadership, better pay, and a higher-quality force. Pushing the illegal traffic from the border towns out into the desert was the easy part and relied primarily on manpower. The rest will require the more sophisticated use of monitoring technology, the deployment of a highly mobile force, and the development of novel interdiction strategies.

Along with an improved law-enforcement agency, there needs to be heightened punishment. For millions of illegal immigrants, getting caught at the border has meant a few hours of inconvenience at worst. After minimal processing, they are returned to the Mexican side of the border and are free to try another crossing immediately. As a result of this revolving door, illegal crossers have come to assume that it might take three or four attempts to get through and that there is no harm in trying as many times as it takes. Instead of rushing to expand the force, Congress should spend some of the money allocated to the Border Patrol to building detention facilities at major crossing points. To the extent possible, people caught crossing should be held for a day or two. This would accomplish two goals. First, getting caught would result at least in disrupted travel plans. Second, and more important, it would give the Border Patrol a fighting chance to identify at least some of the people being apprehended. Since 1994, the Justice Department has been making a determined effort to deport illegal aliens who are serving jail terms for crimes they committed after entering the United States. However, many just return. Border Patrol agents report that they can easily spot the convicts in a group of apprehended aliens—they

have iron-hard muscles from all the time in prison weight rooms and
a lot of tattoos—but rarely have the chance to make a full identification because there is nowhere to hold them. Similarly, Border Patrol
agents can often pick out the professional smuggler in a group of
aliens but have to turn him loose with the rest. An adequate period
of detention would give the agents a chance to get a positive identification of the suspected deportees and smugglers and bring charges
against them as appropriate. This effort would be aided with the
further development of a computerized fingerprint identification
system that the Border Patrol has been testing in the San Diego area
since 1995. Like all such high-tech systems, it will cost far more,
take longer to create, and deliver less than expected, but if a suspect
can be detained for a day or two, the system should eventually have
the potential to allow expedient identifications of the notorious illegals, such as known criminals and smugglers who have been caught
repeatedly.

In addition, Washington should authorize spending for lengthier
detentions and full-scale repatriations—transporting people back
to their homes in the interior of Mexico or Central America—at
least on a limited basis designed to generate the maximum psychological impact in the communities that send out large numbers of
illegal travelers. Women with children or extended families or
teenage men might be targeted for a perfectly benign and legal
regime of detention and repatriation, which would prove enormously costly to the illegal immigrants and their relatives. The
objective would be to disrupt the migratory channels that facilitate
illegal immigration.

As border controls are tightened, the United States must also act
to combat alien smuggling from Mexico. As the difficulty of illicit
crossing increases and smuggling fees go up, larger and more
sophisticated criminal organizations will get into the business of
bringing people into the United States. As noted previously, Congress and the Clinton administration have neglected the investigative sections of the Immigration and Naturalization Service that
combat alien smuggling. While the Border Patrol grew by 2,435
slots between 1992 and 1997, only 680 positions were added to
the investigative force. Faced with considerable criticism of its neg-
ligible efforts on alien smuggling, the Clinton administration
announced in June 1997 that it was launching Operation Global
Reach, but behind this bombastic moniker there was nothing more

than the reassignment of forty-five officers. Adding three hundred or four hundred agents dedicated to a full-scale assault on the criminals who traffic in migrants would be a more significant first step, according to frustrated career officials at the INS. Next, the government could fully follow through on a 1995 interagency report to the White House that pointed out how much more could be done to get help from foreign governments in this effort. For example, the report noted that in much of Latin America alien smuggling is not a crime or, where it is a crime, the existing laws are rarely enforced. While the State Department claims to have increased liaison with governments that allow their territory to serve as safe-transit zones for alien smugglers, much more aggressive steps are justified given that the interagency report estimated that some 300,000 to 400,000 would-be illegal aliens pass through Central America and Mexico every year intending to enter the United States. Cooperation and effective action on alien smuggling should be preconditions for U.S. aid and trade privileges in much the same way that Washington now demands cooperation in antidrug efforts and certifies foreign governments on a yearly basis. Even modest efforts by the Mexican police to thwart smugglers—stopping them from digging holes under the border fence, for example—could make a big difference, according to Border Patrol agents who bemoan the safe haven enjoyed by coyotes on the other side of the line. Mexico, however, has been reluctant to do much that actually interferes with illegal crossings, and it still formally endorses the right of free migration. This is an anachronism left over from an era of revolutionary hostility toward the United States and needs to be rescinded if Mexico expects the United States to continue acting as the chief guarantor of its economic security.

More effective border controls and antismuggling efforts are certain to increase the number of persons entering the country legally with temporary visas who then become illegal aliens by overstaying their allotted time. Simultaneous steps will have to be taken on this front starting with boosting the manpower and technical resources available at U.S. consulates overseas where visas are issued and at the ports of entry where visitors are checked on arrival. One strategic improvement would be an effective system to keep track of when visitors enter and leave the country. Currently, the United States has no way of knowing for sure whether someone overstays a visa. The immigration card some visitors fill out on arrival is slowly and somewhat haphazardly matched with the portion of the card that is supposed to be turned in on departure. Worse yet, there is no method of keeping track of Canadians and Mexicans who enter the country across land borders as visitors, and they account for 90 percent of the 220 million visits the United States registers each year. Bar-code technology or other forms of data management certainly could remedy this situation. If Wal-Mart can account for its inventory, the United States certainly can track its visitors. On entry, every visa or border-crossing card would be swiped over a scanning device, and the same would happen on the way out. A fairly elementary data processing system could produce timely lists of people with expired visas who had yet to leave the country. It would not be necessary to hunt down and deport overstayers. Rather, the goal would be to pose a credible threat that an alien who overstayed would face serious hurdles if he or she ever tried to return to the United States or sought legal immigrant status under any guise. This would apply also to citizens of the several European nations who are not required to obtain a visa to visit the United States but who are only allowed to remain here for specific periods of time. On arrival, an immigration officer would put a bar code on their passports that would then be used to track their movements.

The 1996 immigration law took a step in this direction by imposing a five-year ban on overstayers who are caught and deported, but the deportation system is time-consuming and costly for both the alien and the U.S. government. Again, there is no need to track down and apprehend overstayers. With an effective system to identify them, punishment could be carried out primarily by consular officers who have enough discretion to deny visas or border-crossing cards to a suspected overstayer who fails to explain the lapse. Once a reliable system for tracking visitors is in place, the United States can experiment with punishments. If a five-year ban does not prove a sufficient deterrent, it could be made a lifetime ban. If denying visa privileges to overstayers does not have enough impact, then the ban could be extended to all members of an overstayer's immediate family. An immigrant family that sponsored an overstayer for a visitor's visa would permanently lose all rights of sponsorship. Finally, identifying people who have abused visas would permit enforcement measures against those in immigrant communities who facilitate this kind of illegal activity. A travel agent in a place like

Washington Heights could be held to account if clients routinely disappeared after arriving on tourist visas that he or she had arranged. With an increasing population of Latinos who are legal immigrants or naturalized citizens, overstaying is certain to increase in the absence of credible deterrence. The application of collective punishment to entire families is justified by the simple fact that the family is the primary vehicle for legal immigration. If blood relations are the sponsors for privileges extended by the United States—the grant of permanent residence and eventual citizenship—then those relations can also be an avenue of retribution against those who abuse the immigration system.

If these measures seem punitive, that is the intent, but it is important to note that they are aimed beyond the borders at people who are still trying to enter the country illegally or are just considering it. One of the primary lessons of the El Paso blockade is that a show of force can be used effectively to deter illegal aliens. Like any law-enforcement measures, these efforts can only succeed by modifying expectations in a way that changes behavior. That takes time, but it can be done. Ten years of consistent enforcement could increase the difficulties and the risk of apprehension to the point that would-be illegals would examine many other alternatives before they attempted an unauthorized trip north. If one mishap at the border or at an airport can ruin an entire family's prospect of ever living in the United States, the migrant channels might begin to police themselves. Such measures have never been tried before. But the United States should be willing to be relentless and even severe, because if the strategy succeeds, it may spare the nation from having to carry out harsh law-enforcement measures at home, in the barrios, against people who have been living here for many years and who are likely to have children who are U.S. citizens. The goal must be to aim enforcement outward before undertaking options that affect civil liberties and the quality of life within the country. But even as it tries to reduce the supply of illegal immigrants, the United States must try to decrease the demand, and that will have to happen on American soil.

Just as no one had ever really tried to control the border before the El Paso blockade, no one has ever tried to control sweatshop labor in recent years. In this area, too, a patient, well-funded law-enforcement effort targeted at the worst offenders is certain to have results in the long term. There is no need to aim at an absolute prohibition on the employment of illegal aliens or at a crusade to uplift the entire low-wage sector of the economy. Federal and state governments could accomplish a great deal by attacking workplaces that are characterized by the violation of many laws. These are the kinds of places where employers fail to pay Social Security, to withhold income taxes, to pay overtime, or to observe safety and environmental regulations. These are also the kinds of businesses that often employ illegal aliens. The United States need not tolerate such corrosive servitude, and it is no mystery to anyone—starting with labor and safety officials—where it can be found. That kind of employment occurs in enterprises that are labor-intensive, low-skilled, and produce slim profit margins. This includes landscaping, fruit and vegetable growing, poultry and meat processing, restaurants, garment and some other forms of light manufacturing. Such businesses should be considered the workplace equivalent of high crime areas. As with the strategies that have brought crime down in New York and many other big cities, enough law-enforcement resources need to be concentrated in these high-intensity areas to implement zero-tolerance policies that would be unnecessary and unrealistic if applied to the community at large. This kind of enforcement campaign needs to be accompanied by punishment of a sort that has never been imposed on the employers of illegal aliens. Jail time does not seem an overly harsh penalty for business owners or managers who pay illegal wages and risk the safety of their workers and the health of consumers in the name of profit. Abuses that do not rise to the level of odious criminality could be deterred by the simple forfeiture of assets used in an enterprise that relied on illegal labor. A drywall contractor, for example, might reconsider hiring illegals from a sidewalk labor market if he knew he risked being pulled over by INS investigators who would seize his truck and all his equipment on the spot. Imagine the headlines that would be generated if the U.S. attorney in San Francisco used forfeiture statutes to seize all the land owned by a name-brand California vineyard after it was caught knowingly and persistently using illegal migrant labor instead of merely issuing it a toothless citation, as is so often the case now.

Because they have never been tried before, it is hard to measure the potential impact of highly publicized and deliberately harsh enforcement actions. But both aggressive border enforcement and a concerted attack on sweatshop employment must be undertaken first and given time to have an impact before more intrusive options are considered. Chief among those are various proposals for computer registries and identity systems that would be used to check the eligibility of every person seeking a job and potentially every person seeking a government benefit. Every employer and potentially every hospital administrator and welfare caseworker would have access to a government database that would ostensibly determine if an applicant is an illegal immigrant. The technical ability to accomplish this reliably is years, perhaps decades, away, and that should allow for a broader debate over the purposes of such a registry, because such technology is not likely to be an instrument of immigration policy alone. Once a registry or an identification system is developed, employers and government officials may want it to determine whether a person has a criminal record, is behind on child-support payments, has a history of drunk driving, is a known sex offender, has a record for financial frauds, or simply has a bad credit rating. Clearly, the handling of such information needs to be considered in the context of the potential conflicts between technology and civil liberties, with illegal immigration as a side issue. That debate can develop over time if less intrusive strategies to attack illegal immigration are tried first.

Finally, the most decisive action against illegal immigration needs to be taken within the barrios themselves. Latinos who have decided to make a permanent home in the United States—legal immigrants, new citizens, and the native born—must accept the fact that a large-scale illegal influx is harmful to their long-term interests. Immigrant neighborhoods are necessarily fluid places, but barrios are all the more unsettled when a large part of the community lives under a question mark. The presence of so many people with a limited ability to participate in American civic life dilutes all efforts to build institutions that contend with the problems Latinos encounter here. More broadly, illegal immigration provokes suspicion, even animosity, in many Americans that often carries over to other Latinos, especially the poor. The barrios urgently need public investments in education, health care, law enforcement, and other services to ensure that the second generation finds a fruitful place in American society, but rightly or not, the specter of illegality impedes those investments. Latinos must face up to this if only as a matter of practical politics. Finally, the truth of all immigration is that new arrivals have the greatest impact on those who are close by. Twenty years of research points to the indubitable conclusion that a steady flow of new immigrant workers brings down wages for those who labor in the same job niches and almost no one else. Similarly, overcrowding and the overburdening of public services is experienced most acutely by those who share the same neighborhoods. The first generation tends to accept these ill effects, especially when the other newcomers are siblings, cousins, and close friends. But this dynamic is now changing. The new arrivals are more distant relations to the Latinos who are already established here, and soon it will be their American-born children, just out of school, who are competing with illegal aliens for jobs and housing.

The El Paso blockade suggested several unexpected possibilities, including the possibility that Latino communities might take a new perspective on efforts to control the illegal influx. The blockade was an enforcement effort pointed outward. Any success would result from the deterrent effect it exercised on the south side of the river. Trying to discourage people from ever crossing implies a very different strategy than trying to make life difficult for illegal aliens who are already in the United States. Putting men in uniform on the border is nothing like sending them into barrios or workplaces to conduct roundups. As time passed and the complex, somewhat contradictory effects of the blockade became apparent, the response in the very old, well-established barrios on the north side of the river showed that Latinos will accept even stringent efforts to combat illegal immigration as long as the combat does not take place in their neighborhoods.

Reyes, a short, dark-skinned man known as "Silver" within the fraternal ranks of the Border Patrol, grew up in Canutillo, Texas, a small town a few miles from El Paso. Sitting close to the border, it was home to chile pickers, railroad hands, and other poor, working-class people. Like almost everyone else in Canutillo, Reyes had close relatives who had come over from Mexico and other relatives who still lived there.

For most of Reyes's life, people went back and forth across the border constantly. Fruits, vegetables, restaurant meals, and medicines were often cheaper on the Mexican side, while manufactured goods were more equitably priced on the U.S. side. Every day, many thousands traversed the border legally—70 million crossings a year. Others went illegally. Whether the trip was just for lunch with some cousins, or a season of work, or for a lifetime, the crossing itself was often the least significant part of the voyage.

El Paso's isolation, its intimate proximity to Mexico, and the large proportion of its population made up of Latinos with immigrant roots has set it apart from the rest of the United States. But its casual acceptance of large-scale illegal migration from Mexico has been typical of the nation as a whole through most of the twentieth century. The difference has been only one of scale. El Paso also mirrored the rest of the nation in the way it suddenly reached a psychological saturation point in the mid-1990s.

When Reyes, then forty-eight years old, returned to El Paso in the summer of 1993 as the top Border Patrol agent, he was disheartened by what he found. "It was chaotic. We were not doing our job very well and what we were doing was generating a lot of complaints. This is my hometown, and I guess I figure I understand the place a little, and I was really worried when I got back here that we were headed for a situation that would be totally unmanageable."

The Border Patrol was apprehending as many as fifteen hundred illegal crossers a day, to no effect. Agents tried to catch illegals right after they had crossed, amid warehouses, railroad yards, and adobe slums just behind the border on the U.S. side. The ones they apprehended would be taken to one of the bridges and ordered to cross back to the Mexican side. Most just tried again and got through eventually. The game was played in crowded neighborhoods populated by Latinos, some U.S. citizens, some legal immigrants, and some illegals. Almost all were of Mexican descent and most were poor. As a whole, they were indistinguishable in their dress and in their physical characteristics and often in the language they spoke. Trying to pick out the illegals who instantly melted into this population inevitably led to mistakes, and the Border Patrol's mistakes—stopping U.S. citizens or legal immigrants and demanding that they prove their immigration status—inevitably led to complaints and lawsuits.

One such suit produced a preliminary injunction in December 1992 from U.S. District Court judge Lucius D. Bunton III, who sternly concluded that the Border Patrol routinely "insulted, humiliated, degraded and embarrassed" people who were illegally "stopped, questioned, detained, frisked, arrested, searched, or physically or verbally abused" only because they appeared to be of Hispanic descent. That constituted a blatant violation of their civil rights, and the judge reinforced rules limiting the circumstances under which the Border Patrol could accost people on the streets of El Paso. Soon afterward, the El Paso City Council voted seven to one to create a special commission to resolve complaints against the Border Patrol, in much the same way civilian review boards handle complaints against police departments. The Border Patrol could see trouble coming, and Reyes was sent to fix it. He went home with a mission to mend relations between the Border Patrol and the Latino community he had grown up in. That is what he had in mind when he launched the border blockade, rather than any grand new plans for national immigration policy.

"One of my major concerns in planning the operation," Reyes said, "was to get my agents out of the neighborhoods, out of those situations that had created so much tension with the community. My idea was that if we put our people right up on the line, they weren't going to have contact with anybody but aliens, and that turned out to be right."

Reyes set out to take care of a very local problem in a very isolated desert city. He acted with an intuitive understanding of his hometown and how it had changed over the years, and in particular how attitudes toward the new large-scale immigration had been changing. He sensed correctly that El Paso's Latinos would not object to a crackdown on illegal immigration as long as they did not get caught up in it.

A mariachi band sounded gay tunes, and the buffet tables offered chicken wings, Swedish meatballs, Vienna sausages, and blush wine. Red-white-and-blue bunting and balloons and lots of American flags decorated the El Paso County Democratic party headquarters. In business suits and bright floral-print dresses, carrying attaché cases and cell phones, many of the most influential Mexican-Americans in town had come together for some fundraising and speeches.

There were lawyers, real estate agents, several local-level elected officials, accountants, and many others who had achieved enough success in their own lives that they could make phone calls and write checks for political candidates. They were English-speaking and, by any tangible measure, full participants in the American mainstream, and yet most of those gathered for the political reception had parents or grandparents who had come from Mexico and they themselves had spent time going back and forth across the river. Four months after Reyes took over the river levees, these Latinos were still having a hard time deciding what they thought about the blockade.

In the past, they had spoken out against most efforts to combat illegal immigration. Like Mexican-American leaders nationally, they had complained that the 1986 law prohibiting the employment of illegals caused discrimination against anyone who looked Latino. They had mocked Jimmy Carter's attempt to put up fences along the Rio Grande, deriding it as the "Tortilla Curtain." In El Paso especially, Latinos alleged that it was a hostile act toward a friendly neighbor and too nearly resembled the kind of thing the Soviets would do. Most recently, they had provided the money and legal expertise to fight the federal lawsuit against the Border Patrol's sweeps of El Paso river wards, and they had won. Middle- and upper-class Latinos backed the legal battle and the political fight for the city council commission, even though the Border Patrol was not charging through their neighborhoods and hassling their sons. All that was happening down by the river in poor neighborhoods, but ethnic solidarity prevailed over class differences. The blockade did not provoke the same kind of outrage. No one had called meetings to coordinate protests or to design a legal strategy to fight it and yet no one in the Mexican-American leadership wanted to come out and say they approved of it.

"Everyone here has divided feelings about this," said Alicia Chacón, a grassroots Latino leader who had fought Anglo politicians and become a powerful county commissioner. "We all treasure our connections to Mexico. We all want El Paso and Juárez to prosper together. We all believe that most of the undocumented are basically good, hardworking people. But we also know there are problems, that there are crime problems and there are cost problems, like when an undocumented person ends up in a hospital and the county has to pay for it."

Those two sets of feelings had been easier to keep in balance in the past, when El Paso and Juárez were roughly the same size and the illegal border traffic seemed like a local, readily managed situation. But both the legal and the illegal traffic across the river had grown rapidly for a decade. This had produced big profits for merchants catering to Mexicans, but the streets were not just crowded with shoppers. They were also filled with panhandlers and petty thieves who had crossed the river, as well. During the late 1980s, serious crime, including muggings and burglaries, increased rapidly in El Paso's river barrios and the number of car thefts all over town skyrocketed, with the vehicles regularly showing up for sale on the other side of the river. Juárez had grown to be three times as big as El Paso. Sometimes the Texas city literally choked on the air pollution generated across the border. Untreated sewage from Juárez constantly threatened the Rio Grande.

"The border was a pretty casual thing when I was growing up," Reyes recalled, "because Juárez and El Paso were basically small towns out in the middle of nowhere. But all that's gone now. What we've got now is New York on the Rio Grande."

Mexican-Americans and immigrants of Mexican descent comprise about two-thirds of the nation's Latino population and most of them live within a few hundred miles of the border. Many no longer see Mexico through the benign lenses of ancestry and heritage because they also deal with Mexico as a contemporary and sometimes troublesome phenomenon in their lives.

The border blockade did not solve all the problems between El Paso and Juárez, but it had an immediate effect where it counted most. The panhandlers and street people in downtown El Paso virtually disappeared and the crime rate dropped substantially. Moreover, the number of Mexican-Americans complaining about being stopped and questioned by the Border Patrol fell to zero. In the ultimate borderland, the idea of a hard, cold barrier between the United States and Mexico became not only acceptable but desirable.

"People can see positive effects as a result of what has happened along the river, even if they really are not very comfortable with the idea of endorsing the Border Patrol," said Chacón. Asked why the response to the blockade was so muted compared to the all-out campaign for the lawsuit, the civilian review board, and other measures aimed at Border Patrol abuses, she said, "That was different. That involved the everyday lives of U.S. citizens and legal immigrants who could not drive through certain parts of town without getting pulled over by the Border Patrol because they supposedly looked like foreigners. That became a civil rights issue for every Latino in El Paso. As for the blockade, people have very mixed feelings, but one thing is for sure: This is not an ethnic issue."

Chacón and El Paso's other Latino leaders could have mounted protests against the blockade, but they did not. If ten or twenty thousand marchers had descended on El Paso Border Patrol headquarters a week after the blockade, if even a few hundred protesters had surrounded Border Patrol vehicles on the Rio Grande levees, the history of U.S. immigration policies would be very different. Given Reyes's intentions, it is clear he would not have pressed ahead if the blockade had produced serious protests by El Paso's Latinos. But he read the mood of his hometown correctly and those things did not happen. Having achieved enough stature to make their voices count, the Mexican-Americans of El Paso decided it was not in their interest to speak up loudly on behalf of illegal immigrants. Most Latinos might not like tough enforcement actions on the border, but they were not prepared to go into the streets and get ugly over it. The middle class, the businessmen, and the political leaders were hardly willing to grumble in public, and a good many of them actually liked the idea of the blockade. In 1996, three years after he led his Border Patrol agents to the levees, Reyes was elected to Congress and became the first Latino to repersent El Paso in Washington. As Chacón said, the blockade was not an ethnic issue.

Just as many Mexican-Americans began to view Mexico differently when it became a larger and more difficult presence in their lives, many also viewed immigration differently, especially illegal immigration. Previously, mere proposals to combat illegal immigration provoked effective political mobilizations by Latinos nationwide. With considerable success, they had argued that if legal immigrants and citizens stood the chance of being harmed, then crackdowns on illegal immigration were a civil rights issue. But when the blockade did not produce a reaction in El Paso, it proved that something is changing. That change was also apparent when the East L.A. Latino political leaders distanced themselves from the immigrant Latinos who took to the streets during the Rodney King riots. And the change could be seen when the Miami Cubans hardly bothered to protest the new policies that forcibly returned rafters to Cuba.

At the very least, what happened in El Paso, Los Angeles, and

Miami indicates that illegal immigration will not become the subject of civil rights protests by native Latinos as long as they do not get swept up in the enforcement efforts. Aside from the practical consequences, this suggests a fundamental change in America's ethnic landscape that could have an impact for decades to come.

In El Paso, all Latinos, regardless of immigration status, share very strong bonds of custom, language, and kinship, but after the blockade, a clear break in those ties became apparent. A substantial number of native-born or otherwise well-established Latinos seem less and less willing to spend their political capital freely in defense of Latinos who are illegal aliens. That kind of fissure, if it becomes widespread and permanent, will call into question Latinos' ability to function as a minority group. If they split along lines of economic class and immigration status, then some Latinos will be on their way to joining the white majority by jumping over the color lines in American society, while others will remain permanently nonwhite.

It is important to remember that the logic of the civil rights era assumes that ethnic or racial identity substantially coincides with political identity. Breaking with that logic and excluding illegal aliens from the Latino political identity means breaking with the strategy of minority-group mobilization that has characterized Latino civic life in the Untied States since the Mexicans of south Texas first began battling discrimination in the 1950s.

The blockade and the reaction it provoked, however, proved to be an aberration. It was the work of a hometown boy taking care of a hometown problem. Whatever potential it offers as a model for a Latino response to illegal immigration remains unrealized. Soon, a cruel new logic of exclusion made its appearance all across the country.

◆•◆•◆•◆•◆•◆•◆•◆•◆•◆•◆•◆•◆•◆•◆•◆•◆•

After the Earthquake

◆•◆•◆•◆•◆•◆•◆•◆•◆• Out in the San Fernando Valley, a few exits on the Golden State Freeway from sunny downtown Burbank, in the town of Pacoima, there are thirteen currency exchanges along a half-mile stretch of Van Nuys Boulevard. Little more than storefronts with waiting areas and well-fortified cashiers' windows, these businesses send money earned in California down an electronic channel to hometowns all over Mexico and Central America. The rest of Pacoima's main commercial strip is a hodgepodge of little eateries, storefront churches, and a few retail establishments.

Pacoima is a suburban village where Latinos have come to work suburban jobs. They live in bungalows that once promised prosperity under the sun to migrants who traveled from the dust bowl to the orange groves. Their lifestyles are anything but suburban, however. Out in this part of the San Fernando Valley, many front lawns have been paved over and transformed into parking lots that at night are filled with big American sedans and little Japanese pickups. The bungalows have only two or three bedrooms, but there are four or five vehicles parked out front.

Homes owned and occupied by a married couple and their children are more the exception than the rule. Instead, the bungalows have become communal residences sheltering extended families or members of a few families. Houses are bought with down payments from several people and they are occupied by constantly changing combinations of friends and relatives, depending on the time of year, the availability of work, and other factors that govern the comings and goings. Regardless of who lives in the primary residence, the garages in Pacoima have become dormitories. The big doors are sealed shut and human-size doors have been cut into them. Outfitted with a sink and a toilet, the garages become rental properties where four or five of the most recently arrived immigrants pay for a place on the cement floor. Sometimes whole families make a home out of a garage.

Pacoima is the kind of barrio that is home to many kinds of Latinos. Some neatly tended homes belong to working-class Mexican-Americans who have been there for decades, and their garages are full of Central American illegals who have just come up for a few months' work. Any home is likely to include some people who are U.S. citizens, some who are legal immigrants, some who are illegal aliens, and many whose immigration status is in a state of bureaucratic flux. Pacoima is a Latino melting pot. Like most Spanish-speaking places, it is crowded and busy. It is a place in the suburbs where people have come to work and sleep. Latinos have made it a new kind of American place.

Pacoima changed on January 17, 1994, when it was hit by an earthquake that had its epicenter less than a dozen miles away, near Northridge. Some of the same changes would eventually hit every barrio in the United States.

After the earthquake, broken bricks from tumbled-down chimneys and garden walls filled many of the front-yard parking lots, and tarps covered ruined roofs. On Van Nuys, many of the neon signs seemed out of kilter, windows were cracked, and streetlights hung limp, as if their necks were broken. Businesses had moved out on the sidewalk beneath sheets of blue plastic. Little chunks of concrete lay scattered all over, and everything seemed just a bit broken or in need of repair. After the earthquake, Pacoima looked very much like Tijuana or any other big Third World city, and as far as the United States government was concerned, Pacoima did constitute a place that was set apart from the rest of the nation.

When Congress voted $8.6 billion in emergency relief funds for the Los Angeles area, it added a proviso instructing federal agencies to begin denying illegal aliens any long-term assistance. Usually, disaster victims are allowed to vouch for their identities, even for their home ownership, because they have often lost all their papers. But to implement the congressional ban, which went into effect ninety days after the earthquake, the Federal Emergency Management Agency was ordered to demand documents proving immigration status; INS officers were dispatched to do spot checks on applicants and arrest any illegals found among them.

The new screening procedures marked the first time the U.S. government ever scrutinized the immigration status of applicants for humanitarian aid in a natural disaster. It also marked the first time the federal government used the threat of fines and imprisonment to deter illegal aliens from participating in a benefits program.

Even though the illegals living in the garages and bungalows of Pacoima were as needy as other victims of this natural disaster, Congress defined them as unworthy on the basis of their immigration status. This represented a more drastic closure than the most militant array of Border Patrol agents along the banks of the Rio Grande. Washington created a new category of excluded people, different and apart from all the others who had suffered from the earthquake. Those who were excluded had paid sales taxes with every purchase, paid property taxes on their houses, and had often paid withholding taxes and Social Security. They had lived and worked in the sunny San Fernando Valley without ever being asked to leave, but now suddenly they were deemed unworthy. If they had been in Mexico and lost their homes to an earthquake, they would have been objects of pity, but here they became targets of scorn.

Every society sets a limit on how much poverty or sickness it will allow anybody to endure. And when people are blameless, like the victims of a disaster, the state often steps in to remedy the harm. Decisions about who benefits from this generosity define the national character every bit as much as decisions about who gets into the country. Deciding that illegal aliens could not receive earthquake aid marked a turning point for the United States. Illegals have long been excluded from income-support programs like food stamps and welfare, but no one had tried to keep them from receiving aid that was considered humanitarian, such as inoculations, disaster relief, or prenatal medical care. Now with the earthquake bill, the United States set out to discourage illegal immigration by allowing living conditions to become uncomfortable and even unsafe for those it considered undesirable. The vote on earthquake aid did not set new income limits or otherwise redefine what the government considered a needy case. Instead, the United States created a new kind of exclusion. People could claim aid regardless of whether they worked, paid taxes, committed crimes, or took drugs. But anyone who could not prove that he or she was a citizen or a legal immigrant might be ruled unworthy of the humanitarian help regardless of how badly that person needed or otherwise deserved it.

As the anti-immigrant backlash began to evolve in the last decade of the century, it focused increasingly on the issue of eligibility for public benefits, and of all the harms ascribed to immigration, increased public-sector spending drew the greatest attention. Proposals to exclude newcomers from various social programs garnered even more support than plans to keep unwanted aliens from entering the country. Schools, hospitals, and social-service centers became the favored targets for enforcement actions, rather than borders, airports, or consulates. It began with long-term earthquake aid for illegal aliens, but then California, several other states, and the federal government eventually sought to prevent illegal aliens from enrolling in programs for child abuse prevention, foster care, breast cancer detection, child nutrition, and assistance to the deaf. Instead of applying the lessons of El Paso and deterring illegal aliens from entering the country, the backlash dictated policies designed to make life difficult for those who had already entered the country.

In this anxious atmosphere, the logic of exclusion leaped from illegals to legal immigrants like electricity arcing between opposite poles. The welfare reform law enacted in the summer of 1996 and signed by President Clinton despite his publicly stated reservations barred future legal immigrants from receiving food stamps, Medicaid, disability benefits, welfare, and most other forms of federally funded social services for the first five years they were in the country. The bill also expanded the circumstances under which an immigrant's sponsor would be considered financially responsible for the newcomer's health and welfare. All this applied to people who were coming to the United States according to the rules and presumably were being welcomed into the country. Moreover, the welfare reform law, as enacted, also enforced these provisions retroactively by applying them to legal immigrants who were already in the United States at the time of passage in August 1996. Up to half a million legal immigrants began receiving notice in early 1997 that they would be cut off from disability benefits that had been granted to them because they were not only poor but also old or sick. Counselors at senior citizen centers warned that some of the frailest immigrants, who were incapable of going through the citizenship process, had become despondent when they discovered they were about to lose their only source of income and health care. Several nursing home suicides were reported. Republican leaders in Congress began to relent in 1997 after Republican governors in states with large immigrant populations complained that the GOP would pay a terrible political price for turning destitute immigrants out in the streets. In the budget deal reached with Clinton in June 1997 the Republicans restored disability benefits, known as Supplemental Security Income, to immigrants who were already in the country at the time the welfare reform bill was passed. But the Republicans refused to restore food stamp benefits for legal immigrants already here, even though in the age of welfare reform this program constitutes the last federal safety net, ensuring that people do not starve in the United States no matter how poor they may be. Finally, the budget deal left in place the broad measures in the welfare reform bill that restrict eligibility for food stamps, disability benefits, and other programs for future immigrants and that grant states broad leeway in barring legal immigrants from receiving the benefits that have replaced old-style welfare. As many as 1.5 million legal immigrants, mostly Latino women and children, face the possibility of losing health and welfare benefits regardless of their condition or their plight.

The Republican authors of the prohibitions on aid to immigrants complained that foreigners were using immigration to the United States as a "retirement program." The GOP legislators said they

merely wanted to shut off the "welfare magnet" that allegedly drew
legal immigrants here with the goal of signing up for benefits as
soon as possible. "We do not believe that people who come to this
country for opportunity and freedom should expect a handout,"
said House Ways and Means chairman Bill Archer, a Texas Republican. The easy rhetoric was never accompanied by any evidence that
legal immigrants are drawn to the United States by the prospect of
collecting public assistance. In fact, numerous studies showed that
working-age legal immigrants have no greater propensity to end up
on cash-transfer social programs than comparable sectors of the
native-born population. Refugees are the only exception, and they
rightly constitute a special case both because they usually depart
their home countries under adverse circumstances and because they
come here under the auspices of the U.S. government and are immediately eligible for many forms of assistance. The elderly, not surprisingly, comprise the other category of newcomer often requiring
assistance, but in many cases these are people who have lived and
worked in the United States for many years but were employed in
jobs that did not provide them with adequate income or health-care
insurance in retirement. The rules that keep immigrants from
receiving public health benefits not only set out to cure a problem
that did not exist—the supposed welfare magnet—but it created an
altogether new problem by withdrawing the safety net from people
who had just arrived. An immigrant can come here legally, work
several years, and find himself helpless if he becomes seriously ill or
suffers an accident. There will be no assistance for his family, and
after exhausting private health insurance benefits, he might well be
obliged to leave the country to get further medical care. An immigrant woman could face deportation for seeking welfare after being
abandoned without resources by an American husband.

After the first five years of residence, legal immigrants become
eligible for several programs, but if they were sponsored by a relative, then that relative's income is counted in determining whether
the immigrant is eligible for assistance. Having a middle-class relative will prevent an immigrant from qualifying for social services,
but there are no effective provisions for guaranteeing that the relative will actually help out the newcomer in hard times. This bureaucratic process known as "deeming" (the sponsor's income is deemed
to be the immigrant's) has had a nefarious side effect. For the first

time in American history, this law drew a sharp distinction in civic status between U.S. citizens who are native-born and those who are naturalized immigrants. The native-born know that the government will be there to help if their parents require expensive health care in their old age. At worst, nursing home residents run through all their assets and then effectively become wards of the state through Medicaid. But the 1996 law foreclosed that option for immigrant citizens who have brought their elderly foreign-born parents here to live with them. This is a growing category of people who are American citizens in every way except that they are now exposed to the nightmare of being bankrupted by the costs of their parents' dying days.

In a parallel effort to reduce the number of poor foreigners entering the country, the 1996 immigration law imposed income requirements for sponsoring a relative as a legal immigrant. Sponsors now have to prove they earn at least 125 percent of the poverty level—nearly twenty thousand dollars for a family of four when the law took effect. Like the welfare-reform law, this measure will have a devastating effect on immigrants already here by denying husbands and wives the chance to reunite with one another and their children. Aside from the emotional loss, there will be an economic one as well. Low-income immigrant families survive in the American economy by pooling the wages of several workers, and sponsoring adult relatives is the means by which they expand their income. As many as half of all Mexican and Central American legal immigrants will become ineligible to act as sponsors, according to official estimates.

In enacting the income requirement, Congress ignored the special difficulties of trying to manage a mature migration. The new law will prove self-defeating because many poor Latinos will simply ignore it and bring their loved ones here illegally. Congress's mistake lay in trying to decree a sudden change in a migratory flow that has developed powerful momentum. Rather than order people to give up deeply felt expectations from one day to the next, policies of this sort can be effective only if they are implemented incrementally over the course of several years. If the income requirement had started much lower and then increased every year for five years until reaching the 125 percent of poverty mark, it would have stood a better chance of altering the makeup of immigration over the long term. Immigrants might have come to accept the new rules and adjusted, instead of seeing yet another rule to be skipped over. The income requirement was ably promoted as a way to protect the country from a "poverty class" of immigrants—a theme that resonated with anti-immigrant sentiments. Just as the 1924 law most responsible for ending the European era of immigration barred foreigners considered undesirable by virtue of their nationalities, the 1996 legislation closed the door on immigrants who are unwanted because they are poor.

Each age of closure has its rationale and its rhetoric, and Governor Pete Wilson was the chief author of the backlash that now marks the era of Latino immigration. In the midst of a desperate political campaign, Wilson reformulated the immigration issue in a manner that has had lasting, nationwide impact. He understood that illegal immigration would not reach its full political potency if the issue was framed in terms of unwanted foreigners taking jobs that rightly belonged to Americans. That had been the argument throughout the seventies and eighties, but it never really caught fire, because most voters have no reason to worry about illegal aliens taking their jobs. To be effective, the issue had to seem more threatening and it had to be brought closer to home. Anxiety over public-sector deficits, crime rates, welfare abuse, economic insecurities, and distrust of government were driving the electorate. Wilson's contribution to the backlash was a rhetorical formula that used illegal immigration to hit all those hot buttons at once.

In the television advertisements that propelled Wilson to a come-from-behind election victory in California in 1994, illegal aliens are portrayed in grainy black-and-white film as nefarious figures scurrying over fences and across rivers to enter the country. They are evil, but of a very particular sort. Wilson promoted the idea that illegal immigration constitutes an "unfunded mandate" imposed by greedy Washington. Controlling the border is a federal responsibility, after all, he argued, and when the inept, remote, and corrupt bureaucrats in Washington fail in their mission, state and local taxpayers get stuck providing illegals with public health, education, and other services. Illegal aliens and their children are so numerous that they are bankrupting the nation, he said. At one point in his campaign, Wilson reduced the argument to a simple equation: If

California did not have to care for illegal aliens, the state government could afford to put a computer on every school desk in the state. The tag line on a Wilson television ad summarized the pitch: "Wilson wants to use the money spent on illegals to take care of California's kids."

By portraying illegals as a drain on public resources, politicians could tap into voter anxiety over spending deficits. Suddenly, immigrants, first illegal aliens and then all immigrants, became a direct threat to the well-being of all taxpayers. Rapacious foreigners were accused of gobbling up the commonweal. Their alleged consumption of public benefits became an easy explanation for the otherwise unfathomable demise of such institutions as the California public schools and for the skyrocketing costs of entitlement programs. Spending on immigrants, legal and illegal, was like a tumor that could be cut out to restore the civic body to good health.

But immigrants don't just consume public services. Like everybody else, they pay taxes when they pay for clothes, gasoline, and housing or collect salaries with taxes already withheld. Newcomers are no different than the native born in requiring more from the public sector when they are either very young or very old, and less when they are of working age. All this makes it difficult to reduce the fiscal impacts of immigration to the kind of cut-and-dry statements typical of contemporary political campaigns. A federally commissioned analysis of tax data by the Urban Institute and an exhaustive study by the National Research Council point to a more complex and uncertain reality. Californians are not being simply paranoid or mean-spirited when they complain that immigrants are a drain on the public sector, nor are they entirely accurate. The research council found that every California household headed by a native paid about $1,178 a year, on average, in state and local taxes to cover the cost of services to immigrants, legal and illegal. Spread out nationwide the analysis found that the burden is about $200 per household headed by a native. The burden in California is greater not only because it has by far the largest immigrant population but also because so many of its immigrants are poor and fertile. They earn less, need more services, and have more children in school. As the study notes, these are the characteristics of Latino immigrants. By contrast, immigrants from Europe and Canada made an average net contribution to their local public treasuries. Over the long run, the research council found, these patterns will evolve. As the huge second generation of Latino immigrants moves out of school and into the workforce in the early years of the next century, they will become a desperately needed source of new tax revenues just when retiring baby boomers put a huge strain on Medicare and Social Security. Even looking at the present, however, fiscal impacts cannot be judged in isolation. Like many previous studies, the research council report found that immigration brings distinct economic benefits by allowing domestic workers to do more specialized and productive work and by stimulating new forms of consumption. These benefits are enjoyed most immediately by the same people who must meet the fiscal burden: middle-class natives who live in proximity to large immigrant communities. Eliminating the immigrant population would not automatically reduce taxes in California or anywhere else because it would produce economic losses along the way. In the end all these studies demonstrate the foolishness of performing a cost-benefit analysis on any sector of the population.

In the 1996 campaign, Democrats and Republicans competed with thirty-second television commercials to demonize immigrants and claim credit for defending the American public. A Republican National Committee advertisement that aired in the summer of the presidential campaign told voters "You spend $5.5 billion a year to support" illegal aliens with welfare, food stamps, and other services. Against the obligatory black-and-white images of furtive border jumpers, it claimed such spending had gone up 12.7 percent under the Clinton administration. The whole pitch made it seem as if illegals got money as a result of some deliberate budget process, with line items that could be calculated down to the dollar, when in fact no one knows how many illegal aliens live in the United States or to what extent they use fake documents or other methods to exploit programs from which they have been excluded as a matter of law for years. That did not bother the Republican ad makers, who left viewers with the statement, "Tell President Clinton to stop giving benefits to illegals and end wasteful Washington spending."

The Democratic National Committee asked television stations not to broadcast the GOP ad, dismissing the allegations about illegal aliens' access to food stamps and other benefits as "a blatant and demonstrable falsehood" because proving legal status has been a qualification for those programs for years. But when the Democrats responded with an ad of their own, they, too, broadcast shadowy images of brown-skinned men, except in this case, the ad boasted of a "record number of deportations" under the Clinton administration and a reinforced Border Patrol. Then the Democrats upped the ante. The ad switched the focus from illegal aliens to legal immigrants, castigating the Republicans for opposing a plan to reduce temporary work visas for legal immigrants who are recruited by U.S. companies for computer programming and other specialized tasks. "Republicans Opposed Protecting U.S. Workers" was stamped like a headline across the screen. Sliding from immigration to crime to drug abuse, the ad made immigration a proxy for a gamut of social ills. Having boasted about the administration's crackdown on immigration, legal and illegal, the ad concluded with the announcer's voice wrapping it all in a neat package: "Only President Clinton's plan protects our jobs, our values."

The ad makers may have seized on immigration as a matter of political expediency, but the issue has continued to resonate nationwide for several years because it poses a question without an answer: When should immigrants be granted access to public education, public health care, and the safety net of social programs?

Regarding illegal aliens, the issue of eligibility has always required something of mixed response. There is little dispute that illegals should be denied welfare and other forms of cash transfers as well as food stamps. As a matter of principle people who have entered the country illegally have no moral claim on economic help when they run into hard times here. But as a practical matter, as well as a question of humanitarian concern, illegal aliens have long been granted access to a variety of public health benefits. Providing inoculations to the largest number of people possible is simply the best way to make such programs effective. Preventative medicine, including prenatal care, has been offered without regard to immigration status by many states because of the savings gained in the long run. In addition, hospitals are obliged to grant emergency care to anyone who needs it regardless of their ability to pay or their legal status, and even the most ardent supporters of Proposition 187 never suggested that illegal aliens should be allowed to bleed to death. Certainly allowing illegal aliens eligibility to these health benefits costs the taxpayers something, but if money is the issue, millions—perhaps billions—more can be saved by systematically attacking fraud and abuse perpetrated by medical providers from the corner chiropractor to mighty hospital corporations. One last category of benefits involves the public schools, and until the U.S. Supreme Court reverses itself, the law is clear in stating children cannot be held responsible for their immigration status and therefore cannot be denied the basic education that states mandate for others their age.

Deciding eligibility for legal immigrants involves an entirely different set of concerns because these newcomers are being welcomed to live in the country and the question is whether that entails a welcome to make use of a public infrastructure that has been built up with the taxes of people who have lived here for generations. This is a new issue in American public life because Medicare, Medicaid, food stamps, the state university systems, and many other public institutions did not exist or were in their infancy during the last great era of immigration. Between the start of the Great Depression and the end of the civil rights era, government at all levels assumed new responsibilities to limit the misery suffered by the poor and sick and to ensure that public education offered every child a reasonable opportunity to succeed. Immigration was so low during that entire period that there was no need to discuss the role of the newly arrived. Then Latino immigration began to produce a large number of new claimants on the public sector, and this occurred just as the American middle class began to rebel at the costs of social services and to doubt their purpose. Now a great reckoning must occur. The United States needs to decide whether newly arrived legal immigrants deserve the same generosity offered to the native-born or whether special rules are necessary to limit government spending on them. At issue is the manner in which American society values newcomers.

Ever since the colonial era, immigration laws have attempted to keep out foreigners likely to become a "public charge" by excluding those who were sick, lame, or illiterate or by requiring that most newcomers have a relative or an employer act as their sponsor. During the anti-immigrant backlash at the beginning of the century, the laws governing entry became increasingly stricter, and a growing number of people faced the prospects of rejection by the inspectors at Ellis Island and a forced return home. These provisions always applied to a legal immigrant's condition before entering the country, but now the test comes after the immigrant has lived in the United States for some length of time. Rather than redefining the terms of entry to the country, today's backlash is changing the terms by which a legal immigrant can become a fully integrated member of American society. Newly arrived immigrants are being told that they can no longer count on help from the government when they get old, fall sick, or suffer hard times. Medicaid is no luxury. For the poor and disabled it is often the only means of acquiring medical care. Immigrants will now be allowed into the country, but they will be barred from the institutions that Americans have created to guarantee the common good.

Exclusion from eligibility, however, does not mean exclusion from society. Congress may decree that legal immigrants are no longer eligible for long-term disability benefits even if they have spent a lifetime working in sweatshops with no health insurance, but that will not make them disappear or keep them healthy. The Supreme Court may reverse itself and allow public schools to deny education to the children of illegal aliens, but that does not mean they and their parents will go home. Too many already have a stake here. They have jobs and homes, and every day more Latino immigrants become the parents of native-born children. Instead of leaving, immigrants, especially poor immigrants, could form a new class of people in American society. In this scenario they will be drawn north by the promise of work, but their work will not be rewarded by protection from poverty. When recessions produce widespread unemployment and business losses, whole communities—the barrios—will have to go without the public benefits that cushion the impact of such downturns and keep them from gaining unstoppable momentum. Inner-city public hospitals, already hard-pressed, will soon find themselves beset with a wave of emergency room cases that cannot be turned away but that might have been avoided if immigrants—illegals and poor legal immigrants who might have benefited from Medicaid—had not been cut off from preventative programs and regular treatment. Children will grow up here, only to discover that it is much harder for them to get college loans or scholarship grants because they are foreign-born. These and all other forms of exclusion will create a new kind of underclass of people who live and work here and pay taxes but who are cut off from the institutions and programs designed to give poor people a minimal sense of security and to guarantee that there is a limit to misery in America. Poor immigrants will be allowed into the country but not into the nation.

In old downtown Los Angeles on land not far from where the Spanish monks built their mission, an odd sight developed during the winter of 1994–1995. Crowds of Latinos began forming on the sidewalks in the chilly predawn hours. They lined up and waited for the offices of the Immigration and Naturalization Services to open so that they could apply for citizenship. In Los Angeles and then in every major city across the country, immigrants suddenly rushed to seek naturalized status in such numbers that they quickly overwhelmed the bureaucracy. It started shortly after the election that produced Proposition 187 and the Republican majority in Congress, and it occurred spontaneously, with little direction or encouragement from political leaders or advocacy groups. As months and then years passed and the number of Latinos seeking citizenship remained at flood stage, it became apparent that something fundamental had changed in the mentality of the barrio.

Prior to this boom in naturalization, conventional wisdom held that immigrants in the United States acquired citizenship in proportion to the distance they had traveled to get here. So, Asians and Europeans routinely naturalized almost as soon as they became eligible, usually after five years as permanent legal immigrants. By contrast, Canadians and Mexicans rarely would become citizens even after living in the United States for decades. Along with immigrants from the Caribbean and Central America, they retained intense ties to their homelands and often lived with the dream of returning.

As a result, every barrio had a huge supply of potential citizens. That reservoir had swelled when the immigrants who came in the surge of the 1980s reached eligibility, and then it grew even larger as the nearly 3 million beneficiaries of the 1986 amnesty became eligible. In 1995, applications for citizenship topped a million nationwide, nearly twice as many as the year before. By 1997, the INS was expecting close to 2 million citizenship applications.

The long lines of Latinos seeking U.S. citizenship marked a turning point. Like the Dominicans in Washington Heights after the 1992 riots, Latino newcomers all around the country were shocked out of their sojourner mentality by the anti-immigrant backlash.

Legal immigrants realized that even though they paid taxes like everyone else, they could still lose access to a social safety net that citizens took for granted. The backlash, however, did not generate the kind of counterreaction typical of minority-group politics. Latinos did not protest or march to demand recognition of their rights. They did not mobilize as a group, nor did they generate a telegenic leader who spoke for their interests. The rush to naturalization was a simple act of self-defense, in part because citizenship offered some protection from the loss of benefits. More important, however, it was a declaration by people who had long lived between two lands that they had begun to consider the United States their permanent home.

Latino immigrants will become citizens with the same quiet relentlessness they showed in entering the country, creating communities, and getting jobs. They are also becoming voters. Together with native-born Latinos, they already make up a significant slice of the electorate in New York, Chicago, Los Angeles, and a number of smaller cities. As with the Irish and the Jews early in this century, the Latinos' political importance will be magnified because they are concentrated in a few highly visible places and because they may be able to swing key states in very close races. Southern California has the potential to become a Latino political bastion in the next twenty years even with no further immigration. More than half of all the youths in Los Angeles County are Latinos, and by the year 2010 Latinos will considerably outnumber Anglos in the entire L.A. metropolitan area. All those kids who carried Mexican flags to protest Proposition 187 have only to grow up and the politics of California and the nation will change for a generation or more. Despite the mathematical inexorability of this change, its direction is not clear. There is always the chance Latinos might fail to translate their numbers into real clout. With the exception of the Miami Cubans, Latino voters have gone Democratic so predictably and by such large margins in the past that the new citizens might suffer the fate of African-Americans, who are often taken for granted because Democrats know they have nowhere else to go. Or if the new Latinos fail to articulate a distinct political identity for themselves, they might eventually resemble the Puerto Ricans and become secondary players who are constantly struggling to make themselves heard.

Initially the leaders and candidates will emerge from the ranks of

Mexican-American and Puerto Rican activists who are steeped in minority-group politics, but over time, as immigrants and the children of immigrants enter the arena, it seems likely that Latinos will develop a broader political identity. Their attitudes and agendas will necessarily evolve as a reaction to their experiences with American public institutions, everything from the neighborhood school to Congress. This is perhaps the greatest source of uncertainty about the future, because Latinos are becoming American citizens at a time when America is at best ambivalent about their presence. After the backlash embodied in Proposition 187 and the restrictionist proposals in Washington, many politicians reversed field. The 1996 election produced intimations of how fast the Latino vote was growing, and leaders of both parties grew apprehensive about seeming blatantly anti-immigrant. So, elderly immigrants were not kicked out of nursing homes, and in 1997 a few provisions of immigration law were modified to soften punitive actions against Central Americans who had overstayed temporary permits and illegals in the process of fixing their status. But all that amounted to mollification at a time when a continued economic expansion generated demand for new workers and temporarily relieved some of the nation's anti-immigrant anxiety. Even with sinking welfare rolls and a shrinking budget deficit, new immigrants are still denied access to America's social safety net. Immigration is widely regarded as convenient, even desirable in good economic times, but that is not a commitment to ensuring the successful integration of a large number of newcomers, especially those who most need help from their hosts. The potential for a renewed backlash remains very real, and so it is likely that today's Latino immigrants will establish their political identity in a nation that oscillates between uneasy acceptance and fearful rejection of them.

For the first time since the Voting Rights Act of 1965 opened polling places in the Deep South to blacks, the United States is enfranchising a large new group of people who have been marked as outsiders. This is not primarily a political process or a matter that can be settled with legislation and policy directives. Latino immigrants are on the brink of taking important steps that will define their place in American society for generations to come. Latino newcomers are well along in this process, but much of what they have accomplished thus far has been done quietly. Most Americans hardly noticed the barrios until they grew large. Now the key tasks ahead can only be accomplished loudly and in the public arena. Immigrants must establish links with the United States as vibrant as those they have maintained with their home countries. The barrios must be converted from self-enclosed enclaves into organic American communities intimately connected with the cities around them. Businesses and neighborhood organizations created primarily to facilitate migration and settlement must now turn to long-term goals. And the United States must stop looking at recently arrived immigrants as appendages that can be disposed of when they are unwanted. That means reaching a new understanding of how American society cares for and absorbs people who come from abroad, work hard, remain poor, and fill their homes with children. In the early part of the next century, the new Latino immigrants will become part of the American nation. They are here already. They are not going to leave. It will happen, but the process of integration is never easy or peaceful. There is conflict on the horizon, but beyond the conflict, there may be signs of hope.

❖•❖•❖•❖•❖•❖•❖•❖•❖•❖•❖•❖•❖•❖•❖•

Accept the Fear

❖•❖•❖•❖•❖•❖•❖•❖•❖• Beatte Winkler speaks English in a
lilting but precise voice, and when she
speaks of migration, most of what she says is overlaid with the sadness of Mitteleuropa, that vast land so thoroughly abused by armies
and ideologies for so many generations.

"Accept the fear and look beyond it, that's all there is," said Winkler. As a child, she fled from east to west. As an adult, she headed a
German government office contending with the social strife caused
by immigration. "I have learned that you must accept the fact that it
is natural to fear, even dislike, those who are different, those who
are strangers. It is there in all the everyday conflicts of human life,
conflicts between men and women, between rich and poor. Because
immigrants are so very different, being afraid of them becomes a
way of expressing many other fears. To understand what is happening around you, you must look beyond the fear."

We met in Nuremberg in October 1993, when immigrants all around Germany were under attack—hostels had been set on fire; skinheads were on the march. Winkler, a tall woman with chopped black hair that matched her sharp cheekbones, was alarmed, even disgusted, but she earnestly warned against a confrontational response.

"People who oppose this violence against foreigners should banish terms like *xenophobic* and *racist* from their vocabularies. Even when those words are aimed at a very small number of extremists, the effect is to alienate a very large number of people. Those are the people who have no political voice, who are feeling many negative things they do not know how to express. When they see foreigners, they think that then they see a problem they understand."

It was a frightening thought, the idea of a silent majority that somehow sympathized with neo-Nazis. I asked her exactly what sorts of feelings were troubling these people without a voice.

"In Germany there is a powerful longing for oneness, for homogeneity, for renewal, for some other time long ago when the German spirit was clear and strong. People see immigration as a challenge to that; they see it as an obstacle."

After a pause, she asked me almost plaintively, "And in America, it is the same in some ways, perhaps?"

I was pretty sure then that both yes and no were wrong answers, but that didn't help me much. I could have told her about all the anger in Southern California or all the old intellectuals worried that America could become a multicultural hodgepodge. Or I could have mentioned the proposals to deny citizenship to the American-born children of illegal aliens, just as Germany denies citizenship to the German-born children of its guest workers.

But sitting in an ancient restaurant in the medieval old quarter of the city that Hitler chose as the site of his party rallies, I could not call even the angriest faces of the American backlash into that room decorated with deer antlers and Gothic heraldry. It did not seem to fit. Americans have never thought of themselves as a single people as the Germans do. Although white, English-speaking Christians of European ancestry have set most of the norms for American society, there is still no sense of a *Volk* (a group that shares a common ancestry and culture and that embodies the national identity). Ideas, not biology, are what generate oneness and homogeneity in the United

States, and so long as faith in those ideas has remained strong, the country has shown an extraordinary capacity to absorb people of many nationalities. Then, listening to Winkler more closely and getting past my preoccupation with the ugly side of German history, I could see that what she said made sense in an American context. Fear of immigrants is natural and predictable because they do bring change, but fear of immigrants is also usually a symptom of other anxieties that fester deeper in a nation's heart. America started coming back into focus. Winkler might be right that the challenges posed by immigration—especially to a nation's identity— are much broader than they seem at first. If so, then the solutions are broader, too, and involve much more than hiring more Border Patrol agents or figuring ways to keep immigrants off welfare. Immigration exposes the fault lines in a society. In Germany, the fault lines represent doubts about what kinds of people can be considered German. In the United States, the fissures lie in the concept of equality.

Accept the fear and look beyond it.

On the surface, the United States today does not appear to suffer any large, overt challenges at home or abroad. It now stands astride the world as an unchallenged superpower awash in affluence. Even so, there are times when the nation's self-assurance seems under strain. Every few years a Ross Perot or a Newt Gingrich comes along and captures the electorate's attention with strident promises of drastic change, and every election produces loud complaints about the poor quality of leadership, the degradation of the political process, and an overall decline in civic life. With the number of divorced persons quadrupling over the past twenty-five years, there is a widespread perception that the nation's traditional moral structure is dissolving and popular culture, though wildly successful in commercial terms, is held to account. Even a seemingly endless economic expansion has not fully quelled unease about the long-term prospects. Some people worry that the stock market will crash or that Social Security will go bankrupt. Others fret that they'll never really get ahead. These anxieties have ebbed and flowed for a decade at least and have naturally gained the loudest expression during economic downturns. But they linger most consistently in the white middle-class core of the population. There, in the nation's demographic heartland, special interests, foreign powers, corporate moguls, and minority groups often are suspected of gaining unfair advantage. While the demons vary, the apprehensions always seem to center on the nation's ability to guarantee that all people will be treated equally, especially people who feel that they simply work hard and make no special claims on society. All this points to a latent crisis of confidence lurking near the core of the American identity. That is what you see in the United States if you accept the fear of immigrants and look beyond it. Fear of strangers is a natural thing, but in this case it is also a symptom of larger fears: fear of ourselves, fear of what we have become, fear of what we have lost. That is what lies beyond the fear of foreigners.

Latino immigrants did not cause this distress, and they are not the solution to it. But they will be actors in its unfolding. They are the new people on the scene and so they will serve as catalysts. They fill churches with children. They light up decaying streets with their storefront enterprises. They spark intense and unanticipated forms of competition for jobs, schools, and neighborhoods. All of this represents a kind of energy pulsing through America's cities, but it is largely undirected energy at this point. There is no circuit that readily connects Latinos to a secure place in the United States, and yet there are too many of them to be left outside the body politic. Latino immigration is big enough demographically that at some point the connection will be made, and that implies change in both the newcomers and the nation.

The large-scale movement of people is a symptom of change in any society. It is easy to see that both European immigration and the movement of blacks to the industrial cities occurred during periods of social and economic transformation in the United States. What often gets obscured, however, is what happens after the migration. The process of absorbing newcomers and their progeny also involves broad, usually difficult periods of change. It was true all through the first half of this century as the European immigrants and their children battled for acceptance, and it was true when blacks sought full citizenship during the civil rights era. On each of these occasions, the process of integration evolved as part of a larger crisis. As it incorporated the European ethnics, this nation moved beyond robber-baron capitalism, stifled nativism and isolationism at home, survived the Depression, and helped defeat fascism abroad. Similarly, the civil rights era and its aftermath, despite limitations and tragedies, coincided with a huge change in the status of women, a concerted defense of the environment, the creation of a medical safety net for the elderly, the economic revival of the South, the emergence of the postindustrial economy, and the successful conclusion of the Cold War.

In both these cases, the process of integration was not the sole cause of broader change, but it accompanied change and lent it direction and energy. This history strongly suggests that the integration of newcomers is not simply a matter of opening a door but, rather, of redesigning the structure. The basic elements of the American identity remain the same, but political practices, economic relationships, and social attitudes evolve when the nation brings a large new group of people into the mainstream. That dynamism has been held up as a sign of strength since the early days of the republic because this nation's identity has emerged strengthened by these crises. Latino immigration raises new questions about how the United States guarantees civil rights and economic opportunity. It focuses new attention on ethnic identity and on America's place in the world and the security of its borders. Because the challenge of integrating Latino immigrants touches on so many troublesome subjects, finding a place for these newcomers can promote a cure for this country's crisis of confidence. That is the hope that must lie beyond the fear.

Beatte Winkler's warning about using terms like *racist* to describe fear of immigrants came to mind in the fall of 1994 during the debate over Proposition 187 in California. About a month before the vote, opponents aired a radio advertisement alleging that some of the proposition's backers had secondhand links with an organization that had supported white supremacist views and eugenics research. The ad suggested that voting to deny public services to illegal aliens would be aiding and abetting the spread of racist thinking. That was not an unusual gambit. Many Latino leaders and pro-immigration advocates routinely denounced as racist all sorts of proposals to limit legal immigration or combat illegal immigration. They argue that because most of the people affected would be Latinos or Asians, the proposals would be racist in effect, if not in intent. But in the Proposition 187 campaign and in the immigration debate generally, such charges have lost their credibility and their effectiveness.

Even in its tawdriest manifestations, the Southern California backlash did not resemble the kind of pure and simple racism that the country had manifested in the past. Saying that illegal-alien children should not be allowed to attend public schools is in no way the same as saying that black children cannot attend the same schools as whites. It is not the same as saying that Jews or Italians will not be admitted at certain private universities, as was the case in days gone by. For one thing, when schools were segregated, it did not matter if a child's father was a millionaire or a sharecropper; if the child's skin was black, the schoolhouse door was blocked. In Southern California at the height of the anti-immigrant backlash, schools and universities remained full of Latinos. They were citizens and legal immigrants, and although they were physically indistinguishable from the dreaded illegals, no one dared suggest they be denied admission. What happened in Southern California was not a blanket rejection based on skin color, and anti-immigrant anxieties in American society today cannot be explained simply as eruptions of racism and xenophobia. Even as the United States puts limits on certain types of immigration, non-European foreigners are welcomed directly into professions such as medicine, banking, and the law; meanwhile, foreign students have become the lifeblood of university science departments. Qualified immigrants, regardless of their race, now slip into positions that were steadfastly restricted to white males just a few decades ago. Indeed, the success of highly skilled immigrants, particularly from Asia, has raised questions about whether these newcomers benefit because they are preferred by employers to native-born minorities. Regardless of how that assertion is judged, their success dramatically refutes the notion that simple racial prejudice is the prime motive behind anti-immigrant anxieties.

Forms of exclusion have changed in the United States over the past fifty years. Rejection is simply not as sweeping or as cut-and-dry as it was when racial segregation was a matter of law and unquestioned custom. Racism persists, and it may even be widespread, but it persists primarily as privately held belief, rather than as public behavior that is socially acceptable, let alone legally sanctioned. This momentous change means that new immigrants arrive in an America that is more tolerant than at any other time in U.S. history. More tolerant, but still prejudiced, because this nation has

developed other forms of exclusion that infect both personal attitudes and public policy. The great divide in American society is no
longer only along racial lines. Instead, prejudice derives from multifaceted perceptions that include not only race and ethnicity but
also assessments of an individual's economic and social standing.
All African-Americans experience some basic level of discrimination, but that bias is so much more explicit and punitive against
poor blacks than against middle-class blacks that it takes on an
entirely different quality. In this regard, prejudice today resembles
the kind of biases encountered by European immigrants a century
ago more than it does the sharp racial divisions that were the central
preoccupation of the civil rights movement.

Today multiple markers lead to the conclusion that certain people
live beyond the bounds of the law and that they are a drain on the
commonweal. It is a combination of traits that designates people
not as substandard or unintelligent but, rather, as nefarious and
exploitative. Stigmatization can result from being Latino or black,
being poor, being young, living in a high crime area, and not speaking English well. The penalties include being rejected for jobs,
loans, or housing without regard for qualifications, attending inad-
equate schools, and living in areas that receive no public or private
investment and that are far from where new jobs are being created.

These terms of exclusion reflect a society in which economic
position has acquired renewed salience alongside race and ethnicity. However, economic position is not measured just in terms of
poverty anymore, because it also reflects perceived dependence on
social welfare programs. In the broad rhetoric favored by conservative politicians, the world is divided into two kinds of people:
those who are pulling the cart and those who are in the cart, getting
a free ride. Welfare queens were the original bogeymen in this new
way of defining the nation's outsiders. Pete Wilson squarely placed
illegal aliens in the unhappy category of people inside the cart and
they were joined by legal immigrants after the 1996 welfare-reform
law.

Residential geography has always played a major role in the
expression of bias in the United States because the people with the
power to set the rules usually choose to live in neighborhoods apart
from those whom they consider inferior. Today geography is more
important than before because spatial segregation has not just resi-

dential but also economic implications. The wholesale shift of the middle class to the suburbs has been followed by the movement of economic activity outside the urban core. Good jobs and good neighborhoods are now often concentrated together on the periphery of a metropolitan area. As a result, the landscape is clearly demarcated into zones of privilege and zones of abandonment. Society concentrates its best resources—green spaces, doctors' offices, new schools, and sewer lines—in some areas, while neglecting others. And in the United States, this separation still has an important racial component, because most of the people living in the zones of privilege are white, of course, and those in the zones of abandonment are not.

For the newly arrived immigrant, and particularly for poor Latinos, these multifaceted prejudices represent an obstacle course blocking full integration to American society. They are not impenetrable, but they can present large and imposing challenges during a lifetime. The many Latinos who live in inner-city barrios face these barriers all at once. They are often isolated from the vibrant middle-class mainstream. They contend with the most deteriorated urban environments and they send their children to schools that breed failure. Then they are judged undesirable, and their Americanized children are labeled dangerous. No one single factor—not racism or economic inequality or suburbanization—explains the situation, nor can the condition of poor Latinos be improved by addressing any one source of bias or any one form of neglect. As the problems grow, the search for solutions must broaden, but we are not there yet.

New forms of prejudice are emerging in American society just as the old remedies for poverty and discrimination are in decline. Affirmative-action policies had helped Latinos and blacks gain access to university classrooms and government jobs, but in recent years both the practice of affirmative action and the philosophy that underlies it have come under assault in court cases, administrative actions, and voter initiatives. The most vigorous and effective attacks have developed in California, not surprisingly. Whites, soon to be a minority there, are trying to preserve their dominant position by imposing university admissions policies that pretend to decide access to higher education according to academic merit alone, even though access to an effective elementary and high school education is still decided by race and economic class. Meanwhile, school desegregation is widely considered a failed, happily forgotten means to seek more equitable distribution of assets in the nation's public schools, and there is little progress on initiatives to equalize spending between rich and poor school districts—a distinction that usually mirrors divisions between suburbs and city, white and minority. Whether in the field of education, voting rights, or even workplace discrimination, government is doing less and less to ensure that members of all racial and ethnic groups have equal access to public benefits, and there is no aggressive national commitment to combat discrimination. On another front, the 1996 welfare law ended the sixty-year-old federal guarantee of social benefits for all who needed them. Clinton and the Republicans in Congress buried the concept of entitlement knowing that they would win political approval in the suburban battlegrounds where elections are decided. Now, state and local governments are supposed to figure out what they can do with the poor, and they are under no obligation to look after all of them. Some welfare-to-work programs and the earned-income tax credit, which cuts the income tax burden for the working poor, have shown promise during a period of economic expansion, but it remains to be seen whether they will be effective in a downturn when they are most needed. New forms of poverty and new forms of prejudice now develop in the United States, and the available antidotes are either antiques that have been declared obsolete or experiments of uncertain effectiveness. Immigration is the new and dynamic factor in this unresolved equation. It is producing a demographic change, and that necessarily will result in political and cultural change as society is obliged to find a place for the newcomers. To understand how this process of integration might help the country define a new set of social goals, it is helpful to consider the issue of language.

Throughout the nineteenth century, many public and parochial schools taught immigrant children in their parents' native languages. By 1900, about 4 percent of the nation's elementary school population—more than 600,000 children—received all or part of their instruction in German. The practice ended in the wave of nativism that swept the country during World War I, and education in a language other than English returned to widespread use only after it was detached from immigration and became a concern for American minority groups. With the enactment of the Bilingual Education Act of 1968, Congress recognized claims by Hispanic- and Asian-Americans that children who could not speak English were "educationally disadvantaged." In 1974, the Supreme Court issued a landmark ruling in *Lau v. Nichols*, applying the same reasoning it used to strike down "separate but equal" schools; it mandated help for children with a limited mastery of English.

Both the 1968 law and the 1974 court decision legitimized a grievance, but neither defined a remedy, leaving it up to local authorities to design adequate programs. Since then, educators have generated so many different classroom approaches and so much wrangling over which ones work that no clear, persuasive rationale for bilingual education ever achieved widespread public acceptance. Meanwhile, advocates of multiculturalism further muddied the situation by arguing that the preservation of an immigrant's original language and culture has an intrinsic educational value.

Over the years, bilingual education has become an easy target for enemies of the educational bureaucracy, for those opposed in principle to group entitlements, as well as for those who simply find fault with the program on its merits. Federal funding for bilingual education now falls short of $200 million a year, less than half of what it was a decade ago, even though the number of students with limited ability to learn in English has skyrocketed. With the erosion of political and financial support for bilingual education, what remains is a residue of mistrust that now carries over to almost any public initiatives to assist or educate people who do not speak English. The hostility is now even directed at programs that allow immigrants to fill out tax forms or apply for building permits in a language they can understand. Voters across the country have ordered state and local governments to adopt "official English" policies over the past decade in order to prohibit the use of other languages for government business. Proponents of such measures often argue that minority groups threaten the country with fragmentation and ethnic conflict by seeking special linguistic rights. Meanwhile, many Latino and Asian activists insist their constitutional liberties are threatened by any move to restrict their use of mother tongues. The original intent of bilingual education seems utterly lost in this quagmire. That is just as well; there is no reason to resurrect it.

Language became a civil rights issue three decades ago when the foreign-born represented only 5 percent of the total population, an all-time low in this century. Now that the proportion of foreign-born has nearly doubled, linguistic issues need to be removed from the realm of civil rights so that they can be considered from a different perspective. With at least three-quarters of a million legal immigrants gaining entry every year, the United States has an undeniable self-interest in ensuring that newcomers learn English so they can become productive workers, responsible parents, and eventually effective citizens. Likewise, the nation has obvious reasons for ensuring that immigrant children do not fall behind in their education while they learn English, even if that means teaching them academic subjects in their mother tongue for a while. This kind of transitional program is one form of bilingual education that has demonstrated its worthiness. Society would be ill-served by elementary schools that produced sixth-grade immigrant children perfectly fluent in English but who could not do multiplication. Nonetheless, there is very little public effort to address these broader challenges because of the distortions that arise when minority-group politics are introduced by people on either side of the language issue. Language programs do not need to be justified or disparaged as a right accorded to a minority group. Instead, they can be viewed as training for an important segment of the workforce. Ambitious language instruction programs need not be related to historical grievances suffered by native Latinos or Asians. They can be justified as an investment in the future because they will help the children of immigrants stay in school, adjust to the United States, and make themselves more productive adults.

There is every indication that today's immigrants would be the first to accept this reformulation of the issue. The 1990 census revealed extraordinary linguistic dynamism in the foreign-born population. With so many recent immigrants, it is not surprising that a large majority reported speaking a language other than English at home—88 percent of those who had come to the United States in the previous decade. But at the same time, nearly a third of that same group reported speaking English "very well," and that measure of English fluency increased rapidly to half of all the people who had been here longer than a decade. The acquisition of English is fastest and most widespread among the children of immigrants. Three-quarters of foreign-born youths who had grown up primarily in the United States reported speaking English fluently. Alejandro Portes and another Johns Hopkins sociologist, Richard Schauffler, found in a survey of south Florida youth that "there is little variance in widespread fluency among the second generation," and that "whether second-generation children live in an English-only environment or in one where use of Spanish is widespread, their ultimate preference for the language of the land will be the same." When Mexican immigrants were asked in the National Latino Political Survey whether people residing in the United States should learn English, nearly 95 percent agreed that they should. Immigrants demonstrate their eagerness to learn English by crowding into low-cost English classes almost anywhere they are available. The Los Angeles public schools turned away more than forty thousand adult immigrants from such classes in 1986—the same year California voters approved an "official English" ballot initiative.

Some Americans understandably worry that their nation is becoming a Babel because so many people are speaking so many languages, but all the evidence shows that the primacy of English is not threatened by immigration. The first step in reaching a new perspective on language issues is to accept that evidence. The most adamant proponents of "official English" laws and the most unbending defenders of bilingual education must accept the fact that English is the single common language of the United States, with a permanent, irreplaceable role at the center of the nation's economic, civic, and cultural life. Those who fear a polyglot future need to be patient and supportive while immigrants learn English. Those who dream of a multilingual society—one marked by the permanent presence of distinct linguistic groups—need to recognize that it is not going to happen in the United States, ever.

At a time of large-scale immigration, America's cities will be filled with the sounds of many languages. But as has always been the case, it will be the sound of languages dying. The newcomers are guaranteed the right to speak any way they like and they deserve protection from anyone who would discriminate against them on the basis of their language preferences or their national origins. Yet, changing the goal of bilingual education from the protection of minority rights to the integration of immigrants would require educators to abandon the kind of multiculturalism that has made maintenance of

immigrants' native languages a major goal of some bilingual education programs. Instead, they would have to agree that the only purpose for using a native language in the classroom is to assist in the
students' transition to English. Immigrants should feel free to celebrate their cultural origins, as they often do with parades and festi-
vals. But if immigrants to the United States feel it is important that
their children preserve their mother tongues, then it is up to them
to pass that knowledge along. If they care enough, today's immigrant communities will create programs and institutions of their
own to maintain their linguistic and ethnic heritage, just as the
Europeans did a century ago. Heritage, however, is exactly what it
will be. The public schools must address themselves to the future,
and English remains the inescapable future.

The children of immigrants embrace this future hungrily, but
they need help. They devour the desires fed them by American
popular culture and would like nothing more than to live and speak
like the people they see on television. For most second-generation
Latinos, however, achieving middle-class prosperity requires a long
leap from the simple skills their parents bring with them to the
advanced requirements of work in an information economy. In the
United States today, the most impenetrable barriers to economic
mobility are not to be found in the labor markets, but in the nation's
public school systems. The American workforce is divided up
according to the qualifications of the workers. People of different
races and national origins, who may never see one another in their
neighborhoods or churches, are likely to meet at their places of
work so long as they share the same skills and education. The segregation between winners and losers in American society still bears a
high correlation to race and ethnicity, but most of the segregating
takes place before people look for their first job. Everything
depends on whether or not they attend schools that prepare them
for the more prosperous reaches of the economy. Education is a slow
mechanism for producing economic mobility and guaranteeing
equal opportunity, but it is by far the surest. It takes time to build
effective school systems and time to get results. Considering the
needs of second-generation youth today, the United States is facing
a twenty-year project if it is going to ensure the children of the barrios a fair chance to move up. The alternative is to see many millions
of young people doomed to the poverty and frustration that is a
dropout's certain fate.

The second generation needs more than just an academic education to prepare for the workforce, because these youths are involved
in a multifaceted process of assimilation. Helping them define themselves as Americans in a constructive fashion will require education
strategies that encompass a sense of community building as part of a
school's mission, and some schools are already trying. Hiring bilingual aides to help immigrant parents understand how they can help
their children through school often has proven of immediate benefit
to entire barrios. When such personnel are in place, schools in many
cities have developed a new role as a liaison between immigrant parents and the police and other government agencies. Schools are also
the natural venue for adult English classes, and such programs often
serve to increase parents' involvement in their children's education.
Several cities have experimented successfully with "newcomer
schools" specifically for immigrant children. They offer a program
usually lasting for two or three years that eases the transition into
regular classrooms. There is no need to return to the ideal of "Amer-
icanization" popular in the early decades of the century, which
pressed immigrants to give up any aspects of their native cultures.
Instead, one aim should be to bolster the position of immigrant parents and offer them every possible form of assistance as they face
the challenges of raising children who become Americanized far too
quickly and often in the worst ways possible. More generally,
schools can help the civic society of the barrios toward fuller
engagement with American institutions.

Defining educational goals in terms of economic mobility and the
successful integration of immigrants, rather than a redress of linguistic grievances, would require a departure from the traditional
minority-group agenda that has long defined most Latino political
activism. At the onset, immigrant and native Latinos may need to
part ways on some issues. Mexican-Americans and Puerto Ricans
will continue to seek social justice where they believe it has been
denied to them, as well they should. But immigrants should not
automatically become associated with their struggles. Foreign-born
Latinos, for example, should not receive the same benefits as natives
in affirmative-action programs designed to reduce the effects of
prior discrimination. Disassociating immigrants from affirmative
action might help ensure its survival. That would not imply even
the slightest relaxation of enforcement efforts against contemporary
acts of discrimination. On the contrary, immigration often spawns

prejudice. Since the government has targeted various categories of foreigners for exclusion from work and welfare, it has an added obligation to ensure that overzealous officials and private citizens do not extend this exclusion to anyone who looks or sounds foreign or has a foreign-sounding name. Ensuring that immigrants get the civil rights protections they deserve might be easier if those special needs are considered separately from the minority-group agenda pressed by many native Latinos. Putting the focus on the future needs of the labor force necessarily means moving away from the ideology of identity politics, but it is a move in favor of more ambitious objectives. Successfully integrating the current wave of immigrants and their children eventually will require a new approach to the interplay of political rights, group identity, and social eligibility. But as a first step, this country's Latinos must answer a basic question about who they want to be.

Before public policy can evolve to take account of Latino immigration, the wild card of illegal immigration has to be taken out of play. As noted previously, Latinos have the most to gain by gradually but deliberately closing the doors of their homes, businesses, and communities to illegal aliens. Reducing the illegal influx is an essential precondition to upgrading the low-wage workforce where so many Latino immigrants and their children are employed. A ready supply of illegal alien workers encourages employers to operate outside the bounds of the law and that includes many Latino businessmen who have no compunction about exploiting their neighbors and relatives. Illegal immigration also prolongs the transitory nature of barrio life by maintaining a segment of the population that is largely unable to help forge constructive links to American institutions such as police departments and U.S. political parties. Finally, the steady arrival of new illegals ensures that the barrios are perpetually burdened with their own peculiar underclass of workers often relegated to the worst-paying and least-secure jobs available. These realities need to be accepted first and foremost by Latinos, natives and immigrants alike. An understanding of that sort would play an enormous role in developing humane and effective immigration controls. It would also imply a fundamental change in the way Latinos view their place in the United States.

Several major obstacles, of course, inhibit such a drastic change of heart. Chief among them is the fact that illegal aliens are thoroughly blended into barrio households. They cannot be made to leave without breaking up families and disrupting the fabric of entire communities. But there is reason to believe that this situation can change. The Latino migration to the United States is maturing as millions of Latinos become U.S. citizens and gain the right to sponsor relatives into the country as legal immigrants. Thus the potential size of the *legal* Latino influx will grow ever larger for years to come. If properly managed by both the U.S. government and the Latinos themselves, this should temper the demographic pressure that feeds illegal immigration. With greater opportunities for legal immigration, Latinos should find it possible to reduce the welcome they extend to new illegal aliens. So far no significant Latino leader has dared speak out explicitly against the illegal influx. Influential groups like the National Council of La Raza listed opposition to employer sanctions as the top item on the Latino civil-rights agenda for many years and denounced as an expression of prejudice virtually every proposal to restrict the flow. Faced with Proposition 187, the 1996 immigration and welfare reform laws, and other portents of the backlash, most Latino political figures have accepted increased Border Patrol deployments, but they are still far from admitting that illegal immigration has a corrosive effect on their communities and that the barrios would be better off without it. This change will take time as Latinos gradually recognize the direct harm they suffer and the extent to which illegal aliens are an impediment to the successful integration of legal immigrants.

Widespread illegality is like a lien on a title that keeps a real-estate deal from closing. Until Latinos themselves reject illegal immigration, they can never conclude the essential transaction that will win them acceptance on the basis of their contributions to American society. The American public is not going to invest in making a success of the new immigrants if there is a justifiable suspicion that some large part of the immigrant population is not playing by the rules. Poor Latinos, who clearly have the most to gain, will have the greatest difficulty so long as they fall under this suspicion. In El Paso in 1993, in Miami and in California in 1994, well-established Latino populations took the first step toward a new approach by not protesting loudly against various efforts to shut off the flow of illegal immigration. The next step is to affirm that building up the barrios and establishing a strong economic and political position in the United States must take precedence over the defense of illegal aliens. Eventually, that would put the whole question of group identity in a new light. Rather than living the transient, transnational existence that has characterized the first thirty years of their migration, Latinos would be declaring themselves Americans on their way to making a new home. That has already begun to happen with the rush to adopt U.S. citizenship in recent years, and every such development should elicit a positive response from the public sector and from private groups that have an interest in seeing this enterprise succeed. Whether they are registering voters, cooperating with community policing programs or promoting local economic development, barrio institutions need encouragement and material help. As this process evolves with adjustments on all sides, Latinos will be embracing an identity not dictated by race or ethnicity but shaped by their experience on American terrain and their relationship with the American mainstream. Newcomers will be judged by fellow Latinos in some large measure according to what they contribute to the building of the barrio and not just on the basis of ethnic solidarity. When Latinos evolve a new concept of ethnic identity that emphasizes shared economic and social interests as much or more than ancestral bonds, then the whole concept of race and of group identity will begin to move like a tectonic plate shifting under the foundations of American society.

If the barrios refuse to serve as havens for illegal immigration and the federal government develops effective controls on the influx, if Latinos give up civil rights claims on language and school systems address the needs of immigrant communities, the United States could begin integrating its newest immigrants and that would fundamentally change the way the nation addresses issues of race and economic opportunity. Instead of zones of exclusion like many black and Puerto Rican ghettoes are, the new barrios can become true ports of entry capable of producing young people prepared to move into the mainstream of American life. That prospect alone is worth the cost of developing a true policy of integration. Poor and low-skilled immigrants come to the United States expecting to live at the bottom of the economic ladder, but their children need patience, tolerance, and investments to ensure that they have access to economic mobility. Latino immigrants do not seek nor do they need welfare or work programs. They deserve a basic safety net to get them through severe economic dislocations and to ensure essential health care, and they have a right to be protected from discrimination. The barrios do not need corporations to come in and build new factories or the government to put up public housing. They need more bank lending, small-business programs, public transportation and, of course, better schools. All of these efforts should be directed at connecting the barrios to the nation's economic and political mainstream while developing the civic institutions and the strong families that already exist in these communities.

As imposing as these tasks may seem, they do not demand another large-scale federal intervention like the Great Society or a massive emergency program like the New Deal. Latino immigration is not yet a disaster that needs remedy. Instead, it represents a universe of problems that is growing but that is still manageable. What immigrants and their children need most is access to opportunity so that they can fix their own futures. And yet this is a large enough universe that to succeed with these problems would change the course of American society as a whole in positive directions. Both the challenge and the potential benefit are best measured in the all-important goal of ensuring economic opportunity for the second and third generations. That task is about to get a huge help from demographic trends. More than 30 percent of the Latino population is under fifteen years old, compared with less than 20 percent of the white population. Starting in about 2010 just as the Latino baby boom bursts into the labor market with full force, the post–World War II baby boom will be going into retirement at a rapid clip. Quite simply, there will be jobs for the children of the barrios, but what remains to be seen is whether they will be ready for those jobs.

Since the civil rights movement and the Johnson administration's War on Poverty set out to change the nation more or less simultaneously in the mid-1960s, race has often served as a proxy for class. To speak of the differences between black and white has become a way of talking about the differences between poor and rich, or, more precisely, the differences between those with little

access to upward mobility and those with their fair share. Despite
the fact that there are 16 million poor whites in the United States,
compared with 9 million poor blacks, the face of poverty as popu-
larly perceived has been the face of a black person in recent years.
The far greater concentration of black poverty—a poverty rate of
nearly 30 percent, compared with under 9 percent for whites—is
only one explanation. The identification of black with poor has dis-
torted debates over social issues, whether they concerned welfare
policy, the breakdown of the family, or urban crime. The use of race
as a proxy for class has nurtured prejudice among those who are
happy believing that blacks are poor because they are black. It has
encouraged others to blame white racism for black poverty. Perhaps
worst of all, it has allowed many Americans to avoid a reckoning
with the origins of poverty and the changing causes of its perpetua-
tion.

That equation of race and poverty has begun to break down
because of the growth in the number of poor Latinos—nearly 9 million in 1996, with a poverty rate a little higher than among blacks.
This poverty cannot be blamed on the corrupting influence of the
welfare state or the residual effects of discrimination. Latino immigrants work, but they stay poor, and their plight should force the
nation to find new ways of talking about race and poverty. Many of
the issues that need fresh consideration may seem familiar: why the
children of the poor are so often discouraged rather than enlight-
ened by school, why a young person's economic fate is decided
before the age of twenty, why frustration and moral corruption are
twin evils, and why all of these maladies are so often concentrated
in a single community. Latino immigration now offers the opportunity for a new conversation about these questions without repeat-
ing the tired quarrels of the past. The option will become an
obligation soon, however, because the growth of the Latino population will force renewed attention to the issues of inequality so often
debated and never resolved. It will happen if new and more corrosive forms of alienated poverty develop in the second generation, or
perhaps it will take open conflict between poor blacks and Latinos;
or if the issue of illegal immigration is not resolved, it will happen
amid a vociferous anti-immigrant backlash by working-class whites
and blacks. Regardless of how events unfold in the next two
decades, the process of defining where Latino immigrants fit into
American society and the process of redefining the mechanisms of

social justice in the United States will become one and the same.

It is clear now that the most advanced postindustrial economy in the world has become dependent on a preindustrial servant class. The United States has become accustomed to having Latino immigrants cooking, sewing, raking, and hammering, ever diligent but undemanding. So far, it has been cheap and easy. But like all addictions, this one will exact a price eventually. These workers now live on the margins and are brought into the America of the white mainstream only to work. Their children are rarely even granted that much. They bear the multiple markers of those who are feared and rejected. Paying the price for this dependency on immigrant workers will mean ending their exclusion and making them full citizens in every sense. The United States has done that before with other groups, but never without conflict and never without producing a profound change in the identity of the nation as a whole.

A national identity, just like an individual's identity, develops in stages often marked by crises or challenges, according to Erik H. Erikson, the philosopher-scientist who helped make psychoanalysis a hallmark of twentieth-century thinking. An immigrant himself, Erikson once said that his idea of the identity crisis as a key element of human development emerged from his understanding of immigration's role in the American experience. In his landmark book *Childhood and Society,* first published in 1950, he wrote, "We began to conceptualize matters of identity at the very time in history when they become a problem. For we do so in a country which attempts to make a super-identity out of all the identities imported by its constituent immigrants." Erikson wrote that in the early years of the Cold War when the United States had indeed finally created a "super-identity" that embraced the offspring of the European migration. To get there, however, the country had endured an identity crisis that began with nineteenth-century nativism and ended only when the country unified under the threat of mass annihilation.

Identity has once again become a problem for the United States, and as before, the crisis of reinvention will create a new identity that embraces the nation's new constituents. The presence of so many Latinos ensures that matters of race and language, of poverty and opportunity, of immigration policy and nationality will be central issues in this process.

Like the European ethnics, Latino immigrant workers could

eventually amass enough economic and demographic leverage to earn eligibility for a basic safety net, decent salaries, and enough public education for their children to have a proper chance at upward mobility. But such a settlement cannot be reached through a purely economic process. Like African-Americans, Latino immigrants will also be plaintiffs demanding that society guarantee certain rights and protections. If eligibility to social welfare programs is earned rather than granted, popular support for aiding the poor might flourish again. If freedom from discrimination in employment is considered an essential element of economic productivity, the enforcement of civil rights laws might seem less threatening to white workers.

All of this would oblige minority-group politics to evolve in new directions. Economic concerns would create new communities of interest that would cut across racial and ethnic barriers. Class differences would share some of the same significance now assigned to racial differences. The interplay of rights and eligibility would take a new shape. There would be less pressure to apportion political power and government largesse strictly according to membership in a given minority group, but the nation would have added reasons to affirm that all its people have the guaranteed right to fair pay and a safe workplace. Although Latino immigrants are still heavily concentrated in central cities, they have begun to spread out, creating minibarrios in the suburban peripheries or choosing to live scattered among working-class whites. Their ghettoization will not be as complete as it has been for poor African-Americans, and that means rich, innovative suburban governments will be addressing the challenges of immigrant integration, not just the overburdened city halls downtown. Even modest moves in this direction will break the spatial segregation that is the direst legacy of white flight and that has left the institutions with the least resources to contend with the greatest problems. In this scenario, upwardly mobile Latino immigrants and their children would serve as the vanguard of integration. As they move into the suburban mainstream, they will bring an agenda that pushes the nation toward a more expansive concept of social equality. Dividing lines will blur and break down.

That is an optimistic scenario. It seems equally likely that Latino immigration could become a powerful demographic engine of social fragmentation, discord, and even violence. An increasingly virulent anti-immigrant backlash could produce an equally virulent militancy among Latinos, especially if there are aggressive efforts to round up and deport Latinos from American cities. Even a single accidental shooting could produce martyrs and a cause. Native and immigrant Latinos would bind together in a defensive reaction that could spawn an ethnic identity conceived in alienation from the white mainstream. Locked perpetually into the low-skilled, low-wage job force, Latinos would replace blacks as the face of intergenerational poverty. The migrant channels that link the United States to Latin America would become conduits for a drug trade larger and more intractable than any seen before. A mass migration in response to a catastrophe in Mexico, Central America, or the Caribbean would produce open hostility between the United States and one of its hemispheric neighbors.

These both may be extreme scenarios and the future may be more muddled, both less violent and less successful. At this point, we can be certain that more Latinos will head north, that the United States will change them, and that they will change the United States. We know that in twenty years the children of the barrios will be America's heirs even if we treat them like our bastard offspring today. History teaches that the identity crisis ahead will produce confrontations and that the search for answers will be painful. The new oneness that embraced the European immigrants was forged in war and economic devastation. The belated and partial acceptance of African-Americans came amid marches, riots, and church burnings. The Latino era of immigration will produce its own hot crucible and America will emerge from it with a stronger vision of itself.

Somewhere beyond the beach, a squall looms in the night sky and America the immigrant nation hurtles through the darkness toward the storm of reinvention. Out past the clouds, the beacon still sits atop the hill, showing the way to freedom and to home. That is what you see when you accept the fear and look beyond it.

NOTES

1. Children of the Future

page 3   **Imelda's story:** Author's account of his first encounters with Imelda appeared in the *New York Times,* January 20, 1992.

    6   **Twelve million foreign-born Latinos:** U.S. Census Bureau, *The Foreign Born Population: 1994* (Current Population Reports P20-486, 1995), Current Population Survey, March 1996, FB96CPS.

       Latinos will become the nation's largest minority group: U.S. Census Bureau, *Population Projections of the United States by Age, Sex, Race and Hispanic Origin: 1995 to 2050* (Current Population Reports P25-1130, 1996).

       No single group has ever dominated a prolonged wave of immigration: In the 1890s, for example, Italy, Russia, Austria-Hungary, and Germany had almost equal shares of the influx (around 15 percent each), with Scandinavia, Ireland, and Great Britain not far behind (around 10 percent each).

       The 6.7 million Mexican immigrants: U.S. Census Bureau, *The Foreign Born Population: 1994.*

  12   **More than a third of all Latinos are younger than eighteen years old:** Georges Vernez, Allan Abrahamse, *How Immigrants Fare in U.S. Education* (Rand, 1996).

13–14   **Fertility rates:** U.S. Census Bureau, *Fertility of American Women: June 1994* (Current Population Reports P20–482, 1995). B. Meredith Burke, "Mexican Immigrants Shape California's Future," *Population Today,* September 1995 (Population Reference Bureau Inc., Washington, D.C.).

       The hourglass effect: Philip L. Martin, "The United States: Benign Neglect Towards Immigration," in *Controlling Immigration: A Global Perspective,* eds. Wayne A. Cornelius, Philip L. Martin, and James F. Hollifield (Stanford University Press, 1995). And for statistics on the distribution of education among immigrants: Alejandro Portes and Rubén G. Rumbaut, *Immigrant America: A Portrait,* 2d ed. (University of California Press, 1996).

       About a third of all recent Latino immigrants live below the official poverty line: U.S. Census Bureau, *The Foreign Born Population: 1994.*

  15   **Twenty years ago there were:** U.S. Census Bureau, *Poverty Income in the United States: 1996* (Current Population Reports P60-198, 1996).

15   **In 1996 the workforce participation:** U.S. Census Bureau, *Money Income in the United States: 1996* (Current Population Reports P60-197, 1996).
      William Julius Wilson: William Julius Wilson, *When Work Disappears* (Knopf, 1996), pp. 52, 65.

17   **In the most extensive nationwide study:** James P. Smith and Barry Edmonston, eds., *The New Americans: Economic, Demographic and Fiscal Effects of Immigration* (National Academy Press, 1997), chapter 5.

18   **Mexicans who had been in the United States for thirty years had achieved modest economic gains:** Vilma Ortiz, "The Mexican Origin Population: Permanent Working Class or Emerging Middle Class?" in *Ethnic L.A.*, eds. Roger Waldinger and Mehdi Bozogrmehr (Russell Sage Foundation, 1996).
      Prison guards and professors: Barry Munitz, "Never Make Predictions, Particularly About the Future" (American Association of State Colleges and Universities, 1995).

21   **Sassen's stages of immigration:** Saskia Sassen, *The Mobility of Labor and Capital: A Study in International Investment and Labor Flow* (Cambridge University Press, 1988), p. 13.

2. Looking North

27   **Cuban rafter's crisis:** Author's accounts of Clinton administration policy changes toward Cuban refugees and reports from Cuba on the rafters first appeared in the *Washington Post* in August and September of 1994.

3. From One Man, A Channel

34   **These family networks function as the brokerage houses of migration:** Surveys and analyses on the functions of family networks can be found in the following publications, among others: Wayne A. Cornelius, "Los Migrantes de la Crisis: The Changing Profile of Mexican Labor Migration to California in the 1980's," unpublished paper (Center for U.S.-Mexican Studies, University of California, San Diego, 1989); Cornelius, "Labor Migration to the United States: Development Outcomes and Alternatives in Mexican Sending Communities," Final Report to the Commission for the Study of International Migration and Cooperative Economic Development (Center for U.S.-Mexican Studies, University of San Diego, 1990); Alejandro Portes and Robert L. Bach, *Latin Journey* (University of California Press, 1985); Glenn Hendricks, *The Dominican Diaspora: From the Dominican Republic to New York City—Villagers in Transition* (Teachers College Press, Columbia University, 1974); Sherri Grasmuck and Patricia R. Pessar, *Between Two Islands: Dominican International Migration* (University of California Press, 1991); Oded Stark and J. Edward Taylor, "Relative Deprivation and Migration: Theory, Evidence and Policy Implications," PRE Working Papers Series 656 (Policy, Research, and External Affairs Complex, World Bank, Washington, D.C., 1991).

36   **Immigrant remittances worldwide:** Sharon Stanton Russell and Michael S. Teitelbaum, "International Migration and International Trade," World Bank Discussion Papers No. 160 (World Bank, 1992).
      The money sent home by Mexican workers: Fernando Lozano Ascencio, "Bringing It Back Home: Remittances to Mexico from Migrant Workers in the United States," Monograph Series, 37 (Center for U.S.-Mexican Studies, University of California, San Diego, 1993); J. Edward Taylor,

"U.S. Immigration Policy and the Mexican Economy" (Urban Institute, 1988); *The Binational Study of Migration Between Mexico and the United States* (released in the United States by U.S. Commission on Immigration Reform, September 1997), p. 36.

36   **Irish remittances:** Patrick J. Blessing, "Irish," in *The Harvard Encyclopedia of American Ethnic Groups,* eds. Stephan Thernstrom et al. (Harvard University Press, 1980).

46   **Cheerful servants:** Laurel Brubaker, "The Remarkable Rise of Randall's Food Markets," *Houston Business Journal,* February 23, 1987.

      In-person servers: Robert B. Reich, *The Work of Nations* (Knopf, 1991), pp. 176–77.

50   **The second generation picked up:** H. J. Gans, "Second Generation Decline: Scenarios for the Economic and Ethnic Futures of Post-1965 American Immigrants," *Ethnic and Racial Studies,* April 1992.

51   **A ticket to permanent subordination:** Alejandro Portes and Min Zhou, "The New Second Generation: Segmented Assimilation and Its Variants," *Annals of the American Academy of Political and Social Sciences,* November 1993, p. 93.

      More a danger signal than a first step: Alejandro Portes and Rubén G. Rumbaut, *Immigrant America: A Portrait,* 2d ed. (University of California Press, 1996), p. 268. See also Alejandro Portes et al., *The New Second Generation* (Russell Sage Foundation, 1996). In his theory of "segmented assimilation" Portes argues that different groups of second-generation youth have sharply different experiences of assimilation and that inclusion in these segments is determined by the parents' experiences. Poor immigrants who suffer discrimination and fail to build strong communities are likely to produce a second generation that develops the "adversarial stance" toward education and work typical of American minority youths. Portes and Zhou (see above reference) cite Haitians in Florida as an example. On the other hand, immigrants who build strong social networks among themselves and are more successful economically are more likely to produce a second generation that assimilates successfully. Chinese and Koreans are cited as examples of this. However, the experience of the Houston Maya and of the Dominicans in Washington Heights suggests that there are grave dangers of downward assimilation even among immigrants who build strong communities.

      In "Second Generation Black Immigrants in New York City," published in *The New Second Generation,* Mary C. Waters, a sociologist at Harvard, cites her research among Jamaicans in New York to argue that assimilation can be segmented within ethnic groups as well as among them. Some second-generation Jamaicans assimilate to a black underclass existence, while others maintain strong ethnic ties and experience economic gains. A variety of factors, from family structures to perceptions of economic opportunity, come into play, according to Waters.

4. Day People, Night People, Madres

61   **In the final analysis:** Rubén G. Rumbaut, "The Crucible Within," in Alejandro Portes et al., *The New Second Generation* (Russell Sage Foundation, 1996), p. 168.

62   **The Flats was pretty good bottomland:** For an account of the establishment of the Mexican community in Los Angeles, see Ricardo Romo,

East Los Angeles: History of a Barrio (University of Texas, 1983). See also Roger Waldinger and Mehdi Bozogrmehr, eds., *Ethnic L.A.* (Russell Sage Foundation, 1996).

69   **The American ethos:** Nathan Glazer and Daniel P. Moynihan, *Beyond the Melting Pot* (Massachusetts Institute of Technology, 1970), p. xcvii.

70   **Ethnic identity in a stratified society:** Frank D. Bean and Marta Tienda, *The Hispanic Population of the United States* (Russell Sage Foundation, 1987), p. 16.

5. *Living by American Rules*

78   **Los rinches:** For accounts of Mexican-American experiences in South Texas, see Rodolfo Acuña, *Occupied America: A History of Chicanos* (HarperCollins, 1988); Matt S. Meier and Feliciano Rivera, *The Chicanos: A History of Mexican Americans* (Hill and Wang, 1972), and T. R. Feherenbach, *Lone Star: A History of Texas and the Texans* (Macmillan, 1987).

83   **Norris v. Alabama** 294 US 587 (1935).

84   **Hernández v. Texas** 347 US 475 (1954).

86   **Failure to understand this history:** Michael Lind, *The Next American Nation: The New Nationalism & The Fourth American Revolution* (The Free Press, 1995), pp. 115–16.

6. *Branding the Babies*

89   **In his memoir:** Martin Anderson, *Revolution: The Reagan Legacy* (Hoover Institution Press, 1988).

95   **The government made no credible effort:** Interviews with INS officials, INS documents, "INS Enforcement Deficit Tied to Law," and GAO testimony as reported by author in the *Washington Post*, February 2, 1995.

96   **The California garment industry:** "Labor Abuse Rampant in State Garment Industry," *Los Angeles Times*, April 15, 1994.

97   **Operation Jobs:** Stephen Barr, "Foundation Awards Honor 15 Creative Government Programs," *Washington Post*, October 26, 1995. In one of the delicious ironies of the employer sanctions saga, Operation Jobs received an Innovations in American Government award from a Harvard University program sponsored by the Ford Foundation. Over the previous twenty years, the Ford Foundation had granted many millions of dollars to organizations that had fought employer sanctions at every turn, such as the National Council of La Raza and the Mexican-American Legal Defense and Education Fund. Perhaps the foundation decided to honor the INS in recognition of the fact that employer sanctions had finally been rendered meaningless.

99   **Remembered the policemen:** William Branigin, "Illegal Population Grows to 5 Million," *Washington Post*, February 2, 1997.
      INS has no specific enforcement: *Immigration and Naturalization Service Monitoring of Nonimmigrant Overstays* (U.S. Department of Justice, Office of the Inspector, Report Number I-97-08, 1997).
      5 million illegals: Immigration and Naturalization Service Office of Public Affairs, "Estimates of the Unauthorized Immigrant Population

Residing in the United States: October 1996" (Department of Justice, 1997).

100   **Enjoying an inchoate federal permission to remain:** *Plyler v. Doe* 102 S. Ct. 2382 (1982).
      Zoë Baird: *Wall Street Journal,* January 20, 1993; *New York Times,* January 15, 1993.

101   **The cigar box deal:** Interview with Jerry Tinker, Kennedy's chief aide on immigration matters and a member of Congress who witnessed the event.

102   **Barbara Jordan and cuts in legal immigration:** Interviews with administration and congressional officials, and commissioners and staff of Jordan's Commission on Immigration Reform.

104   **In 1997 a team of twenty experts:** *The Binational Study of Migration Between Mexico and the United States* (released in the United States by U.S. Commission on Immigration Reform, September 1997), p. 53.
      The study's demographic estimates: *Binational Study of Migration,* pp. 8–9.

105   **The debate on immigration:** *Binational Study of Migration,* p. 53.

7. Save Our State

107   **Barbara Coe:** Author's account of Barbara Coe's role in launching the Proposition 187 campaign and other coverage of the 1994 election season in California appeared in the *Washington Post,* August–November of 1994.

109   **Demographic change in Southern California:** Roger Waldinger and Mehdi Bozogrmehr, eds., *Ethnic L.A.* (Russell Sage Foundation, 1996).

8. Los Angeles: People in Motion

124   **A border is a dividing line:** Gloria Anzaldúa, *Borderlands/La Frontera, The New Mestiza* (Aunt Lute Books, 1987).

9. Houston: Cantina Patrol

134   **Jews:** Nathan Glazer, *American Judaism* (University of Chicago 1972); Arthur A. Goren, "Jews," in *Harvard Encyclopedia of American Ethnic Groups* (Harvard University Press, 1980).
      Latino National Political Survey: Rodolfo O. de la Garza et al., *Latino Voices: Mexican, Puerto Rican, and Cuban Perspectives on American Politics* (Westview, 1992).

10. New York: From Stickball to Crack

139   **Fuck your canoes:** The joke is Ed Vega's.
      El Barrio: For accounts of the early years of the Puerto Rican migration to New York, see Joseph P. Fitzpatrick, S.J., *Puerto Rican Americans* (Prentice-Hall, 1987); Nathan Glazer and Daniel P. Moynihan, *Beyond the Melting Pot* (Massachusetts Institute of Technology, 1970).

141   **All the streets are alive:** Piri Thomas, *Down These Mean Streets* (Vintage, 1967), p. 14.

143   **Barely off the bottom:** On Puerto Rican poverty and economic participation, see Department of City Planning, *Puerto Rican New Yorkers* (New

York City, 1994); Clara E. Rodriguez, *Puerto Ricans: Born in the USA* (Westview, 1991); Frank D. Bean and Marta Tienda, *The Hispanic Population of the United States* (Russell Sage Foundation, 1987); Roger Waldinger, "Changing Ladders and Musical Chairs: Ethnicity and Opportunity in Postindustrial New York," *Politics & Society* 15, no. 4 (1986–1987); Angelo Falcón, *Puerto Ricans and Other Latinos in New York City Today: A Statistical Profile* (Institute for Puerto Rican Policy, 1992); Angelo Falcón and John Santiago, eds., *The "Puerto Rican Exception": Persistent Poverty and the Conservative Social Policy of Linda Chavez* (Institute for Puerto Rican Policy, 1992); Clara E. Rodriguez, Virginia Sanchez Korrol, and Jose Oscar Alvers, eds., *The Puerto Rican Struggle: Essays on Survival in the U.S.* (Puerto Rican Migration Research Consortium, 1980).

145   **The people in this book:** Oscar Lewis, *La Vida–A Puerto Rican Family in the Culture of Poverty–San Juan and New York* (Random House, 1965), xxvi, xlv.
      Latino and black immigrants are: Richard J. Herrnstein and Charles Murray, *The Bell Curve* (Free Press, 1994), p. 360.

146   **Mexicans in the United States are likely to be unskilled:** George J. Borjas, *Friends or Strangers: The Impact of Immigrants on the U.S. Economy* (Basic Books, 1990), pp. 8, 114, 223.

151   **Circular migration:** Edwin Melendez, "Los que se van y los que regresan: Puerto Rican Migration to and from the United States, 1982–88," unpublished paper (Department of Urban Studies and Planning, Massachusetts Institute of Technology, 1992).

155   **The continuous recourse to migration:** Roger Waldinger, *Still the Promised City? African Americans and New Immigrants in Postindustrial New York* (Harvard, 1996), p. 4.
      Just as with the first generation: Ibid., p. 23.

156   **Conservative writers:** Linda Chavez, *Out of the Barrio: Toward a New Politics of Hispanic Assimilation* (Basic Books, 1991).

11. Miami: A Barrio Without Borders

160   **The creation myth of Cuban Miami:** For accounts of the Cuban migration to Miami see Alejandro Portes and Alex Stepick, *City on the Edge: The Transformation of Miami* (University of California, 1993); Guillermo J. Grenier and Alex Stepick, eds., *Miami Now! Immigration, Ethnicity and Social Change* (University Press of Florida, 1992); David Reiff, *Going to Miami: Exiles, Tourists and Refugees in the New America* (Little, Brown, 1987).
      For if the go-go '80s: Cathy Booth, "¡Miami!" *Time*, September 6, 1993.
176   **In June 1990:** *City on the Edge*, pp. 141, 176–7.

12. New York: Teetering on the Heights

179   **Up on Manhattan's high ground:** Author's first reportage on the bodega economy and other aspects of the Dominican migration to New York appeared in the *Washington Post* from 1993 to 1996. See also Ramona Hernández et al., "Dominican New Yorkers: A Socioeconomic Profile, 1990," unpublished paper (Dominican Studies Institute, City University of New York, 1995); New York City Department of City Planning, *Newest*

New Yorkers (New York City, 1992, 1997); Ramona Hernández and Silvio Torres-Saillant, "Dominicans in New York: Men, Women, and Prospects" (Dominican Research Monographs, Dominican Studies Institute, City University of New York, 1994).

194   **TE RECORDAMOS:** On the Kiko Garcia incident, aside from extensive coverage in the *New York Times* and other publications, see Sonia Bu et al., "Washington Heights Outbreak of a Crisis: Analysis of the Events and Outlook Within the New Context" (Centro de Estudios Dominicanos, 1992). This author conducted extensive interviews with senior officers of the NYPD on condition that they not be identified.

197   **The Treasury Department announced:** Benjamin Weiser, "Cash Transfers to Be Monitored in Effort to Track Drug Money," *New York Times,* September 5, 1997.

201   **This is Giuliani time:** Dan Barry, "Second Officer Faces Charges in Torture Case," *New York Times,* August 16, 1997.

13. Los Angeles: From the Churn to the Burn

206   **The number of Mexican-born people:** For accounts of the Latino migration to Los Angeles and the demographic and economic changes that accompanied it, see Roger Waldinger and Mehdi Bozogrmehr, eds., *Ethnic L.A.* (Russell Sage Foundation, 1996); Saskia Sassen, *The Mobility of Labor and Capital: A Study in International Investment and Labor Flow* (Cambridge University Press, 1988); Mike Davis, *City of Quartz* (Verso, 1990); Rebecca Morales and Frank Bonilla, eds., *Latinos in a Changing U.S. Economy* (Sage, 1993); Edwin Melendez et al., *Hispanics in the Labor Force* (Plenum, 1991).

215   **Janitors and economic restructuring:** Richard Mines and Jeffery Avina, "Immigrants and Labor Standards: The Case of California Janitors," in Jorge Bustamante et al., *U.S.-Mexico Relations: Labor Market Interdependence* (Stanford University, 1992).

228   **I try my best to be an advocate:** George Ramos and Tracy Wilkinson, "Unrest Widens Rifts in Diverse Latino Population," *Los Angeles Times,* May 8, 1992.

14. The City That Worked

235   **One day in 1975:** As observed by this author, who was then covering Daley for the City News Bureau of Chicago.

236   **About the time Daley was born:** Patrick J. Blessing, "Irish," in *The Harvard Encyclopedia of American Ethnic Groups,* eds. Stephan Themstrom et al. (Harvard University Press, 1980).

237   **The day of unalloyed welcome:** William S. Bernard, "History of U.S. Immigration Policy," in *The Harvard Encyclopedia of American Ethnic Groups.*

15. From the Burn to the Backlash

243   **On a sultry summer morning:** This author's account of black–Latino relations in South Central L. A., written with coauthor, Gary Lee, first appeared in the *Washington Post* as "Latino–Black Rivalry Grows: Los Angeles Reflects Tensions Between Minorities," October 13, 1993.

246   **Blacks and Latinos in the Los Angeles economy:** For an extensive
       analysis of this subject, see Roger Waldinger and Mehdi Bozogrmehr,
       eds., *Ethnic LA* (Russell Sage Foundation, 1996); Rebecca Morales and
       Frank Bonilla, eds., *Latinos in a Changing U.S. Economy* (Sage, 1993); and
       Edwin Melendez et al., *Hispanics in the Labor Force* (Plenum, 1991). Data
       is from U.S. Department of Commerce, Bureau of the Census, 1990 Census
       of Population, "Detailed Occupation and Other Characteristics From the
       EEO File," 1992. For an analysis of the post-riot situation, see Kevin L.
       Kearns, "L.A.: You Can't Put a City Back to Work Without Real Jobs,"
       Washington Post, September 6, 1992.

248   **Account of Danny Bakewell activities:** interviews with author.

251   **Latino letter in response to Bakewell:** Bob Baker, "Latinos Short-
       changed in Riot Aid, Group Says," *Los Angeles Times,* September 15, 1992.

260   **Frank L. Morris:** Frank L. Morris, *Cast Down Your Bucket Where You
       Are: Black Americans on Immigration* (Center for Immigration Studies,
       1996), pp. 3–6.

16. Closing the Doors

269   **At the height of the 1994 campaign:** Robert Suro, "California Crack-
       down Vowed," *Washington Post,* September 18, 1994; Steve McGonigle,
       "Crackdown Announced on Illegal Immigration," *Dallas Morning News,*
       October 14, 1994.
       The United States border enforcement: *The Binational Study of Migra-
       tion Between Mexico and the United States* (released in the United States by
       U.S. Commission on Immigration Reform, September 1997), p. 28.

270   **A series of surveys conducted in Mexico:** *Binational Study of Migra-
       tion,* p. iii.

280   **Border patrol and civil rights:** U.S. District Court judge Lucius D. Bun-
       ton III, preliminary injunction in *Murillo et al. v. Musegades* (EP-92-CA-
       310-B), December 1, 1992.

17.   After the Earthquake

288   **Effects of welfare reform:** "Immigrants and Welfare," *Research Perspec-
       tives on Migration* (Carnegie Endowment for International Peace and the
       Urban Institute, September 1996).

291   **Effects of income requirements:** Celia W. Dugger, "Immigrant Study
       Finds Income Limit Bar to Uniting Families," *New York Times,* March 16,
       1997.

293   **The research council found:** James P. Smith and Barry Edmonston,
       eds., *The New Americans: Economic, Demographic and Fiscal Effects of
       Immigration* (National Academy Press, 1997), chapters 5, 6.

18. Accept the Fear

311   **Bilingual education:** James Crawford, *Bilingual Education: History, Poli-
       tics, Theory and Practice* (Crane, 1989); Alejandro Portes et al., *The New
       Second Generation* (Russell Sage Foundation, 1996); Alejandro Portes and
       Rubén G. Rumbaut, *Immigrant America: A Portrait,* 2d ed. (University of
       California Press, 1996).

321   **Super-identity:** Erik H. Erikson, *Childhood and Society* (Norton, 1950).
      In an autobiographical essay published in 1970 as he was retiring from
      Harvard, Erikson wrote of his idea of identity crisis: "I do not remember
      when I started to use these terms; they seemed naturally grounded in the
      experience of immigration and Americanization." He explained that he
      personally underwent what he considered "a test of my American iden-
      tity" during a grave personal crisis. It was when he resigned from his first
      real professorship, a job at Berkeley, rather than sign a McCarthy-era loy-
      alty oath. "[W]hen we foreign born among the non-signers were told to
      'go back where we came from' we suddenly felt quite certain that our
      apparent disloyalty to the soldiers in Korea was, in fact, quite in line with
      what they were said to be fighting for." Erikson, "Autobiographical Notes
      on the Identity Crisis," *Daedalus,* Fall 1970.

ACKNOWLEDGMENTS

My first thanks go to three friends who helped launch this book but did not live to see it completed. As deputy national editor of the *New York Times,* Jeffrey H. Schmalz helped me formulate several of the major themes that guided this project from the start. He would have been one of the great newspaper editors of our generation if he had been granted a full life. Don Schanche of the *Los Angeles Times* was the best traveling companion a foreign correspondent could ever want, and he always pushed me to look beyond the day's story. Jerry Tinker, majority counsel to the Senate subcommittee on immigration, was more than a great source; he was a great teacher.

Much of the reporting and the early writing of this book was supported by fellowships or grants from the Twentieth Century Fund, the Alicia Patterson Foundation, the Woodrow Wilson International Center for Scholars, and California State University. I am deeply grateful to these institutions and absolve them of any responsibility for the outcome.

Esther Newberg of ICM adopted this project in its infancy and lent me support and good advice at every turn. Jonathan B. Segal, senior editor for Alfred A. Knopf, vastly improved my work with incisive criticism, high standards, and a sharp pencil. I am indebted to them as a writer but also as a reader because they each have done so much to fill my shelves with great nonfiction.

My editors at the *Washington Post* have been unfailingly understanding while I labored on this book. Karen DeYoung, assistant managing editor for national news, told me I had to press forward when all I had was a three-page précis of a proposal, and Len

Downie, the executive editor, offered to help me get it done. The amazing thing about their encouragement is that it came while I was still working for the *Times*. In 1994, two years after those first conversations, I went to work at the *Post* full-time and have made a very happy home there ever since.

While I was out wandering the barrios, a great many people helped with introductions and by sharing their knowledge of their communities. I am lucky that they are too numerous to list here and I am grateful to everyone who took the time to help me. Special thanks go to several colleagues who helped with research or shared sources: Maureen Balleza of the *Times* in Houston, David González of the *Times* in New York, Cathy Booth of *Time* magazine in Miami, and Gary Lee of the *Post,* with whom I spent time exploring South Central Los Angeles. I benefited greatly from the wisdom and generosity of Antonio González of the Southwest Voter Registration and Education Project in Los Angeles; Ed Vega, the author, who brought the tragedy of the Puerto Rican migration to life on long walks through El Barrio, and Dr. Rafael Lantigua of Columbia-Presbyterian Hospital, who introduced me to Washington Heights and sat with me in his office for many hours while I tried to sort out the meaning of the Dominican experience there.

I was extremely lucky to have explored California during research and teaching stints at several campuses of California State University, an institution that is very close to the great challenges confronting that state. Many faculty members and administrators helped with everything from locating migrant workers to hunting down books. I am especially grateful to Barry Munitz and his wife, Anne, for their friendship. My thanks also go to Joy Phillips, Ruben Armiñana, Steven Arvizu, Rosemary Papalewis, Jaime Regalado, Victor Rocha, and Maria Nieto Senour.

Several scholars and public officials in the field of immigration have been generous with their time as I tried to learn about the subject. I am especially indebted to Demetrios Papademetriou for being a great friend and interlocutor. I am also thankful to Frank Bean, Alex Aleinikoff, Doris Meissner, Rodolfo de la Garza, Rick Swartz, David Martin, Saskia Sassen, Phillip Martin, Michael Teitelbaum, Roger Waldinger, Alejandro Portes, Wayne Cornelius and Aristide Zolberg. No student has ever had such an extraordinary collection of tutors.

I received helpful suggestions from several colleagues at the *Post* who read parts of this manuscript—my thanks go to Glenn Frankel, Ann Grimes, Liz Spayd, and Robert McCartney. I am also grateful to Richard C. Leone, president of the Twentieth Century Fund, and Michelle Miller, the editor of the two policy papers I wrote for the fund, for helping me develop a line of analysis on this difficult subject.

Dozens of Latino immigrants all across the country welcomed me into their lives and endured my questions. Their sagas of coming to a new land are reflected in every page of this book, and I thank them for being so generous.

Finally, I am forever indebted to my children, Giulia and Michael, and my wife, Mary, for their extraordinary patience and sacrifice in allowing me to pursue this dream and for the sustenance of their love.

INDEX

A Note About the Author

Roberto Suro, the son of a Puerto Rican father
and an Ecuadorean mother, was born and raised
in the Washington, D.C., area. He began a career
as a newspaper reporter in Chicago, where he first
wrote about immigration. In 1978, he became a
correspondent for *Time,* eventually doing tours in
its Chicago, Washington, Beirut, and Rome
bureaus. From 1985 to 1993, he worked as a
bureau chief for the *New York Times,* first in
Rome and then in Houston. In 1994, he became
a staff writer at the *Washington Post.* He is the
author of two Twentieth Century Fund papers on
immigration: *Remembering the American Dream:
Hispanic Immigration and National Policy* and
*Watching America's Door: The Immigration Back-
lash and the New Policy Debate.* He lives in Washington, D.C., with his wife and their two children.

A Note on the Type

The text of this book was composed in Apollo, the first typeface ever originated specifically for film composition. Designed by Adrian Frutiger and issued by the Monotype Corporation of London in 1964, Apollo is not only a versatile typeface suitable for many uses but also pleasant to read in all of its sizes.

Composed by NK Graphics,
Keene, New Hampshire
Printed and bound by Berryville Graphics
Berryville, Virginia
Designed by Anthea Lingeman

DISCARDED

DATE			